ADDITIONS AND CORRECTIONS

TO THE

W.P.A.

INVENTORY

OF

HAMILTON COUNTY, OHIO:

CINCINNATI

Jana Sloan Broglin

HERITAGE BOOKS
2025

HERITAGE BOOKS

AN IMPRINT OF HERITAGE BOOKS, INC.

Books, CDs, and more—Worldwide

For our listing of thousands of titles see our website
at
www.HeritageBooks.com

Published 2025 by
HERITAGE BOOKS, INC.
Publishing Division
5810 Ruatan Street
Berwyn Heights, MD 20740

Copyright © 2025 Jana Sloan Broglin

(Originally Titled)
INVENTORY OF THE COUNTY ARCHIVES OF OHIO
Prepared by
The Ohio Historical Records Survey Project
Division of Women's and Professional Projects
Work Progress Administration

No. 31. HAMILTON COUNTY (CINCINNATI)

Columbus, Ohio
The Historical Records Survey
1937

International Standard Book Number
Paperbound: 978-0-7884-4932-1

County Offices and their Records

PREFACE
2nd Edition

In 1929 after the stock market crash along with the Great Depression, crop failures and drought, which followed, President Herbert Hoover and his successor Franklin D. Roosevelt formulated relief projects, the most successful was the establishment of the Works Progress Administration (WPA).

Established as the Works Projects Administration in 1935, the WPA was the largest of the many programs developed during Roosevelt's "New Deal." In 1939, the agency's name was changed to Works Progress Administration, and continued as such until its demise in 1943.

The Federal Writers' Project, a division of the WPA (known as Federal Project Number One), created jobs for many unemployed librarians, clerks, researchers, editors, and historians. The workers went to courthouses, town halls, offices in large cities, vital statistics offices and inventoried records. Besides indexing works, many records were transcribed. One of these many projects was the *Inventory of the County Archives* which has benefitted genealogists and historians. The inventories listed the records, either by volumes or file boxes and years per record type, within the office. Although the WPA oversaw this project, the information for each volume of records may differ significantly by the information submitted.

For information regarding three of the "New Deal" projects designed to get people working, see: CCC (Civilian Conservation Corps), WPA, and NYA (National Youth Administration) see: CCC: **https://en.wikipedia.org/wiki/Civilian_Conservation_Corps;** NYA **https://en.wikipedia.org/wiki/National_Youth_Administration;** and WPA: **https://en.wikipedia.org/wiki/Works_Progress_Administration.**

The information herein is verbatim except for obvious spelling errors. Records listed may have met the requirement for retention and have been destroyed as per the records retention act, while other records are considered permanent records. (*See:* **https://codes.ohio.gov/ohio-revised-code** Ohio Revised Code, sections 149.31 and 149.34). Records once considered "open" to the public, such as lunacy, idiotic, and juvenile cases, may be "closed" due to a revision of state laws. However, the records may be opened to family members with adequate proof of lineage.

PREFACE
2nd Edition

The addresses and website section of this edition list an up-to-date location guide to each office mentioned, if located.

This project was to encompass all of Ohio's 88 counties although approximately 30 of these inventories have been located while others may be missing or never done.

Mention is made of the Ohio State Archaeological Society now known as the Ohio History Connection, 800 East 17th Avenue, Columbus, Ohio, **www.ohiohistory.org.**

Jana Sloan Broglin
Fellow, Ohio Genealogical Society
Swanton, Ohio
2025

PREFACE
1st Edition

The Survey of State and Local Historical Records, under the national direction of Dr. Luther H. Evans, was initiated as a nation-wide undertaking in January 1936, as a part of the Federal Writers' Project of the Works Progress Administration. General regulations and procedures applicable to all project units in the forty-eight states have been followed in Ohio. The Survey began operations in February 1936, under the technical supervision of Dr. William D. Overman, State Archivist and Curator of History, Ohio State Archaeological and Historical Society. In the sixteen districts of the Works Progress Administration in Ohio, the project was organized and operated by the district supervisors of the Writers' Project. In November 1936, the Survey became an independent part of the Federal Project No. 1, but its administration and operation in Ohio remained unchanged.

The objective of the Survey in Ohio has been the preparation of complete inventories of the records of the state and of each county, city, and other local governmental unit. Although a condensed form of entry is used, information is given as to the limiting dates of all extant records, the contents of individual series, and location of records in statehouse, county courthouse, or other depository.

The *Inventory of County Archives in Ohio* will, when completed, consist of a separate number for each county in the state. The units of the series are numbered according to the respective position of the county in an alphabetical list of the counties. Thus, the inventory herewith presented for Hamilton County is No. 31. The inventory of the State archives and of municipal and other local records will constitute separate publications.

The principle followed in the inventory of county records has been to place a record in the office of origin rather than in the place of deposit. The records are arranged with those of the executive branch of the county government first, followed by judicial, law enforcing, fiscal, and miscellaneous agencies. Minor agencies are placed in the general arrangement according to function rather than according to constitutional or statutory responsibility to a major subdivision. The legal development of each office or agency has been treated in a prefatory section preceding the inventory of the records of the office.

The survey in Hamilton County, under the direction of Harry Graff, district supervisor, was started in February 1936 and completed in July 1937. The project employed an average of eighteen editors, journalists, and clerks. Fieldworkers under the immediate supervision of Howard Sagmaster carefully inventoried all county records. Hearty co-operation has been encountered among county officials.

Indicative of the value of the inventory is the fact that the director of the Bureau of Municipal Research is compiling a chronological index to those records which trace the growth of civic functions. For the completeness and accuracy of the inventory, the project personnel in Hamilton County have been entirely responsible; the state office staff, under Dr. Overman and John O. Marsh, state supervisor, edited the legal histories and prepared the final manuscript.

The various units of the *Inventory of County Archives* will be issued in mimeographed form for free distribution to state and local public officials and public libraries in Ohio, and to a limited number of libraries and government agencies outside the state. Requests for information concerning particular units of the *Inventory* should be addressed to The Historical Records Survey, 337 South High Street, Columbus, Ohio.

James G. Dunton
State Director
The Historical Records Survey

Columbus, Ohio
October 1, 1937

ADC . . . . Aid to Dependent Children
ad valorem tax . . . . according to value
adm. . . . . administration
am.. . . . . amended
Arch. . . . . Archaeological
Art. . . . . Article
c. . . . . copyright
capias . . . . a warrant or order for arrest of a person
typically issued by the judge or magistrate in a case.
CCC. . . . . Civilian Conservation Corps
certiorari. . . . . to be more fully informed
chap(s). . . . . chapter(s)
comp. . . . . compiler
Const. . . . . Constitution
ed(s). . . . . editor(s)
et al. . . . . (et alii), and others
et seq . . . . and the following
(et) passim . . . . and here and there
ex officio . . . . as a result of one's status or position
et seq. . . . . and following
fee simple . . . . full and irrevocable ownership
G. C. . . . . General Code
habeas corpus . . . . protection against illegal imprisonment
ibid. . . . . the same reference
loc. cit. . . . . *(loco citato)* in the place cited
N. P. . . . . The Ohio NISI PRIUS REPORTS
n. p. . . . . no place of publication shown
NRS. . . . . Nonresident Service
n. s. . . . . new series
nolle prosequi . . . . notice of abandonment by a
plaintiff or prosecutor of all or part of a suit or action
NYA . . . . National Youth Administration

O. L. .... *Laws of Ohio*
op. cit. .... (*opere citato*) In the work cited
posse comitatus............ a group of citizens called upon to assist the sheriff
praecipes.................................... a written request for action
prima facie .... on the first impression
pro rata... in proportion
procedendo .... sends case from appellate court to a lower court
pt. .... part
PWA .... Public Works Administration
quo warranto............................. by what authority or warrant
replevins .... return of personal property
                                    wrongfully taken or held by a defendant
R. S. .... Revised Statutes
SS .... State Service
sec(s)....................................... section(s)
sic .... thus, following copy
supersedeas............. a stay of enforcement of a judgment pending appeal
TS .... transient service
v. .... versus
venires....................... a group of people summoned for jury duty
vol(s). .... volume(s)
WPA .... Works Progress/Projects Administration
writ .... a formal, legal document, a decree
x .... by
— .... current, to date
4-H .... (Four - H)

ABBREVIATIONS, SYMBOLS, AND EXPLANATORY
NOTES

Each chapter or section of "County Offices and Their Records" consists of an essay describing the legal status and functions of one department of county government and an inventory of the records of that department.

Each record constitutes a separate entry. Entries are arranged under topical headings and subheadings.

Each entry sets forth, insofar as applicable, the following:

1. Entry number. Entries are numbered consecutively throughout the inventory.

2. The exact title as it appears on the record, or if the record has no title a supplied title in brackets. If the title of the record is non-descriptive, misleading, or incorrect an additional title (in capitals and lowercase letters), also enclosed in brackets, has been supplied.

3. Dates show inclusive years or parts of years covered by the record. Breaks in dates indicate that the record is missing or was not kept between dates shown. A dash in place of the final date indicates an open record. If no current entries have been made the date of the last entry is noted. Where no statement is made that the record was discontinued at the last date shown, it could not be definitely established that such was the case. Where no comment is made on the absence of prior and subsequent records, no definite information could be obtained.

4. Quantity, given in chronological order wherever possible.

5. Labeling. Numbers and letters within parentheses indicate labeling on volumes, file boxes, or other containers.

6. Variations in title. The current or most recent title is used but significant variations are shown with dates for which each was used.

7. Change of agency. Occasionally a record is discontinued as a county record and kept by some other agency.

8. Description. A statement of the nature and purpose of the record and of what the record shows. As the contents of a record may vary, over time the description may differ somewhat from the record at any one period. Wherever feasible, changes in content are shown with dates. In map and plat entries the names of author and publisher and the scale are omitted only when not available.

9. Arrangement. Records said to be alphabetically arranged are frequently alphabetized only as to initial letter of the surname. This is true especially where there is a secondary arrangement.

10. Indexing. Self-contained indexes are described in the entry. Separate indexes constitute separate entries with cross references to and from the record entry.

11. Nature of recording. Changes are indicated with dates.

12. Condition. No statement is made if good or excellent.

13. Number of pages. Averaged for the series.

14. Dimensions show size of volumes, maps, file boxes, or other containers and are expressed in inches in every instance. The dimensions of volumes are given in order of height, width, and thickness; of file boxes in order of height, width, and depth.

15. Location. Rooms referred to are in the county courthouse unless some other building is specified.

Title line cross references are used to complete series where a record is kept separately for a period of time or in other records for different periods of time. They are also used in all artificial entries which are made to show, under their proper office, records kept in the same volume or file with records of another office. In both instances, the description of the master entry shows the title and entry number of the record from which the cross reference is made. Dates shown in the description of the master entry are for the part or parts of the record contained therein, and are shown only when they vary from those of the master entry. Artificial entries show only title, dates, and description.

Separate third paragraph cross references from entry to entry, are used to show prior, subsequent, or related records which are not a part of the same series. If, however, both entries are under the same subject headings, no third paragraph references are made. "See also" references from subject headings refer to entries in the same department which contain records logically belonging under that heading but which have been classified under an equally appropriate heading.

Hamilton, second largest county in the state in population, and the second to be proclaimed a county (January 4, 1790) is the southwestern most subdivision of the state of Ohio. Cincinnati, a city of 451,160 population, is the county seat. With an area of 407 square miles, the county is bounded on the south by the Ohio River, on the west by Dearborn County, Indiana at the southwestern corner by the great Miami River; on the north by Warren and Butler Counties (formed from its own territory in 1808); and on the east by Clermont County and the Little Miami River, beyond which, from the northeastern corner of the county, runs a narrow strip of Warren County.

For some time before the close of the Revolutionary War, and thereafter, the states of Massachusetts, Connecticut, and New York laid claims under the Old colonial grants, two parts of the territory now occupied by the state of Ohio. The state of Virginia claimed the whole of the territory Northwest of the Ohio River, under the colonial charters granted by King James I, in 1608, 1609, and 1611, and by the right of conquest of General George Rogers Clark in 1788-1799. (B. A. Hinsdale, *The Old Northwest,* N. Y., 1888, 192-193). These conflicting claims were settled when all the states ceded their rights to the United States; and Virginia, after much controversy, was allowed to retain the territory between the Scioto and Little Miami Rivers, which came to be known as the Virginia Military District. (*Ibid.,* 242-245).

The Ohio land embraced in the Virginia Military District is composed of Adams, Brown, Clinton, Clermont, Highland, Fayette, Madison, and Union Counties; portions of Scioto, Pike, Ross, Pickaway, Franklin, Marion, Delaware, Hardin, Logan, Clark, Greene, Champaign, and Warren Counties; and that portion of Hamilton County lying east of the Little Miami River in Anderson Township. (Henry A. Ford and Kate B. Ford, comps., *History of Hamilton County,* Cleveland, 1881. 35).

The Congress Lands, by far the largest partition of land in the history of land titles in Ohio, comprised all that territory lying in Hamilton County west of the Great Miami River, viz.: Whitewater, Harrison, and Crosby townships. The immense tract of which these lands are part was surveyed and marketed by direct sales from the Treasury Department of the Government, then called the "board of treasury," as soon as practicable after passage of a Congressional Ordinance to that effect, May 20, 1785, when the several states claiming ownership had all made deeds of cession to the United States, and the title had been cleared and perfected by Indian treaties. (Hinsdale, *op. cit.,* 255).

Following the Ordinance of 1785, which provided for the survey and sale of public lands (Hinsdale, *op. cit.,* 258), the historic Ordinance of July 13, 1787, which established the Northwest Territory (Hinsdale, *op. cit.,* 262-279), and another measure granting authority to the government "board of treasury" to contract for the sale of public lands (Hinsdale, *op. cit.,* 276), means were provided for a civilized settlement of that territory in the southern part of Ohio now known as Hamilton County.

In the meantime, in 1786, the region between the two Miamis was explored by Major Benjamin Stites, trader of Redstone, Pennsylvania. With supplies for settlers, he had arrived at Limestone (Maysville), Kentucky, in the midst of consternation over the theft of horses by Indians from the North. Heading an organization to recover the horses, Stites trailed the Indians across the river into the upper Miami country. Stites did not find the horses, but he did find a country so beautiful and fertile that he determined to start a settlement here and walked to New York to ask congress for a land grant.

Stites interested John Cleves Symmes, Congressman from Trenton, New Jersey, who visited the country with five companions the following summer. As enthusiastic as Stites, Symmes returned home, and on October 2, 1787, secured a contract for land between the two Miamis, which on survey proved to be 600,000 acres. Of this land, for which he had paid sixteen and two-thirds cents an acre, he sold, 20,000 acres to Stites.

In January 1788, the entire section 18 in the fourth township and first fractional range, and the fractional number lying between it and the river was purchased by Matthias Denman, of New Jersey. (Deed recorded March 17, 1821, Hamilton County Recorder's office).

By the winter of 1788-1789 scattered white settlements surrounded the Miami Purchase. On November 18, 1788, Major Benjamin Stites founded Columbia, the first white settlement in the new country, about three-quarters of a mile west of the Little Miami River. (Beverly W. Bond, Jr., *The Civilization of the Old Northwest, 1788-1812,* N.Y., 1934, 12). Major Stites erected several blockhouses for the eighteen men; and one sergeant was dispatched to the scene by the government for the protection of the settlers. One month after Stites settled at Columbia, a party composed of immigrants from New York, New Jersey, and Kentucky arrived at the cove opposite the emergence of the Licking River into the Ohio and founded Losantiville (a Latin-French compound signifying "the village opposite the mouth of the Licking"). (S. B. Nelson & Co., pub., *History of*

Cincinnati and Hamilton County, Ohio, Cincinnati, 1894, 31). The third settlement, organized in February 1789, by Judge Symmes and a party of sixty persons from New Jersey, was called North Bend, because it was at the northernmost bend of the Ohio River between the Muskingum and the Mississippi. (*Ibid.,* 18).

On January 2, 1790, General Arthur St. Clair arrived at Losantiville to establish headquarters for the Northwest Territory, of which he was the newly appointed governor. He found a cluster of log cabins along the river front and a backwoods fort (Fort Washington) on the plateau just above.

On January 4, the governor renamed the settlement Cincinnata (later the name was changed to Cincinnati) in honor of the Society of Cincinnati, of whose Pennsylvania branch he was president (Rev. Charles Frederic Goss, *Cincinnati the Queen City, 1788-1912,* 2 volumes, Cincinnati, 1912, I, 91) and proclaimed as a county that vast area comprising about one-eighth the present state of Ohio. The name Hamilton was given to the county by Judge Symmes, in honor of his friend Alexander Hamilton, then Secretary of the United States Treasury. (Bond, *op. cit.,* 61).

On the day Hamilton County was proclaimed, commissions were issued by the governor for a county court of common pleas and a court of general quarter sessions of the piece. William McMillan, William Goforth, and William Wells were appointed judges of the court of common pleas and justices of the court of general quarter sessions of the peace. Three other justices were also appointed at this time – Benjamin Stites, John Gano, and Jacob Topping. John Brown was commissioned to sheriff and Israel Ludlow was made prothonatary [sic] to the court of common pleas and clerk of the court of general quarter sessions of the peace. (Clarence Edwin Carter, *The Territorial Papers of the United States*, Washington, 1934, III 294-295). On May 24, William Burnet was appointed recorder of deeds; and constitutional government for the county was thus established. (*Ibid.,* 343).

The boundaries established by the governor's proclamation were as follows: "Beginning on the Bank of the Ohio River at the Confluence of the Little Miami & down the said Ohio River to the Mouth of the big Miami & thence up said Miami to the standing Stone Forks or Branch of said River & thence with a Line to be drawn due East to the little Miami & down said little Miami River to the Place of Beginning." (*Ibid.,* 294-295). In 1796, by proclamation of Governor St. Clair, Hamilton County's boundaries were extended along the Ohio River just west of the Scioto River, and to the North and West to Wayne's Treaty Line, at Detroit. By 1815, however, this area, 5,000 square miles, had been reduced and ten additional counties carved from the territory originally known as Hamilton County. (Ford and Ford, *op. cit.*, 68-69).

Hamilton County, like other counties created from the Symmes (or Miami) Purchase, was settled largely by emigrants from New Jersey, Pennsylvania, New England, and Virginia. The population of the county increased from 15,285 in 1810 to 80,145 in 1840. (*Population, U. S. Eleventh Census,* 1880, pt. i, 35).

These intensely religious pioneers were diligent in establishing houses of worship. Baptist and Methodist congregations, established at the close of the eighteenth century, were soon supplemented by congregations of Presbyterians, Lutherans, and Friends. By 1850 there were 156 churches in the county. The Methodist led in number with thirty-eight houses of worship; the Presbyterians came next; and several other denominations including Congregationalists, Christians, Lutherans, Moravians, and Jews had meeting houses. (*U. S. Seventh Census,* 1850, 870-879). Seventeenth century puritanism still survived, and the choice topics of the pulpit were the joys of death and the horrors of hell. Cards and billiards were, of course, prohibited by law. (Mrs. [T. A.] Trollope, *Domestic Manners of the Americans,* 2 volumes, London, 1832, I, 101-109).

An important element of the population comprised the Germans who, after the unsuccessful political upheavals of 1830 and 1848 in Europe, fled to America and founded homes, in some ways similar to those in Europe, in the Miami Valley. (*Ohio State Journal,* November 8, 1842. Interesting biographical sketches of some of the early German immigrants settling in Cincinnati, many of whom were graduates of universities in their fatherland, appear in Gustav Philipp Koerner's *Das Deutsche element in den Vereinigten Staaten von Nordamerica, 1818-1848,* Cincinnati, 1880, 177-225). In time Cincinnati became the most European city in Ohio, and in its customs, language, manners, and habits was as much European as American. Indeed, when Frederika Bremer visited Cincinnati in the fifties she found the Germans residing over the Rhine (north and east of the canal) living as they had in their fatherland; drinking beer, practicing music, and still pondering "*über die Weltgeschichte.*" (Frederika Bremer, *The Homes in the New World,* 2 volumes, N. Y. 1853, II 165-166; Edward Dicey, *Six Months in the Federal States,* 2 volumes, London, 1863, II, 55). The strait-laced puritanism manifest in Cincinnati during the earlier years of its existence was somewhat softened by the presence of the German settlers, who, as in their native land, considered Sunday to be a day of recreation as well as a day of worship. (For a resume see *Columbian and Great West,* September 2, 1854; Cincinnati *Gazette,* June 5, 1849).

The steady influx of the foreign-born soon aroused in the ardent nativist fear of dangers which might result from unrestricted immigration. Greater alarm was occasioned by the fact that many of the newcomers were communicants of the Catholic faith. The need for the large German Catholic population for services in German had been met in St. Peter's Cathedral (dedicated December 17, 1826) by the holding of German masses at an assigned hour (11 A. M.). In 1834, the cornerstone of the first German Catholic Church west of the Alleghenies was laid in Cincinnati. (*Catholic Telegraph*, April 19, 1834). The construction of additional Catholic churches to accommodate the ever increasing communicants of that faith was terrifying to the older stock, who immediately suspected that the Pope was attempting to colonize the Mississippi Valley. (Lyman Beecher, *A Plea for the West*, Cincinnati, 1835, 51-53; *Presbyterian of the West*, August 4, 1842; *Catholic Telegraph*, April 19, 1834.). The forensic duel between the two religions, beginning in the late thirties as a result of a debate between Archbishop Purcell and Alexander Campbell as to the merits and demerits of Catholicism, continued to be waged with varying degrees of intensity in the following decades, and finally was culminated in the formation of the American party in the middle fifties. Having, as its tenets, America for the Americans, stricter naturalization laws, and war to the hilt on Romanism, this party proved to be a convenient haven for old-line Whigs rather than a purely nativistic organization. Succeeding decades saw the addition of large numbers of immigrants to the population of the county. However, the foreign population of Cincinnati has steadily declined from 42 percent in 1839 to 6 percent in 1930. (Cincinnati *Gazette*, December 6, 1839; *Population. U. S. Census*, 1930, III, pt. i, 521.) The antagonism between religious and racial groups, although evidenced again in the nineties and following the World War, has steadily declined. (For an interesting study in war hysteria see Carl Wittke, *German-Americans and the World War, Ohio Historical Collections*, V, Columbus, 1936).

The growth and population was accompanied by a similar increase in manufacturing. After the opening of the Ohio River to navigation (1816), the construction of the Ohio Canal (1827), and the laying of railways, the industrial growth of the county was rapid. (For an account of the early commercial and business activities of Hamilton County see *The Ohio Gazetteer*, Columbus, 1819, 45, 82; *ibid.*, 1833, 130; Cincinnati *Gazette*, June 17, July 21, 1828). By the decade of the fifties Cincinnati, known as the gateway to the west because of her strategic position, was a well-known manufacturing center producing clothing, furniture, soap, pottery, and wagons for the markets of the South and Southwest. (*Annual*

Report of the Commissioner of Statistics, 1857, no. 8, 506-507.) Cincinnati likewise developed into the chief packing center of the west, a position which she held until the decade of the sixties. (Cincinnati *Gazette,* October 13, 1852.) At the same time, the city became an important wholesale center and Cincinnati "drummers" were visiting the markets not only of the South, but of the newer North and Northwest. Indeed, fear of a possible cancellation of the usual southern orders caused many Cincinnatians to attempt to curb the abolitionist propaganda, which, beginning in the thirties, was causing a gradual tightening of political and of sectional lines. "The Southern feeling is too strong in this city; the interest of her merchants, her capitalists, and her tradesmen, are too deeply interwoven with a Southern country; commercial and social intercourse between her citizens and the citizens of the South Western states are too intimate," wrote the editor of the Cincinnati *Republican,* "to admit the successful operation, of a Society, tending to separate the ties which connect the city with those States, and withdraw from her their confidence and trade." (Cincinnati *Republican,* January 18, 1835.)

Regardless of the efforts of the pro slavery groups to check the abolitionist crusade by expelling the free negroes [sic] from Cincinnati in 1829 by destroying the abolitionist press of James G. Birney in 1836 and by prohibiting anti-slavery meetings, Cincinnati furnished a portion of the scene and topic for the outstanding propaganda novel of the period, *Uncle Tom's Cabin,* which, according to James Ford Rhodes, was one of the most potent factors in crystallizing the anti-slavery sentiment in the North, and assuring the election of Abraham Lincoln in 1860. (Cincinnati *Gazette,* October 28, November 27, 1829; Cincinnati *Republican,* August 1, 1836; James Ford Rhodes, *History of the U. S. from the Compromise of 1850.* 7 volumes, N. Y., 1893-1906, I, 279-285.) Besides the commercial interest which opposed the agitation of the slavery issue there were the old-line Whigs, who, following the dissolution of their party in 1854, still placed their union-saving sentiments above sectional party lines and labored, as members of the American party and later as Republicans, for a preservation of the Union.

Although Cincinnati lost its economic supremacy in the nation, following the War between the States, to such rapidly developing communities as New York, Chicago, and St. Louis (after the construction of the trunk line railways), the city continues to be one of the important industrial centers of the United States. According to the census of 1930, her 2,018 manufacturing establishments, employing 85,421 men, produce annually products valued at $729,019,066. (*Manufacturing. U. S. Fifteenth Census,* 1930, III, 398.)

As a result of the early industrialization of Cincinnati, Hamilton County became a center of the labor movement. As early as 1827 the laboring men of Hamilton County established co-operative stores, and in 1836 they began to publish in Cincinnati a weekly paper known as the *Workingmen's Friend*, which was devoted to the interest and instruction of the working classes. (Cincinnati *Republican,* June 22, 1836.) Labor unions, established during the thirties and forties, were successively destroyed by the panics of 1837 and 1857. Following the War between the States, Hamilton County labor leaders, as those in other industrial counties of the nation, again affected combinations to promote the interests of labor. The railway unions, militant during the earlier years of their success, participated in the first general railway strike in 1877. It was not, however, until the decades of the eighties and nineties that labor, like capital, was able to organize on an extensive scale. During this period Cincinnati became a center of action for labor politicians, who were attempting to solve the problem of the farmer and the factory worker by political action. Although the industrial tranquility of the county has been occasionally marred by recurring minor strikes and lockouts, the relations between capital and labor have been, in the main, satisfactory. (For a discussion of the labor movement in the briefest compass, see Samuel P. Orth, *The Armies of Labor, The Chronicles of America Series,* XL.)

The county is well supplied with schools, libraries, and newspapers. The University of Cincinnati, begun in 1858, and formally established by legislative act in 1870, and Xavier University established in 1831 and incorporated by the legislature in 1842 (40 O. L., 84), are but two of the institutions of higher learning.

The population of the county had advanced, from 313,374 in 1880, to 409,479 in 1900, to 450,732 in 1910 (*Population, U. S. Thirteenth Census*, 1910, III, 406.) According to the census of 1930, the population of the county was 589,356. (*Population, U. S. Fifteenth Census*, 1930, III, pt. ii, 521.)

Ohio counties were laid out to fit the needs of an agricultural society of the nineteenth century. The last Ohio county was created in 1851 and there have been no changes in boundaries for over half a century. The counties now range in population from 10,000 to 1,200,000. Approximately seventy of Ohio's eighty-eight counties may be considered rural. (R. E. Heiges, *The Office of Sheriff in the Rural Counties of Ohio*, Findlay, Ohio, 1933, 52.) The average population is 30,000 but over half of the people live in eight large urban counties.

The county is a creation of the state for the execution of state policy and has such powers as the state confers on it. It has, however, had to provide an ever-increasing number of local services similar to those rendered by municipalities and its legal status is therefore changing. The county eventually may become relatively less the agent of the state and tend to approximate the municipal corporation in the character of its activities and in its legal status. (Report of Governor's Commission, *The Reorganization of County Government in Ohio*, 1934, 3, 28-29.)

The board of county commissioners is the central feature of the structure of the county government. The functions of this board touch either directly or indirectly every other branch and department. The board is the agency in whose name actions for and against the county are brought. This board is empowered to determine certain policies for the conduct of county affairs such as adoption of the budget, establishment of services left optional by law, and the authorization of improvements. Thus in a limited sense it constitutes the legislative branch. The board also functions as a central administrative body although much of the administration, centered in other elective offices, is beyond its control. The county auditor was originally made secretary of the board and still functions as such in the majority of the counties. Later provisions of the law permitted the board to appoint its own clerk, thus removing this duty from the auditor. (*Ibid.*, 58-59.)

There are three types of financial functions performed by county officers and employees: tax administration, handling of the fiscal affairs of the county, and the trusteeship of funds held for individuals in court procedure. The principal financial authorities are the board of commissioners, auditor, and treasurer. The commissioners levy taxes, appropriate funds, and authorize payments. The auditor's primary duties are the keeping of accounts, issuance of warrants, valuation of real estate, and preparation of the tax list. The treasurer collects taxes, receives and has custody of county moneys, and disburses upon warrant from the auditor. (*Ibid.*, 71).

There are three strictly clerical officers whose work consists mainly of the preparation and custody of records: recorder, clerk of courts, and judge of the probate court. All three have some part in the recording of documents and instruments affecting the title of property and of other documents presented for record. The last two have as their principal duty the keeping of court records: the clerk of courts serving both as clerk of the court of appeals and the common pleas court, and the probate court looking after its own records. (Report of Governor's Commission, *op. cit.,* 179.)

It is the duty of the recorder to copy, index, and file documents authorized to be recorded in his office. These consist almost entirely of chattel mortgages and instruments affecting the title to real estate. (Report of Governor's Commission, *op. cit.,* 180.) The system of recording is prescribed by statute. With the exception of a few urban counties recording is done by typewriter with considerable use of printed forms. The photographic method of copying is now in use in Clark, Cuyahoga, Hamilton, Lucas, Montgomery, and Summit Counties.

The principal records of the clerk of courts are prescribed by statute. They include an appearance docket, execution docket, journal of the orders of the court, complete record of case papers, a system of indexes, and the file of original papers. The clerk is responsible for a variety of non-judicial record work, of which the filing and indexing of automobile bills of sale is the major item. At present the clerk acts as the agent of the state for the sale of hunting and fishing licenses and also issues auctioneers' and ferry licenses.

The probate judge is by statute the clerk of his own court. The Constitution permits the combination of the probate and common pleas courts in counties of less than 60,000 population. In this case the judge of common pleas becomes ex officio the clerk of the probate division and two separate offices are retained for keeping of records. Such mergers now exist in three counties: Adams, Henry, and Wyandot. (Report of Governor's Commission, *op. cit.,* 182-183.)

Listed below, with amendments, are some notable provisions adopted at the conventions of 1851 and 1912 which affected the organization of county government:

"Laws may be passed to secure to mechanics, artisans, laborers, subcontractors and material men, their just dues by direct lien upon the property, upon which they have bestowed labor or for which they have furnished material. (Art. II, sec. 33. 1851.) "All nominations for elective state, district, county and municipal offices shall be made at direct primary elections or by petition as provided by law. . ." (Art. V, sec. 7, 1912.) "The General Assembly shall provide by general law for the organization and government of counties, and may provide by general law alternative forms of county government. No alternative form shall become operative in any county until submitted to the electors thereof and approved by a majority of those voting. . .Municipalities and townships shall have authority, with the consent of the county, to transfer to the county any of their powers or to revoke the transfer of any such power, under regulations provided by general law, but the rights of initiative and referendum shall be secured to. . .every measure. . .giving or withdrawing such consent," (Art. X, sec. 1, amendment adopted 1933.)

"Appointments and promotions in the civil service of the state, the several counties, and cities, shall be made according to merit and fitness, to be ascertained, as far as practicable, by competitive examinations." (Art. SC, sec. 10, 1912.)

"Elections for state and county officers shall be held on the first Tuesday after the first Monday in November and the even-numbered years." (Art. XVII, sec. 1, amendment adopted 1905.)

The aim of the survey has been to make information available regarding the records which have accumulated over a period of more than 130 years. Survey workers have not made a study of the functions of the county offices with a view toward recommending any reorganization of county government but in the report of the governor's commission (*op. cit.,* 186-187) recommendations were made bearing upon the records system as follows:

1. County charters and optional forms of government should provide for a department of records and court service to take over the functions of the recorder and clerk of courts, the non-judicial record work of the probate court, and functions of sheriff as a court officer. (See also Heiges, *op. cit.,* 55-66.)

2. The issuance of licenses should be transferred from clerk of courts to department of finance.

3. Wider use should be made of the photographic process of recording in larger counties.

4. Legislation should be adopted permitting destruction of chattel mortgages and automobile bills of sale after they have ceased to have effect.

5. The requirements of the system of indexes of cases in the clerk's office should be eliminated from the code and only the index of pending suits and living judgments should be required.

6. Provisions should be made in the rules of the common pleas court for service of process by mail and that method should be brought into general use. (See also Heiges, *op. cit.,*60-61.)

Following the report of the governor's commission a new law (116 O. L. 132-133) was passed in 1933 permitting any county to adopt a charter or an alternative form of government, as provided in section 3 of Article X of the Constitution of Ohio, if it does not interfere with or restrict in any manner a charter which has been adopted by any municipal government. The electors may establish by charter provision a civil service commission or personnel department. In April 1935 (116 O. L. 134) the legislature also provided that the electors of any county may establish by charter provision a county department of health.

Hamilton County built its first courthouse in compliance with an act of the Territorial Legislature, passed in 1792, which required every county to erect a "courthouse, jail pillory whipping-post, and several stocks, constructed of such materials and to such dimensions and on such plans as directed by the judges of the court of common pleas. (Theodore Calvin Pease, *Laws of the Northwest Territory 1788-1800, Illinois State Bar Association Law Services* I, Springfield, 1925, 78.) Erected in 1802, the courthouse was a crude limestone building on the public square, near the southwest corner of Fifth and Main Streets, fronting on Fifth.

The building, which cost $3,000, was constructed, after a plan furnished by Judge Turner of the court of common pleas, in the shape of a parallelogram, with a frontage of 42 feet and the depth of 55 feet. The walls, including the parapet, were 42 feet high. The jail, of one story, 16 feet square, and constructed of logs, faced on Fifth Street west of the courthouse, with a whipping-post and pillory a little to the front. (Henry A. Ford and Kate B. Ford, comps. *History of Hamilton County, 1789-1881,* Cleveland, 1881, 232-233.)

During the War of 1812 this first courthouse was used as a barracks for soldiers. In 1814 it was destroyed by fire. Deciding to change the location of the courthouse, the county commissioners accepted a large tract of land at the corner of Court and Main Streets. A new (second courthouse) building, imposing for neither size nor beauty, was immediately begun; but it was not finished until 1819. (*Ibid.,* 233.)

The courthouse was situated, "itself and appurtenances, on a circular plat of ground about two hundred feet in diameter. . .It was a substantial and spacious structure, about 62 feet in length, east and west, and 56 feet in breadth, north and south, and elevated to the cornice, 50 feet, to the summit of the dome or cupola on the center of the uprising, four-sided roof, 120 feet, and to the top of the spire, 160 feet. It contained two fireproof rooms in which the clerk of the Court of Common Pleas, and the Supreme Court, and the Recorder of Deeds kept their offices. On the first floor over the basement with a large, spacious and commodious courtroom. . .This great room extended the whole length of the building, and was nearly 30 feet in width." About 1838 another, smaller courtroom was constructed in the old courthouse. This was in the second story, immediately above the larger room, and was occupied by the old superior court. The old courthouse also contained a sheriff's office not very large but convenient, a county commissioner's office, a grand jury room, and several other jury rooms.

"After some years, the necessities of increased business requiring it, there were two separate buildings erected on Main Street on the front line of the square, one north and one south of the line of the courthouse, the former one occupied by the Treasurer, Auditor, and County Commissioners' office, and the latter by the Clerk of Court of Common Pleas and the County Surveyor." (Judge [A. G.] Carter, *The Old Courthouse: Reminiscences and Anecdotes*. Cincinnati, 1880. 7-11.)

On Monday, July 9, 1849, fire again destroyed the county courthouse. After the fire, the courts, county offices, and law library found a temporary home in a large brick building of four stories on the northwest corner of Court Street and St. Clair Alley. (*Ohio Statesman*, July 12, 1849; Cincinnati *Enquirer*, July 10, 1849.) The county offices were accommodated on the second floor; the four rooms housing the supreme court, the court of common pleas, the superior, and the commercial courts were on the third floor, together with the law library, which at that date was very small. (Cincinnati *Gazette*, July 14, 1849.) Note papers of importance were lost in the fire. (Cincinnati *Enquirer*, July 11, 1849.) After the court of common pleas was reorganized in 1852, the entire third floor was utilized by this court. The superior and the commercial courts were provided with space on the second floor of a building across the alley on Court Street, the two structures being connected by a bridge across the alley. (Ford and Ford, *op. cit.*, 235.)

By the time the new courts had begun operation under the constitution of 1851, the lower story of the courthouse (third), was completed sufficiently for the courts, at the discretion of the county commissioners, to move from the temporary quarters to rooms in the new building. The judges objected to moving. One of the common pleas court judges issued a peremptory order to the sheriff that other quarters for the courts should be obtained. The sheriff accordingly rented on the northeast corner of Ninth and Walnut Streets a large building which he fitted up for the courts. (Ford and Ford, *op. cit.*, 235.)

After frequent delays occasioned by change of plans and conflicting views as to style and utility, the new courthouse (Cincinnati Gazette, September 17, November 7, 15, 1851; April 2, 1852) was finally completed, and in 1857 the courts and the county offices moved into their new quarters. (Cincinnati *Gazette*, January 8, July 1, 1857.) The building, which stood at Court and Main Streets upon the site of the old courthouse, had a front length and a depth of 190 feet and was 60 feet high, with three stories above the basement. (Ford and Ford, *op. cit.*, 235).

The ground floor of the building was occupied by the county treasurer, coroner, sheriff, and surveyor, with apartments in the rear corners allotted to the recorder and the clerk of courts for storage of records. The second floor housed the offices of the auditor, recorder, clerk of courts, probate court, and grand jury. On the third floor were offices of the courts of common pleas, superior court, and law library. Considered, at the time, to be a structure of great beauty, this building, constructed of stone and brick at a cost of $695,253, was thought to be fireproof, but in 1884 it, too, was destroyed by fire, in what has come to be known as the great "Courthouse Riot." (Cincinnati *Enquirer*, March 30, 1884.)

Kindled in the auditor's office by an angry mob, the fire spread rapidly to the probate courtroom, then to the clerk's and recorder's offices. In the meantime, the sheriff's and coroner's records had been completely destroyed by the surging mob. "In these offices," stated the *Enquirer*, "were stored the records of the county since its formation, over one hundred years ago, now all gone up in smoke, and never can be replaced." (Cincinnati *Enquirer*, March 30, 1884.)

After viewing the ruins, a reporter of the Cincinnati *Enquirer* wrote: "It is an incalculable loss. It is a loss, not a visible property, which may be replaced, but of intangible property which can never be. It is a loss which Hamilton County will feel for centuries hence, which will fatten unborn generations of lawyers, which will make many a poor man, many a widow and orphans sweat drops of agony as the property on which they relied for support is taken from them because they cannot prove the title by which their hold was good previous to 1884. If all the money and bonds in the County Treasurer's were taken it could be replaced. If every other piece of property belonging to the city or county were today smoking and ruined; if half the city lay in ashes, all could be replaced. But the County Records—never. Consider what property it was that the crowd so madly tore and threw into the flames. Records a century old; records of the infant Village of Cincinnati; transcripts from the United States Courts of instruments of the highest use to the citizens of their county, the proceedings of the Courts for a hundred years, of wills probated, of marriages and deaths—records in which many a title to property hang. All gone forever! The splendid Law Library—one of the finest in the land, one of the most complete, in which almost every law book published in the English Language could be found. It is only a matter of history now that it ever existed. It was not a destruction of paper and leather, as the destroyers imagined when they hurled the written books from their places. It was the vanishing of intangible property which will cost thousands of present and future citizens all their peace of mind. If the courthouse had only been made fireproof as the jail is." (Cincinnati *Enquirer*, March 30, 1884.)

The next building to house the county government, and imposing edifice in the Romanesque style, was regarded as a great work of architecture. At the time of first use, in 1887, this fourth courthouse was deemed adequate to accommodate county offices for many years to come. But, as time went on and county business increased to the point where space for the proper transaction of business was found inadequate, the need for a new courthouse became imperative; so that in 1915 work upon a fifth structure, the present courthouse, was commenced. Because of labor troubles and litigation, more than four years were required to complete the building, and it was not until September 1919, that the county offices moved into their present home. (Cincinnati *Enquirer*, June 26, 1935.)

The present courthouse is not only one of the largest buildings in Cincinnati, but it is also one of the most beautifully designed county buildings in the country. It occupies a plot one city block square, bounded by Central Parkway and Main, Court, and Sycamore Streets. Erected at a cost of $3,500,000, the building is a massive Grecian structure of rusticated masonry and Ionic columns. (Cincinnati *Enquirer*, June 26, 1935.)

Commissioners. Practically all records prior to 1884 were destroyed by the courthouse fire of that year. Extant records, generally in good condition, are housed in metal cabinets or on metal shelves. No additional space or filing equipment is needed at the present time.

Recorder. Records in the main offices, well-preserved and readily accessible, are housed on steel shelving and in steel filing cabinets, the more valuable of which are kept in a vault. Records housed in the basement storeroom are not in good condition and are covered with dust. There is ample room for expansion. No additional shelving or cabinets are needed at present. There are wooden tables and chairs for the accommodation of users in both the main offices and in the basement storeroom. Lighting, both artificial and natural, is good in the main offices but poor in the basement.

Deeds of the Symmes Purchase have been reproduced several times. The restored volumes, in good condition and easily accessible to the public, are housed in steel filing cabinets.

Clerk of Courts. Records, which include those of the common pleas, domestic relations, supreme, superior, insolvency, district, circuit, and appeals courts and the grand and petit juries, in custody of the clerk of courts are housed in Rooms 123, 328, and 329 of the courthouse, and in Rooms 113, 122, and 126, and in the attic storage in the Cincinnati City Hall.

Steel filing cabinets and steel cases with roller shelving are provided in Rooms 328 and 329 of the courthouse. There is ample space and equipment in Room 329, except in the automobile division, which is in need of both additional space and files. Room 328, likewise, is very crowded, with no space for much-needed additional equipment.

Assignment Commission. Records, generally in excellent condition, are housed in steel filing cabinets and a fireproof vault. There is ample space for expansion.

Probation Department. No additional filing equipment is required for records of the probation department. Present quarters, however, are crowded, and an additional thousand square feet of office space is recommended for the proper handling of cases.

Probate Court. Records of the probate court are generally in good condition and filed in an orderly manner. Most of the records are in volume form, properly indexed. All are housed in fireproof steel cabinets. Much improvement has been made during the past year in arranging and filing the records and in making them more readily accessible. There is adequate space and equipment to accommodate only records added during the next three or four years.

Older records, stored in steel cabinets in the basement, are in fair condition. No additional space is needed at present.

Jury Commission. Records, housed in steel filing cabinets in Room 415 of the courthouse, are in good condition and both neatly and efficiently arranged. There is ample space and adequate equipment to file the records for many years.

Prosecuting Attorney. Records, generally in good condition, are housed in steel cabinets and filed in logical order. There is adequate filing space, and no additional room will probably be needed for many years. However, for more efficient filing, several cabinets are needed at the present time.

Records prior to 1917 cannot be found. It is the opinion of incumbent officials that the records were moved to temporary quarters during construction of the present courthouse, and have not since been located.

Coroner. Records. Records are in good condition, properly indexed, and conveniently arranged upon shelves in steel filing cabinets. With the exception of a few records kept in the basement storeroom (particularly those dating from the courthouse fire of 1884), the archives are in a good state of preservation. The space available for the filing of records will be ample for some time.

Sheriff. Records are housed in Rooms 222 and 223 and in the county jail office on the sixth floor of the Hamilton County Courthouse. While affording considerable space for the routine work of this division, the quarters are inadequate for the proper filing, care, and preservation of records.

With the exception of records of the present sheriff and his immediate predecessor, and such other records that by law must be kept open for inspection, the archives are housed in a fireproof vault in the rear of Room 222. While this vault is commodious and well arranged for the filing of records, the space is used also as a storeroom for an assortment of gaming devices, liquor, clothing, and other articles held as evidence making it impossible properly to file and care for the records.

Records filed in the vault and outer offices, dating back to the riot and fire of 1884, are generally in excellent condition. A few volumes, preserved from the fire, are carefully wrapped and filed separately. These are practically worthless for reference, however, since their condition is such that they may not be handled without being completely destroyed.

Records in the jail office, sixth floor, consisting mostly of registers showing commitment, release, and social and criminal history of prisoners, are in excellent condition.

To facilitate reference and research work, it is suggested that the sheriff's office adopt a more complete indexing system. As in other important departments of county government, the sheriff's office also should be provided with storage quarters, removed from the office proper, to ensure more efficient filing and preservation of records.

Treasurer. Records are in good condition and, excepting those housed in the vault, are readily accessible. Most of the records are housed in steel cabinets and filing cases. Sales tax receipts and cashier's memoranda are kept in cardboard boxes in the vault. While these do not provide a fire hazard, it is suggested that steel shelves and cabinets be installed for more efficient filing. As a result of a completed WPA project, much improvement has been affected in the filing efficiency and accessibility of records in the basement storeroom. Space and equipment are not needed at present in the main offices, but are required in the basement quarters shared with the auditor.

Auditor. There are five general divisions of the auditor's office, all of which, with the exception of the general office and sealing and weights divisions, consist of several departments. The auditor has custody of the records of the budget commission and board of revision. Records in all offices are generally in good condition.

The bureau is adequately equipped with fireproof steel shutter cabinets. In these files are housed tax duplicate volumes, plat books, and other records used in the daily routine of the office. A large basement is used for filing of the older records and any others not handled in the regular routine. These records, housed in steel cabinets, are generally in good condition.

A spacious concrete and steel vault is provided for the storage of the more valuable records and any personal property of taxpayers.

A modern, extensive card index system, housed in steel filing cabinets, is readily accessible for the convenience of the public. Several clerks are assigned to keep this current record.

There is adequate space in this bureau for the addition of records for the next few years. Every care is taken to preserve an orderly filing arrangement, and to guard against loss, fire, and other hazards.

Purchasing Department. Records prior to 1932 have been destroyed, under provision of the law which permits the destruction of records following their certification by the state examiner.

All records are housed in identical filing cabinets, measuring 11 x 13 x 25, excepting addressograph and vendors' records which are kept in a steel cabinet, 20 x 24 x 42. Being standard, records of specifications are not dated.

The archives are generally in good condition. Additional space and equipment are required for more efficient filing, as the records are crowded in order to give space for the examination of merchandise to be purchased.

Board of Control. Records are housed in the basement storeroom of the superintendent of buildings.

Sinking Fund Trustees. Records, housed in steel filing cabinets, are in excellent condition. There is no separate office for this board; its records are kept in the auditor's office. No additional filing cabinets or space is needed. There is ample space for research work.

Board of Education. Most of these records, which are generally in good condition and readily accessible, are housed in steel cabinets and cases. No additional space is required at present.

Hillcrest and Glenview Schools. Records of the Hillcrest School for problem girls, which is in Wyoming, Ohio, are kept in the offices of the secretary to the superintendent, the parole and record officer, and the doctor. The first two offices are in the Administration Building and the last is in Cottage A.

All records are in excellent condition, properly filed in alphabetical order, and housed in wooden filing cabinets of the regulation type. Record space is ample for present needs. Better to safeguard records from fire hazard, steel filing cabinets should replace those of wood.

Few records of the school are preserved. The custom is to destroy all "unimportant" records after a number of years.

Records of the Glenview School, neatly arranged and well-preserved, are housed in steel filing cabinets. No additional space is required.

Board of Health. These quarters consist of an office (Room 404), 30 x 25 feet, and a storage room (Room 401), 8 x 14 feet, both of which are in a crowded condition. Approximately seventy-five percent of the bureau's records are housed in Room 401. Expansion is a vital need in Room 404, because of the accumulation of public school medical records. The storeroom, crowded with bundles of early records, requires steel cabinets for better filing. Many of the current records, now kept in cardboard or wooden boxes and filing cases, should likewise be transferred to steel cabinets. No facilities are provided for the use of the records.

Tuberculosis Hospital. Records, kept in the offices of the superintendent of the hospital, are in good condition.

County Home and Chronic Disease Hospital. Records, in excellent condition, are neatly housed in steel filing cabinets. No additional space or filing equipment is required. Accommodations for the use of the records are adequate.

Department of Public Welfare. Records for approximately the past two years are in good condition. Because of frequent changes in the method of keeping records, however, they are in many cases difficult to follow through without the guidance of an employee familiar with the various systems which have been used.

The major portion of the records are kept on the first floor of the main office building, Twelfth Street and Central Parkway, Cincinnati, Ohio; relief records, however, are housed at 411 Lincoln Park Drive.

For 1934 and previous years, there is no apparent plan for keeping records, with the exception of case records housed in the main office. Records other than case histories are incomplete, sometimes merely as bundles tied together and stored haphazardly in scattered cabinet sections.

The main office has ample space for present and future requirements and the filing equipment is generally fireproof and adequate.

Soldiers' Relief Commission. Records, in excellent condition and in good order, are housed in steel filing cabinets. No additional filing space is needed.

Blind Relief Commission. Records are neatly kept and housed in steel filing cabinets. No additional space or equipment is needed.

Aid to Dependent Children. Records are generally in good condition, their arrangement neat but inefficient because of crowding. They are housed in steel filing cabinets. Additional space and more adequate filing equipment is greatly needed.

Board of Elections. Records, in excellent condition, are housed in steel filing cabinets. Some records, such as ballots and poll books, are destroyed after the lapse of a limited time. There is ample space both for filing records and for accommodation of the public.

Permanent registration of voters is limited by law to certain urban communities, which include Cincinnati, Norwood, and St. Bernard.

Civil Service Commission. Records, kept neatly and in excellent condition, are housed in steel filing cabinets. No additional space or equipment is needed. Accommodations for research work are ample.

Engineer. The archives of the county engineer's office are in excellent condition. Housed in Rooms 209 and 225 in steel filing cabinets in wall racks of the roller type, records are readily accessible to the public.

While space for the filing of records in Room 209, the surveying division is adequate, the records here, predating those in the general office division and of greater historical value, are well preserved. It has been suggested that these records be filed in a vault, better to protect them from various hazards.

Most of the records in Room 225, the general office division, a series of five rooms accommodating the engineering, drafting, and sanitary departments, date to 1919, when the county engineer's office was made a district division of county government and its records removed from the offices of the county commissioners. These quarters are spacious; records are well cared for and readily accessible.

While a single record in this department antedates 1800, when the office was established by statute most of the other records date from the time of the courthouse riot and fire of 1884. Explosives fired in the riot were touched off immediately beneath the county commissioners' offices, where records of this department were on file. It was in this section of the building that the greatest damage was done.

Regional Planning Commission. Additional space and more equipment is necessary for the proper care and housing of the records. This single office, 25 feet square, in which this important division of the county government is required to transact business and to house its many valuable records, is inadequate. Filing space for the large amount of records measures but 117 linear feet. The office, in fact, is so crowded that there is no accommodation whatever for reference to records.

Board of Park Commissioners. Records, housed in steel filing cabinets, are in excellent condition. No additional filing equipment or floor space is needed at present. Chairs and tables are provided for use in referring to the records.

Conservancy District Board. Records of this board are housed at Dayton, Ohio.

Superintendent of County Buildings. Records in the basement storeroom of the superintendent of buildings are in good condition, but they are piled indiscriminately on maintenance supply shelves. All records are heavily covered with dust. Access to these records may be had on application to the superintendent of buildings.

Agricultural Society. Records, in excellent condition, are efficiently filed, being conveniently arranged for reference. Office space and filing equipment are adequate for requirements.

Dog Warden. In good condition, records are housed in steel filing cabinets. No additional filing equipment or space is needed. Accommodations for the public are adequate.

Hamilton County like other counties along the river front, has suffered from innumerable floods. The most serious floods (those of 1832, 1847, 1884, 1913, and 1937), although they left death and destruction in their wake, destroyed no county archives. Indeed, during the flood of 1847, the courthouse, favorably located and beyond the reach of the 63 foot crest, served as a haven of refuge for flood sufferers. (*Liberty Hall and Cincinnati Gazette,* February 23, 1832; Cincinnati *Gazette,* December 17, 1847; Cincinnati *Commercial Gazette,* February 15, 1884; Cincinnati *Commercial Tribune,* April 1, 1913; Cincinnati *Times-Star,* January 28, 1937.)

The records of Hamilton County, accumulating for years, have been successfully housed in five courthouses. During the early years of the nineteenth century many of the records were destroyed by fire, while many later records were destroyed by well-meaning officials, who, in their attempt to provide additional space for current records, were unable to distinguish between the important and the unimportant materials of the past. At present the records are well housed and are available, for the most part, to students and investigators. Although the records are well arranged, there is a growing need for systematic classification of documents and an index system whereby the documents may be easily and quickly found.

33

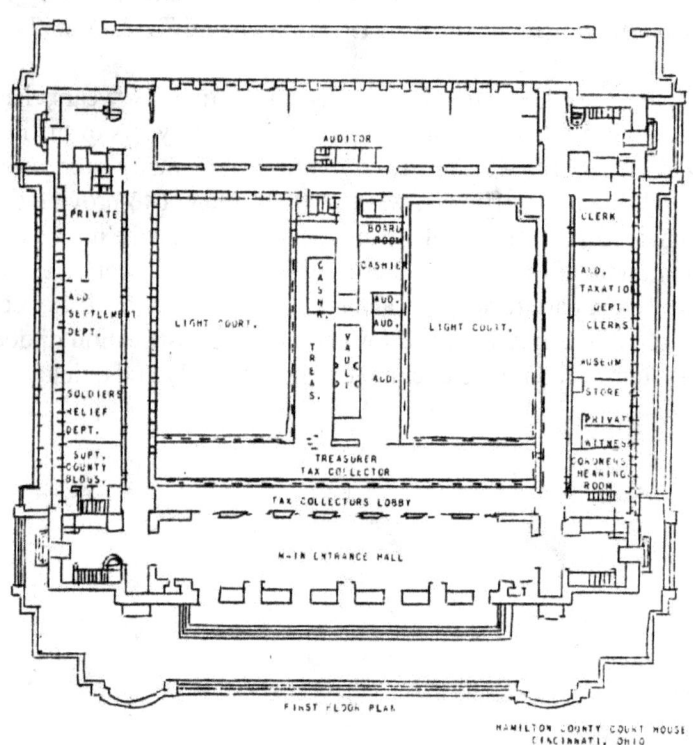

FIRST FLOOR PLAN

HAMILTON COUNTY COURT HOUSE
CINCINNATI, OHIO

34

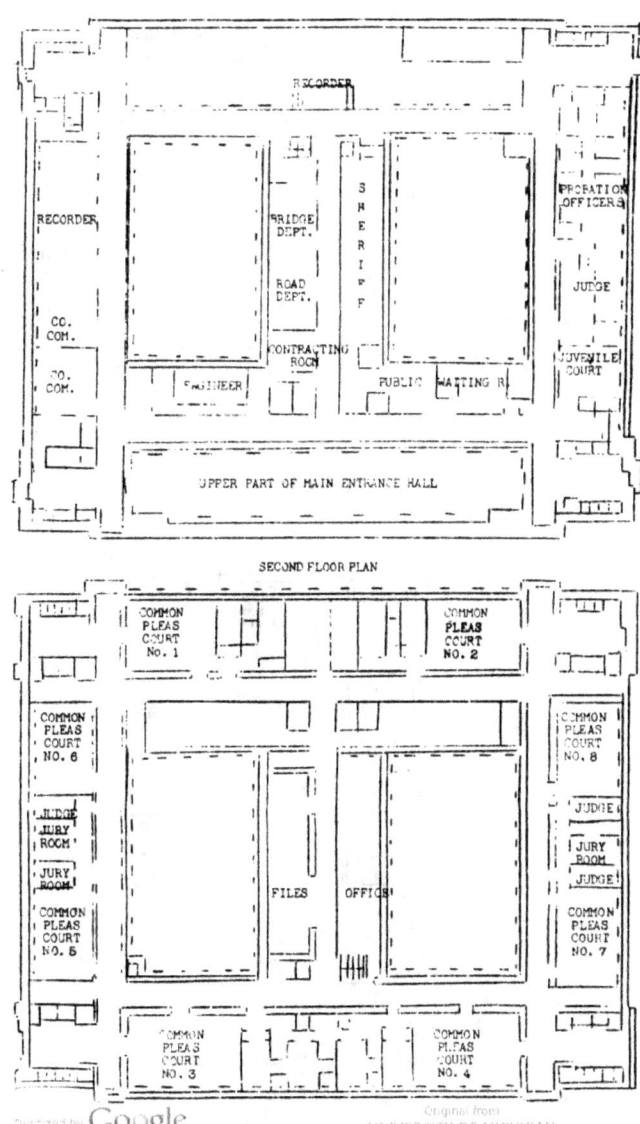

SECOND FLOOR PLAN

35

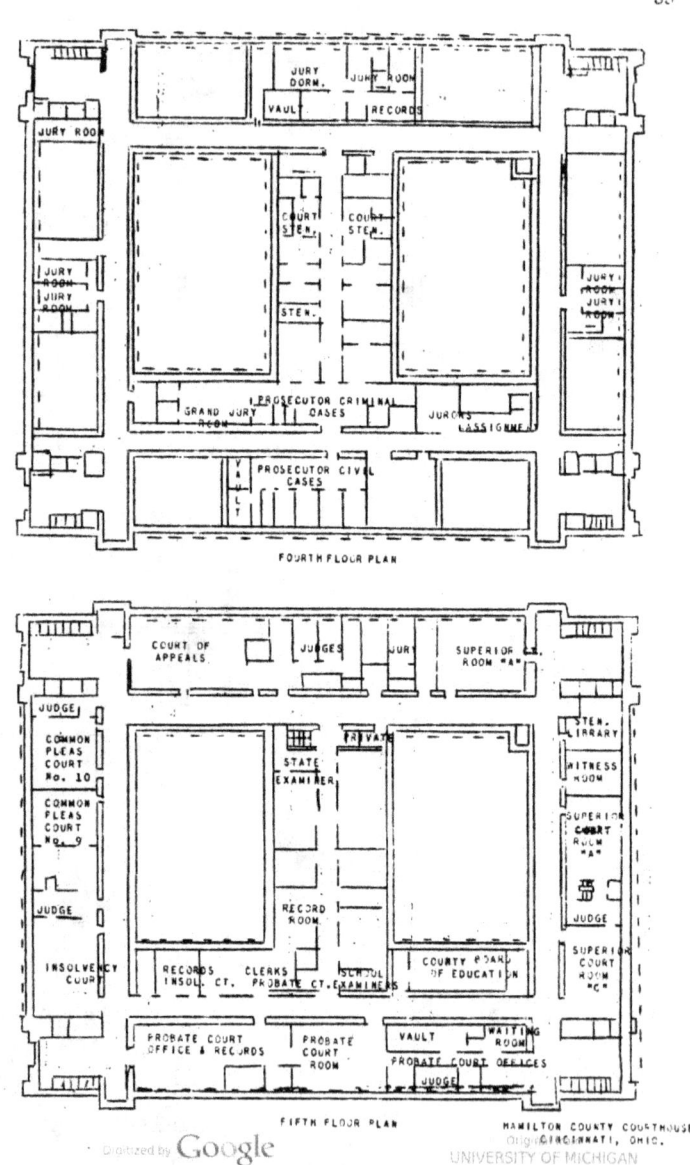

FOURTH FLOOR PLAN

FIFTH FLOOR PLAN

HAMILTON COUNTY COURTHOUSE
CINCINNATI, OHIO.

36

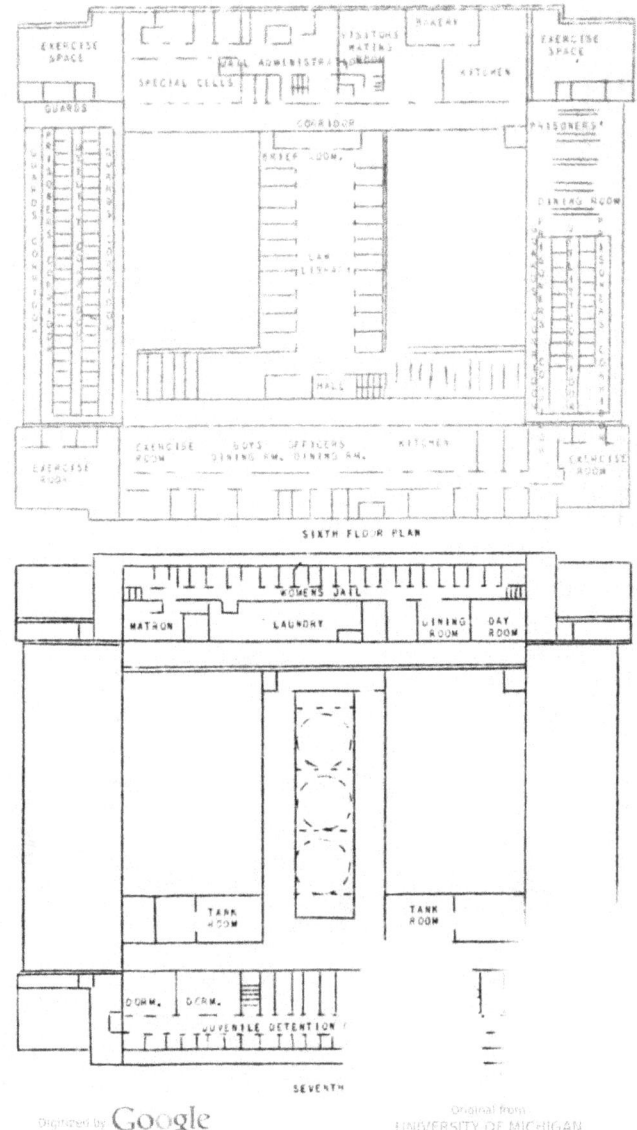

SIXTH FLOOR PLAN

SEVENTH

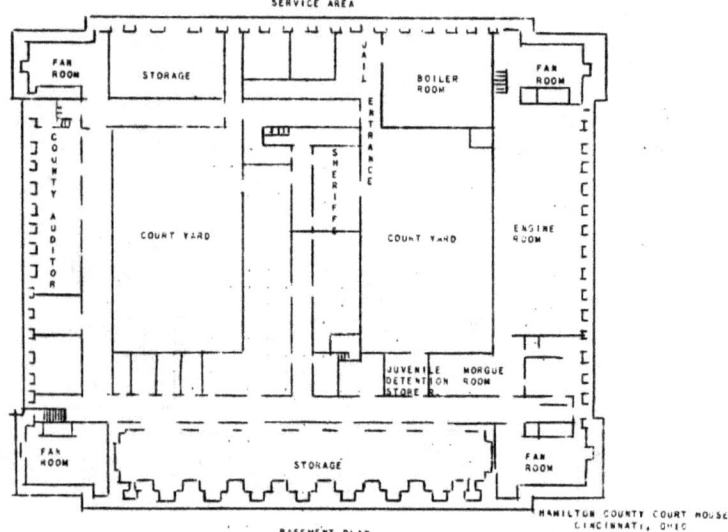

BASEMENT PLAN

The local governmental system for the Northwest Territory comprising the present state of Ohio, established the office of county commissioners. Created by the territorial act of 1792, this office consisted of two appointed commissioners who were directed to compile a tax list, levy taxes for the county, and to draft plans for, and supervise the construction of a "court-house, jail pillory whipping-post, and several stocks." (Theodore Calvin Pease, *Laws of the Northwest Territory 1788-1800, Illinois State Bar Association, Law Series*, I, Springfield, 1925, 78.)

The governmental system established in 1802, under the first constitution of Ohio, made no provision for the office; it exists because of statutory enactment. By an act of the legislature passed in 1804, the territorial office was recreated and was to be composed of three members elected for a three-year term. (2 O. L. 150.) Four years later the commissioners were made a corporate body invested with the power to sue and be sued. (5 O. L. 97.) They were required to keep a record of their proceedings, assess taxes for the support of the county, appoint a county treasurer, and supervise the construction of bridges. (8 O. L. 48.) They were paid at a per diem rate. Moreover during the same period they were given the task of constructing courthouses, jails, and offices for the clerk of courts, court of common pleas, sheriff, auditor, and treasurer. (2 O. L. 154-157; 29 O. L. 316.) Of these earlier duties the commissioners retain all but one: that of appointing a county treasurer. However, since 1831 they have been authorized to examine and compare the accounts of the county treasurer and the county auditor and to examine the condition of county finances.

Besides the duties regarding construction and finance, the commissioners were given the task of constructing local highways when so authorized by the legislature. During the first thirty years of Ohio history the duties of the commissioners in this respect were local in nature. But as the system of road construction expanded they were given the additional duty of converting free turnpikes into state roads. (44 O. L. 74.) During the forties and fifties private companies were authorized by the legislature to construct plank roads. (*Ibid.*, 126-127.) When, in 1857, these companies were caught in the stringency of a financial depression, the county commissioners were authorized to purchase their holdings. If such a transaction were made, the transfer signed by the president of the company was to be deposited with the county auditor. (54 O. L. 198.) In the seventies the commissioners, although earlier subjected to regulatory measures by the legislature, were prohibited from levying taxes for roads to exceed three mills on the dollar on the taxable property in the county. (69 O. L. 111.) Later, in 1885, they were authorized to levy taxes not to exceed five mills on the dollar on all taxable property in the county for the maintenance and upkeep of roads which had been damaged by excessive wear or from other causes. (G. C. sec. 7419.)

With the development of modern means of transportation, scientific principles were applied to road construction and maintenance. Although the county surveyor, now the county engineer, had in earlier years furnished the commissioners with estimates for bridge construction, it was not until the latter part of the nineteenth century that they were authorized to utilize his scientific knowledge in road construction. (78 O. L. 285; 98 O. L. 245-247. See also page 255.) At the opening of the present century the surveyor was directed to appoint, with the consent of the commissioners, a maintenance engineer, to supervise the repairing of improved roads in the county. (108 O. L. pt. i. 497).

Although the county commissioners have never been closely associated with the administration of criminal justice, their earlier duties regarding the construction of county jails qualified them, in the earlier period, for additional duties in this respect. During the middle of the nineteenth century the commissioners of Cuyahoga County were authorized to employ on construction work persons confined in the county jails. (37 O. L. 54.) While this provision was repealed by the criminal code, adopted in 1853, other earlier functions applicable to all counties were continued. Since 1843 the commissioners have provided equipment and fixtures for places of incarceration, food, and clothing for prisoners; and have appointed a jail physician. (41 O. L. 74; 87 O. L. 186.) Since 1869 they have been authorized to offer a reward for the detection or apprehension of any person charged with a felony in the county. Moreover, since 1892, the commissioners, in any county where there is no workhouse, may, under certain conditions, release or parole an indigent person confined in jail. (89 O. L. 408; 113 O. L. 203.) With the extension of modern crime into the rural areas, in the form of small-town bank robbing, the commissioners were given the duty of furnishing motorcycles to the sheriff and his deputies in an attempt to compete with the high-powered equipment used by modern gangs. One of the latest functions, in this respect, is the contracting with radio stations for the broadcasting of descriptions of fugitives from justice. (G. C. sec. 13431-1.)

Besides providing for those who have violated the laws of the county, the commissioners were given the duty of caring for persons, who, because of poverty or physical or mental defects, became public charges. Since 1816 they have established and maintained poorhouses. (14 O. L. 477.) Since 1913 they have been authorized, in any county containing a city which has an infirmary, to contract with the director of public safety for the care of the county's indigent. (G. C. sec. 2419-1.) In 1933 the commissioners were designated as a board to administer the state law providing aid for the aged. (115 O. L. pt. ii, 431-439. See also page 204.) Two years later, in 1935, the commissioners were authorized to provide noninstitutional support, care, assistance, or relief for the indigent in the county and were authorized to establish a suitable agency or office for such purposes. (116 O. L. 134. See also page 184.) Since 1908 the commissioners have been authorized to issue warrants for the relief of the blind. (G. C. sec. 1963. See also page 322.)

In addition to furnishing financial aid to the civilian population the commissioners were authorized (1886) to levy a tax for the relief of indigent Union soldiers, sailors, or marines of the Civil War, or, if such veterans were deceased, for their dependents. (83 O. L. 232.) In 1919 the provisions of the original act were amended to include indigent veterans of the World War. (108 O. L. pt. i, 633. See also page 229.) The commissioners were authorized also, in 1884, to defray the funeral expenses of any honorably discharged Union soldier, sailor, or marine who died in poverty. Ten years later, the provisions of the act were extended to include the mother, wife, or widow of any soldier, sailor, or marine—or any war nurse. (90 O. L. 177. See also page 229.)

The humanitarian duty of caring for the county's dependent and neglected children was delegated to the county commissioners. Since 1866 they have been authorized to establish and maintain children's homes. At the beginning of the present century, when the treatment of children was undergoing a remarkable change, they were authorized to place dependent and neglected children in private homes or institutions where they would receive food, clothing, and medical and dental treatment. (109 O. L. 533.) The development of the juvenile court system added new responsibilities. In order to completely segregate juvenile offenders from adults being tried in the regular criminal courts, the commissioners were authorized to provide a separate building, to be known as the "juvenile court."

By the authority conferred upon them to construct public buildings, the commissioners were given duties regarding educational advancement. Since 1871 they have been authorized to accept bequests for the construction of county libraries, and since 1913 to issue, after submitting such questions to the voters, bonds for the construction of libraries, or to contract with existing libraries for the use of people in the county. (G. C. secs. 2454, 2434-1; 110 O. L. 242.) Moreover during the same period they were authorized to provide and maintain civic centers in the county and to employ an expert director to supervise and administer them. (G. C. sec. 2457-4.)

Other duties not closely related to the original duties of the commissioners have been added from decade to decade. For example, in 1850 they were authorized to subscribe for one leading newspaper of each political party in the county and caused them to be bound and deposited with the county auditor as public archives. (48 O. L. 65.) An amendment to the original act, passed in 1923, provided for the preservation of such newspapers for a period of ten years, after which they may be removed to the Ohio State Archaeological and Historical Society. (110 O. L. 4.) Besides this, they have been authorized to promote historical research by appropriating annually a sum not to exceed $100 to defray the expenses of compiling and publishing historical data for historical societies not incorporated for profit. (G. C. sec. 2457-1.)

During the early years of the twentieth century the commissioners were given the duty of providing facilities for county sanitation, which, in previous years, had been sadly neglected. In 1917 they were authorized to lay out, establish, and maintain one or more sewer districts within the county, and to employ a sanitary engineer to aid them in the performance of their duties. In counties having a population exceeding 100,000, commissioners were authorized to create and maintain a sanitary engineering department. Since 1917 no sewer or sewerage treatment works may be constructed outside an incorporated municipality by any person, persons, firms, or corporations until the plans have been approved by the commissioners. (G. C. sec. 6602-1; 107 O. L. 440.)

During the same period the commissioners were authorized to provide facilities for the treatment of tuberculosis. In 1913 they were empowered to appoint, with the approval of the state department of health, one or more instructing and visiting nurses to visit homes or places wherein there was a case of tuberculosis, and since 1917 have been authorized to establish tuberculosis dispensaries and provide by tax levies the necessary funds for their establishment and maintenance. (G. C. sec. 3153, 3153-5.) Meantime, they were instructed to cooperate with the commissioners of other counties for the establishment of a district tubercular hospital. (100 O. L. 87.) Ten years later, the commissioners in any county having more than 50,000 population, with the consent of the state department of health, were directed to "provide the necessary funds for the purchase or lease of a site and the erection and equipment or the lease and equipment of the necessary buildings thereon for the operation and maintenance of a county hospital for the treatment of persons suffering from tuberculosis." (G. C. sec. 3148-1; 108 O. L. pt. i. 253; 109 O. L. 212.) The management and control of such a hospital were vested in the commissioners.

Finally the county Commissioners have acted in a supervisory capacity over other county officials. Since the middle of the nineteenth century they have been authorized to compare the annual reports and statements made to them by the prosecuting attorney, clerk of courts, sheriff, and treasurer, and to take measures to rectify errors, correct discrepancies, and record in their journal the results of such examinations. (G. C. sec. 2504; R. S. 886; 48 O. L. 66.) Such reports are filed with the county auditor who served as secretary to the county commissioners until 1908. Since that date the purchasing clerk has acted as secretary to the commissioners and has custody of their official acts and proceedings. (See page 176.) Moreover, in the latter part of the same century the commissioners were given their present duty of visiting and reporting on the sanitary conditions and the treatment of inmates in hospitals, detention homes, private asylums, or any institution exercising a reformatory or correctional influence over individuals. These reports, filed with the county prosecuting attorney, are open to the inspection and examination of the public. (G. C. sec. 2499; 92 O. L. 212.)

The county commissioners offer a typical example of an office which, designed primarily for an agricultural society, has expanded to meet the needs and requirements of modern society. At present the commissioners are elected for a four-year term. (108 O. L. pt. ii, 1300.)

Journals and Reports

1. MINUTES HAMILTON COUNTY COMMISSIONERS
1884——. 86 volumes. (15-100). Prior records destroyed in courthouse fire
of 1884.

Record of all business transacted by county commissioners with exception of that
pertaining to county infirmary. Chronologically arranged. Alphabetical index by
names of institutions, departments, or individuals concerned in back of each
volume. Handwritten and typed. Volumes average 600 pages. 18 x 13.5 x 3. County
Courthouse, Room 204.

2. MINUTES OF HAMILTON COUNTY INFIRMARY
1913——. 8 volumes. (18). Prior records missing.

Record of all business transacted by county commissioners pertaining to county
infirmary. Chronologically arranged. Alphabetical index by names of departments,
firms, or individuals concerned in back of each volume. Handwritten and typed.
Volumes average 600 pages. 18 x 13.5 x 3 . County Courthouse, Room 203.

3. MINUTES OF GENERAL HOSPITAL
1924-1927. 1 volume.

Record of all business transacted by county commissioners pertaining to general
hospital. Chronologically arranged. Alphabetical index by names of departments,
firms, or individuals concerned in front of volume. Handwritten and typed. 600
pages. 18 x 13.5 x 3. County Courthouse, Room 203.

For subsequent records see entry 1.

4. MINUTES OF SANITARY ENGINEER
1925-1931. 6 volumes. (16).

Record of all business transacted by county commissioners pertaining to the
sanitary division, county engineering department. Chronologically arranged.
Alphabetical index by name of county departments, projects, firms, or individuals
concerned in front of each volume. Handwritten and typed. Volumes average 600
pages. 18 x 13.5 x 3. County Courthouse, Room 203.

For subsequent records see entry 1.

5. TRANSCRIPT OF RESOLUTIONS
1908-1911. 1 volume.
Record of resolutions adopted by county commissioners. Chronologically arranged. Alphabetical index by names of institutions, county departments, projects, firms, or individuals concerned in back of volume. 1000 pages. 14 x 9.5 x 2. County Courthouse, Commissioners' storeroom, basement.
For subsequent records see entry 1.

6. RECORD OF DEPARTMENT INVENTORY
1911—. 17 volumes. 1913-1919 missing.
Record of inventories made by county department heads and reported to county commissioners listing equipment, furnishings, fixtures, and supplies on hand. Chronologically arranged. Alphabetical index by names of institutions or departments in front of each volume. Handwritten and typed. Volumes average 600 pages. 14 x 9 x 2. County Courthouse, 1911-1912, 1 volume, Commissioners' storeroom, basement; 1920—. 16 volumes, Room 204.

7. GENERAL REPORT OF STATE EXAMINER
1902-1934. 1 volume. Filing of subsequent reports is in arrears.
Record of examinations of all county departments. Chronologically arranged. Alphabetical index by name of departments in front of volume. Typed. 400 pages. 13 x 8 x 1.5. County Courthouse, Room 204.

Business Administration of Office

8. DEPOSITORY SECURITIES
1909—. 5 volumes.
Record of securities deposited by banks covering deposits of county funds listing name of bank, name of surety, date, amount of bond, attestation, and signatures of bank official. Alphabetically arranged under initial letters of names of depositories. Alphabetical thumb tab index attached to margins. Handwritten on printed forms. Volumes average 500 pages. 16 x 10.5 x 2. County Courthouse, 1909-1915, 3 volumes, Commissioners' storeroom, basement; 1916—. 2 volumes, Room 202.

9. MISCELLANEOUS EXPENSE ACCOUNTS
1917-1920. 2 volumes. (1-2).
Accounts of monies spent by county commissioners for miscellaneous items. Chronologically arranged. No index. Handwritten. Volumes average 300 pages. 11 x 8 x 1. County Courthouse, Commissioners' storeroom, basement.
For subsequent records see entry 1.

10. LEGAL NOTICE, ACCOUNT BOOK
1894—. 5 volumes.
Accounts for legal advertising in newspapers. Chronologically arranged. No index. Handwritten. Volumes average 200 pages. 12 x 8 x 1. County Courthouse, 1894-1914, 1 volume, Commissioners' storeroom, basement; 1915—, 4 volumes, Room 203.

11. EXPENSE ACCOUNT, COUNTY COMMISSIONERS
1887-1894. 8 volumes. Discontinued.
Itemized expense accounts of county commissioners listing date, account number, and amount. Numerically arranged by account numbers. No index. Handwritten. Volumes average 100 pages. 17 x 12 x 5. County Courthouse, Superintendent of building, basement storeroom.

12. DOCKET OF BILLS FILED
1913-1929. 2 volumes. Discontinued.
Miscellaneous bills covering expenditures authorized by county commissioners. Chronologically arranged. No index. Typed. Volumes average 600 pages. 18 x 13.5 x 3. County Courthouse, Commissioners' storeroom, basement.

Miscellaneous

13. PERSONAL BONDS
1915-1927. 1 volume. Discontinued.
Record of official bonds given by county employees listing name of surety or bonding company, amount of bond, signature of person bonded, date and notarial seal. Chronologically arranged. No index. Handwritten on printed forms. 600 pages. 14 x 8.5 x 2.5. County Courthouse, Commissioners' storeroom, basement.

14. ROAD CONSTRUCTION BONDS
1912-1915. 4 volumes (16-19). Prior records missing.
Record of contract response listing names of contractor and company, signature of contractor, attestation, signatures of commissioners, and specifications of contract. Alphabetical index by names of contractors or firms in back of each volume. Handwritten on printed forms. Volumes average 300 pages. 22 x 12 x 2. County Courthouse, Commissioners' storeroom, basement.

For subsequent records see entry 1.

15. STOCK LEDGER
1880-1897. 3 volumes. (1-3). Discontinued.
Inventory of office supplies. Chronologically arranged. No index. Handwritten. Volumes average 400 pages. 15 x 12 x 1. County Courthouse, Commissioners' storeroom, basement.

16. LEGAL NEWSPAPER CLIPPINGS
1896—. 6 volumes.
Clippings of legal notices from newspapers. Chronologically arranged. No index. Printed. Volumes average 200 pages. 14.5 x 9.5 x 3. County Courthouse, 1895-1927, 3 volumes, County Courthouse, Commissioners' storeroom, basement; 1928—. 3 volumes, Room 203.

17. CORRESPONDENCE
1885—. 62 file boxes.
Miscellaneous correspondence of official nature pertaining to activities of county commissioners in matters of finance, taxation, road and bridge construction, and institution and department management. Chronologically arranged. No index. Handwritten and typed. 42 file boxes, 18 x 11 x 5; 20 file boxes, 24 x 15 x 2. County Courthouse, 1885-1931, 42 file boxes, Room 203; 1932—, 20 file boxes, Room 204.

The office of county recorder, although not unknown as an early English institution for the registration of land titles, developed colonial America, where, because of the mobility of the restless pioneers, changes in land titles were frequent and some system was needed to protect purchasers against previous encumbrances. Public land registers, established in most of the colonies during the colonial period and continued by the states following independence, provided a model of land registration for the territory of which the present state of Ohio was then a part. Thus the office of county recorder was established by an act of the Northwest Territory passed on August 1, 1795. Adopted from the Pennsylvania code, this act provided for the appointment by the governor of a recorder in each county whose principal duty was to recording of deeds. (Pease, *op. cit.*, I, 197-199.)

When Ohio entered the union, in 1802, no constitutional provision was made for the continuation of the office, but the legislature during its first session passed an act providing for a recorder in each county to be appointed by the judges of the court of common pleas for a seven-year term. (1 O. L. 136.) The recorder continued to be an appointed officer until 1829, when, by an act of the legislature, he became elected for a three-year term. (27 O. L. 65.) The tenure of office remained at three years until the constitutional amendment of November 7, 1905, which provided for the election of all county officers in the even-numbered years. (*Ohio Const.*, Art. XVIII, sec. 2.) The term of office was fixed at two years, and so continued until the amendment of 1933, which extended the tenure of the incumbent until January 1937, at which time the recorder, elected at the regular election in November 1936, began to serve a four-year term. (115 O. L. 191.)

The first county recorder was directed by statute to record "all deeds, mortgages and conveyances of lands and tenements," lying within his county, and also all instruments and writings which are required by law to be recorded. (1 O. L. 137.) In 1805 he was directed to record all plots and maps of newly laid-out villages and new subdivisions of towns and villages. (3 O. L. 213-215.) In 1835 he was permitted, when authorized by the county commissioners, to transcribe from the records of other counties all deeds, mortgages, and other instruments of writing for the sale or conveyance of lands, tenements, or hereditaments affecting land titles in his county. (33 O. L. 8; 35 O. L. 10-11.)

Since the establishment of the office many duties besides those of recording land titles have been added. The present practice of recording powers of attorney began in 1818. (16 O. L. 155-156.) Although the mechanics of Cincinnati were authorized to file mechanics' liens with the recorder as early as 1823, it was not until 1840 that the privilege was extended to all laborers of the county. (21 O. L. 8-10; 38 O. L. 15-16.) Successive acts in 1865, 1872, 1881, 1884, 1888, 1904, and 1923 added new duties in the recording of soldiers' discharges (62 O. L. 59), copies of certificates of compliance authorizing companies not incorporated under the laws of Ohio to transact business in the state, and certified copies of renewal as granted by such companies to their agents (69 O. L. 32, 150; 97 O. L. 405), limited partnership agreements (8 O. L. 179), partition fence records (97 O. L. 140), and federal tax liens. (110 O. L. 252.) The recording of chattel mortgages and conditional sales began in 1846. Such instruments were to be deposited with the township clerk where the mortgagor was a resident. In all townships, however, in which the recorder maintained his office such instruments were to be deposited with him. (44 O. L. 61.) Since 1906 chattel mortgages have been filed with the county recorder exclusively. It is provided that in order to be valid against subsequent mortgages, the chattel mortgage must be deposited with the county recorder of the county where the mortgagor resides at the time of its execution, and to retain its validity the mortgage must be renewed every three years. (G. C. sec. 8565.) In 1936 the legislature passed an act authorizing the recorder to destroy such instruments six years after the time of refiling has expired. (116 O. L. 324.)

In the latter part of the nineteenth century an important extension of the method of recording land titles was provided by an act of the general assembly. The "Torrens System," as provided by the act of 1896 (92 O. L. 220), was declared unconstitutional by the supreme court of Ohio as contrary to section 16 of the bill of rights of the state constitution. (56 O. S. 575.) The present act, passed in 1913 (amended in 1913 and 1915), provides for the examination of land titles by the recorder and the issuance, if the title proved to be held in fee simple, of a certificate of title by the courts. The official certificate becomes the title of ownership and is indefeasible. However, in the event an interest is found in the land, after the issuance of the certificate, a claim is allowed to the legal claimant from a fund created for that purpose at the time of registration. (G. C. secs. 8572-34 - 8572-56; 106 O. L. 225; 115 O. L. 445-447.) This system, although adopted by a few counties, is not used as widely as it might be because of the difficulty of replacing the traditional complicated system.

The recorder, like other county officials, has been required to keep records of the business of his office. Although records were prescribed in earlier years, it was not until the middle of the nineteenth century that the legislature, looking forward to some uniformity in land registration, enacted measures prescribing the form and contents of such records. Since 1850 the recorder has been required to keep a record of deeds in which is recorded all deeds, powers of attorney, and other instruments of writing for the unconditional sale of land, tenements, or a hereditaments (48 O. L. 64.) The same year saw the beginning of a record of mortgages in which was recorded all mortgages, powers of attorney and other instruments of writing by which land, tenements, or hereditaments "shall or may be mortgaged" or otherwise conditionally sold; and a record of plats in which was to be recorded all plats and maps of town lots and of the subdivisions thereof, and of other divisions or surveyed lands, in like regular succession according to the priority of their presentation. (48 O. L. 64.) Since 1851 the recorder has been required to keep a separate record of deeds and mortgages denominated as "Record of Deeds" and "Record of Mortgages." (49 O. L. 103.) Fourteen years later began the separate recording of leases in which the recorder was, and is, required to record all leases and powers of attorney for the execution of leases. (62 O. L. 170.) The present practice of keeping a daily register of deeds and a daily register of mortgages had its beginning in 1896. In this record are entered in alphabetical order the names of the grantors of all deeds and mortgages affecting real estate. (92 O. L. 268.)

Although indexes had been prepared in earlier years, the present system of indexing had its beginning in 1851 and took practically its present form in 1896. (49 O. L. 103; 92 O. L. 268; 102 O. L. 277.) At present, the recorder, at the beginning of each day's business, is required to make and maintain a general alphabetical index, direct and reverse, of all names of both parties of all instruments recorded by him. The indexes show the kind of instrument, date, range, township and section, survey number and number of acres, or the lot and sublot numbers and the part thereof, of each tract or lot of land described in any such instrument of writing; the name of each grantor is entered in the direct index under the appropriate letter and followed on the same line by the name of the grantee; the name of each grantee is entered in the reverse index under the appropriate letter and followed on the same line by the name of the grantor. (G. C. sec. 2764.)

Since 1859 the county commissioners have been authorized to provide sectional indexes to the records of all real estate in the county, beginning with some designated year and continuing through a period of years as may be specified. (G. C. sec. 2766; 64 O. L. 256; 76 O. L. 49; 102 O. L. 289.)

The present duties of the recorder do not differ, from those prescribed in the middle of the nineteenth century. His records, in large bulky volumes, are open to the inspection of the public, and are transferred to his successor.

Record and Index Division

The record and index division was established by the county recorder to execute certain powers conferred on his office by statute. (R. S. 1143; G. C. 2757.) The function of this division is to record and index all deeds, mortgages, and other legal documents in the recorder's office.

Real Property Transfers

Deeds, Mortgages, and Wills

18. GENERAL INDEX TO DEEDS AND MORTGAGES
1787— 357 volumes and 128 duplicates (arranged in 7 series: 1787-1859, 1-23; 1860-1871, 1-28; 1872-1886, 1-36; 1887–1903, 1-58; 1904-1918, 1-66; 1919-1927, 1-61; 1928—, 1-85).
Index listing names of mortgagors and mortgagees; grantors and grantees, and volume and page numbers of record. These volumes also serve as an index to township survey maps. General Index to Deeds, 128 volumes, were salvage from courthouse fire of 1884 and have been transcribed. Alphabetically arranged by names of mortgagors and mortgagees, grantors and grantees. Typed on printed forms. Volumes average 400 pages. 18 x 12 x 2.5. County Courthouse, 1878—, 357 volumes, Room 217; 1787-1884, 128 volumes, Recorder's storeroom, basement.

19. DEEDS
1787—. 1,722 volumes, and 310 duplicates. (1787-1822, 36 volumes, A-Z; 1823—1,686 volumes, 20-1705).
Record of all deeds recorded in Hamilton County showing names of grantor and grantee, body of deed, seal, and recording. These include records of leases and incorporation of churches until 1844 and of mortgage releases until 1859. A record of mortgages was included between 1799 and 1857. 188 volumes of deeds and 122 volumes of deeds and mortgages were salvaged from courthouse fire of 1884 and were transcribed. Chronologically arranged 1787-1908, handwritten; 1909-1929, typed; 1930—, photostats. Volumes average 640 pages. 18 x 12 x 2.5. County Courthouse, 1787—, 1,722 volumes. Room 217; 1787-1884, 310 volumes, Recorder's storeroom, basement.

20. INDEX TO DEEDS
1787—. 53 volumes. (1-53).

Index to deeds listing names of grantors and grantees and volume and page numbers of record. Alphabetically arranged by names of grantors and grantees. 1787-1929, handwritten; 1930—, typed. Volumes average 600 pages. 18 x 12 x 2.5. County Courthouse, Room 217.

21. DEED REGISTER
1883— 47 volumes.

Record of deed registrations in Hamilton County listing names of grantee and grantor, record book number and page number, and receipt signature of grantee or grantee's agent. Alphabetically arranged by names of grantees and grantors. For index see entry 18. 1883-1911, 22 volumes, handwritten; 1912—, 25 volumes, typed. Volumes average 630 pages. 18 x 12 x 2.5. County Courthouse, Room 217.

22. SYMMES PURCHASE DEEDS
1787-1819. 47 volumes.

Restored records of Symmes Purchase deeds filed with the county recorder of Hamilton County giving details of property transfers, dates, names of contracting parties, and signatures. These records are included in the regular deed record, entry 19. One volume (A) is the earliest restored record available. Chronologically arranged. No index. Handwritten and typed. Volumes average 160 pages. 32 x 14 x 2.5. County Courthouse 1787-1817, 2 volumes, Recorder's office; 1818-1819, 2 volumes, Recorder's storeroom.

23. CEMETERY DEEDS
1859—. 4 volumes and 1 duplicate.

Record of cemetery lot purchases listing name of purchaser, name of cemetery, and lot number. The duplicate volume, 1874-1883, was one of the volumes salvaged from the fire of 1884 which was later transcribed. Chronologically arranged. No index. Handwritten. Condition poor. Volumes average 500 pages. 19 x 12 x 3. County Courthouse, 1859—, 4 volumes, Room 217; 1874-1883, 1 volume, Recorder's storeroom, basement.

24. DEEDS AND MORTGAGES

1884—. 170 file boxes. Prior records destroyed in courthouse fire of 1884. Original deeds and cancelled mortgages uncalled for by owners. Alphabetically arranged by names of grantors and grantees. No index. Handwritten on printed forms. 5 x 1 x 24. County Courthouse, Room 217.

25. MORTGAGES

1799—. 1,502 volumes. (numbering varies). Record of all real estate mortgages recorded in Hamilton County showing names and signatures of mortgagor and mortgagee, location and description of property, lot number, date of recording, and amount of mortgage. Between years 1799 and 1857 mortgages recorded in same volume as deeds. Alphabetically arranged by names of mortgagors and mortgagee. For index see entries 18, 26, and 27. 1799-1906, handwritten; 1907-1929, typed; 1930—, photostats. Volumes average 640 pages. 18 x 12 x 2.5. County Courthouse, Room 217.

For mortgage records, 1799-1857, see entry 19.

26. INDEX TO MORTGAGES

1799—. 42 volumes. (1-42). Index listing names of mortgagor to mortgagee and names of mortgagee to mortgagor on opposite pages; also volume and page numbers of record. Alphabetically arranged by names of mortgagors. 1799-1930, handwritten; 1931—, typed. Volumes average 600 pages. 18 x 14 x 2.5. County Courthouse, Room 217.

27. CARD INDEX TO MORTGAGOR

1928—. 160 file boxes. Record initiated 1928. Index listing name of mortgagor and volume and page numbers of record. Alphabetically arranged by names of mortgagors. Handwritten. 1 x 7 x 24. County Courthouse, Room 216.

28. DAILY MORTGAGE REGISTER

1884—. 36 volumes. (1884-1901, 11 volumes, 1-11; 1902—, 25 volumes. labeled chronologically.). Prior records destroyed in courthouse fire of 1884. Register listing names of mortgagor and mortgagee, amount of mortgage, mortgage index volume and page numbers, date of recording, and signature of person recording mortgage. Chronologically arranged. No index. 1884-1911, handwritten; 1912—, typed. Volumes average 360 pages. 18 x 12 x 1.5. County Courthouse, Room 217,

29. MORTGAGE RELEASES
1892—. 21 volumes. (1-21).
Record of releases and discharges from lien and operation of mortgages giving names of mortgagor and mortgagee, location and description of property, date of release, and notarial seal. Volume 1, for index see entry 60. Volumes 2-21, alphabetical index by names of mortgagors in back of each volume. 1892-1910, handwritten; 1911-1930, typed; 1931-1933, typed and photostats; 1934—, photostats. Volumes average 640 pages. 18 x 12 x 2.5. County Courthouse, Room 217.

30. ASSIGNMENTS
1907-1928. 3 volumes.
Record of mortgage assignments listing names of mortgagor and mortgagee, volume and page numbers of record, and amount of mortgage. Chronologically arranged. No index. Handwritten. Volumes average 400 pages. 18 x 12 x 1.5. County Courthouse, Room 217.
    For subsequent records see entry 32.

31. CANCELLATIONS
1920-1928. 9 volumes.
Record of mortgage cancellations listing names of mortgagor and mortgagee, volume and page numbers of record, amount of mortgage, and lot number. Alphabetically arranged by names of mortgagors and mortgagees. No index. Handwritten. Volumes average 400 pages. 18 x 12 x 2.5. County Courthouse, Room 217.

32. CANCELLATIONS AND ASSIGNMENTS
1929—. 8 volumes.
Record of assignments and cancellations of mortgages listing names of mortgagor and mortgagee, volume and page numbers of record, amount of mortgage, recording fee, date, and signature of party calling for original instrument. Chronologically

arranged. No index. Typed. Volumes average 640 pages. 18 x 12 x 2.25. County Courthouse, Room 217.

33. WILLS
1904—. 1 volume.
Record of certificates of portions of wills designating disposition of certain properties showing portion of will and property disposed of in certain cases, will book and page numbers, deed book and page numbers, court seal, amount of fee, and date of recording. Chronologically arranged. Alphabetical index by names of testators in back of each volume. 1904-1912, handwritten; 1913—, typed. 400 pages. 18 x 12 x 2.5. County Courthouse, Room 217.

Leases

34. LEASES
1844—. 225 volumes, and 1 duplicate (1-225).
Record of long, short, and perpetual leases showing names of lessee and lessor, description and location of property, terms, agreements, stipulations, and authority under which lease was made. 1867-1868, 1 volume has been transcribed. Alphabetically arranged by names of lessees. 1844-1908, handwritten; 1909-1930, typed; 1931—, photostats. Volumes average 325 pages. 18 x 12 x 2.5. County Courthouse. 1844—, 225 volumes, Room 217; 1867-1868, 1 volume, Recorder's storeroom, basement.

35. INDEX TO LEASES
1844—. 4 volumes (1-4).
Index showing names of lessors and lessees and volume and page numbers of record. Alphabetically arranged by names of lessors and lessees. Handwritten. Volumes average 400 pages. 18 x 12 x 2.5. County Courthouse, Room 217.

Liens

36. MECHANICS' LIENS
1843—. 50 volumes (1-49, 1 volume labeled Mechanics Liens Against Contractors).
Record of all liens or claims placed against property for labor or materials used in

the construction or repair of buildings. Railroad liens were included after 1885. Alphabetically arranged by name of lien holders. Alphabetical index in back of volumes 1-49. Duplicate volume, 1884-1891, no index. 1843-1909, handwritten; 1910-1929, typed; 1930—, photostats. Duplicate volume condition four. Volumes average 355 pages. 18 x 12 x 2.5. County Courthouse, 1843—. 49 volumes, Room 217; 1884-1891, 1 volume, Recorder's storeroom, basement.

37. RAILROAD LIENS
1883-1885. 1 volume.
Record of suits and claims against railroads in Hamilton County. Alphabetically arranged by name of lien holders. No index. Handwritten. 625 pages. 18.5 x 13 x 3. County Courthouse, Recorder's store room, basement.

For subsequent records see entry 36.

Atlases, Maps, and Plat Books

38. CINCINNATI ATLAS
1883-1884. 1 volume.
Atlas containing maps of sections of Cincinnati showing railroads, thoroughfares, parks, cemeteries, and wards by numbers. Prepared by E. Robinson and R. H. Pidgeon. Published by Robinson Company, New York. No index. Printed and colored. Scale, 1 inch equals 150 feet. 28 pages. 20 x 29 x 3. County Courthouse, Room 217.

39. CINCINNATI AND HAMILTON COUNTY ATLAS
1869. 1 volume.
Atlas containing maps of Hamilton County, townships, and suburbs of Cincinnati showing thoroughfares, cemeteries, and parks. Included are an outline and railroad map of the United States and engravings of Longview Hospital, Cincinnati, Ohio. Prepared by R. H. Harrison and assistants. Published by C. O. Titus Company, Philadelphia, Pennsylvania. No index. Printed and colored. Scale, 1 inch equals 1-1/5 mile. 38 pages. 18 x 29 x 3. County Courthouse, Room 217.

40. HAMILTON COUNTY ATLAS
1883. 1 volume.

Maps listing sections of Cincinnati by townships and suburbs showing thoroughfares, parks, and cemeteries. Prepared by George Moessnger and F. Bertsch. Published by American Photo Lithograph Company, New York. No index. Printed with some portions shaded. Scale, 1 inch equals 2-2/5 mile. 13 pages. 37 x 24 x 3. County Courthouse, Room 217.

41. MAP OF ANNEXATIONS TO CITY OF CINCINNATI
1902-1930. 1 map.

Map showing annexations, dates of annexations, and thoroughfares. Revised 1913, 1914, 1926, 1927, and 1930. Prepared by E. W. Wulfekoetten. Published by Department of Highways, Cincinnati, Ohio. Blueprint with annexations outlined in color. No scale. 42 x 48. County Courthouse, Room 217.

42. OUTLINE MAP OF CINCINNATI
1884. 1 map.

Map showing thoroughfares, townships, section numbers, public buildings, cemeteries, parks, railroads, suburbs, and northern section of Kentucky opposite Cincinnati. Prepared by E. Robinson. Published by A. H. Mueller Company, Philadelphia, Pennsylvania. Printed and colored. Scale, 1 inch equals 1200 feet. 36 x 48. County Courthouse, Room 217.

43. CINCINNATI MAP
1903. 1 map.

Map showing section numbers, parks, thoroughfares, townships, cemeteries, suburbs, estates, and railroads. Prepared by William Peete. Hand drawn with subdivisions, parks and cemeteries in color. Scale, 1 inch equals 500 feet. 60 x 120. County Courthouse, Room 217.

44. CINCINNATI AND VICINITY MAP
1913. 1 map.

Map showing township numbers, fractional range numbers, and incorporated villages; also villages in Kentucky opposite Cincinnati with indications of parks, thoroughfares, cemeteries, and railroads. Prepared by J. A. Stewart. Published by C. E. Stewart Map Company, Cincinnati, Ohio. Printed with some incorporated

places shaded and some outlined in color. Scale, 1 inch equals 1000 feet. 84 x 96.
County Courthouse, Room 217.

45. GREATER CINCINNATI MAP
1930. 1 map.

Map showing boundary lines, street railways, railroads, bus lines, street numbers,
public and parochial schools, and police and fire stations. Map has a south
extension showing Woodside, Lakeside Park, Crestview Hills, Erlanger, and
Elsmere; a west extension showing Cleves and North Bend. Published by National
Map Company, Indianapolis, Indiana. Printed. Scale, 1 inch equals 2.5 miles. 36 x
48. County Courthouse, Room 217.

46. HAMILTON COUNTY MAP
1855-1865. 1 map.

Outline map of Hamilton County showing the thoroughfares, railroads, townships,
estates, and fractional ranges. Prepared and published by American Photo
Lithograph Company, New York. Printed with townships and villages outlined in
color. No scale but shows table of distances from Cincinnati to outline villages. 48
x 30. County Courthouse, Room 217.

47. HAMILTON COUNTY MAP.
1883. 1 map.

Map showing township numbers, fractional ranges, and thoroughfares. Prepared by
G. Moessinger and F. Bertsch. Published by American Photo Lithograph Company,
New York. Printed with townships outlined in color. 1 inch equals 2-2/5 mile. 30
x 48. County Courthouse, Room 217.

48. HAMILTON COUNTY MAP
1914. 1 map.

Map showing incorporated villages of Cincinnati and outlying townships. Prepared
by J. H. Stewart. Published by Stewart Map Company, Cincinnati, Ohio. Printed
with incorporated villages outlined in red and townships in other colors. Scale, 1
inch equals 2000 feet. 60 x 84. County Courthouse, Room 217.

49. TOWNSHIP SURVEY MAPS
1927. 14 volumes (labeled by names of townships).
Maps showing subdivisions, estates, thoroughfares, township section and fractional range numbers, and index book and page numbers for Anderson, Colerain, Columbia, Crosby, Delhi, Green, Harrison, Miami, Millcreek, Springfield, Storres (Cincinnati), Spencer, Sycamore, Symmes, and Whitewater Townships. Prepared by county engineer. For index see entry 18. Photo stats with estates outlined in color. Volumes average 38 pages. 24 x 30 x 2.5. County Courthouse, Room 217.

50. PLAT BOOKS
1850—. 36 volumes and 11 duplicates (1-36).
Record of plats showing surveys, subdivisions, easements, sewers, and right of ways. Eleven volumes were salvaged from courthouse fire of 1884 and have been transcribed. Prepared by county engineer. 1850-1928, hand drawn; 1929—, photostats. Average 73 pages. 23 x 18 x 2.5. County Courthouse, 1850—, 36 volumes, Room 217; 1860-1884, 11 volumes, Recorder's storeroom, basement.

51. PLAT BOOKS INDEX
1850—. 46 shutters and 8 volumes which are duplicates.
Cards listing name of plat, subdivision, plat book and page numbers. Two volumes have been transcribed. Alphabetically arranged by names of subdivisions. Typed on cards. Shutters, 16 x 8. Volumes average 400 pages. 18 x 16 x 2. County Courthouse, 1850—, 46 shutters, Room 217; 1850-1884, 2 volumes, Recorder's storeroom, basement.

Corporations

52. TRADERS' RECORD
1884-1886. 5 volumes. (1-4, 9). Volumes 5-8 missing. Discontinued. Prior records destroyed in courthouse fire of 1884.
Record of individuals and partners engaged in business in Hamilton County showing firm name, names of owners or partners, residence, and type of business. Chronologically arranged. Alphabetical index by names of traders in front of each volume. Handwritten. Volumes average 450 pages. 17 x 12 x 2. County Courthouse, Recorder's storeroom, basement.

53. RECORD OF PARTNERSHIP AGREEMENTS
1846—. 2 volumes.

Record showing all partnership agreements recorded in Hamilton County recorder's office. Chronologically arranged. For index see entry 60. Handwritten. Volumes average 600 pages. 20 x 14 x 3. County Courthouse, Recorder's Office. Room 213.

54. CHURCH RECORDS
1844—. 7 volumes. (1-7).

Record of Articles of Incorporation of churches in Hamilton County showing names of applicants, dates of incorporations, and seals and signatures of parties concerned. Chronologically arranged. For index entry 60. 1844-1910, handwritten; 1911—, typed. Volumes average 640 pages. 18 x 12 x 2.5. County Courthouse, Room 217.
 For prior records see entry 19.

Miscellaneous

55. POWERS OF ATTORNEY
1848—. 15 volumes. (1-15). Prior records missing.

Record of powers of attorney showing names of principal and agent and agreement between parties. Chronologically arranged. For index, volumes 1-10 see entry 56. Volumes 11-15, alphabetical index by names of principals and agents in back of each volume. 1848-1915, handwritten; 1916-1930, typed; 1931—, photostats. Volumes average 640 pages. 18 x 12 x 2.5. County Courthouse, Room 217.

56. INDEX TO POWERS OF ATTORNEY
1848-1881. 1 volume and 1 duplicate.

Index to volumes 1-10, entry 55, listing names of principals and agents and book and page numbers of record. One volume has been transcribed. Alphabetically arranged by names of principals and agents. Handwritten. Volumes average 450 pages. 15 x 12 x 2.5. County Courthouse, 1848-1881, 1 volume, Recorder's storeroom, basement; 1848-1881, 1 volume, Room 217.

57. SOLDIERS' AND SAILORS' DISCHARGES
1865—. 8 volumes (1-8).

Record of official discharges from army and navy listing name of soldier or sailor, date of entry into service, date of discharge, and service number. Until March 1919, the record lists only soldiers' discharges; after that date, sailors' discharges are also included. Alphabetically arranged by names of soldiers and sailors. For index see entries 58 and 60. 1865-1911, handwritten; 1912-1926, typed; 1926—, photostats. Volumes average 640 pages. 18 x 12 x 2.5. County Courthouse, Room 217.

58. INDEX TO SOLDIERS' AND SAILORS' DISCHARGES
1865—. 1 volume.

Index listing name of soldier or sailor, discharge number, and volume number of record. Alphabetically arranged by names of soldiers and sailors. Handwritten. 300 pages. 18 x 12 x 2.5. County Courthouse, Room 217.

59. MISCELLANEOUS RECORDS
1859—. 8 volumes. (1-8).

Miscellaneous record of wills, certificates, apprenticeships, patent Deeds, money receipts, bond affidavits, agreements, and mortgage releases until 1892. Arranged alphabetically with a subject division. For index, volumes 1-2, see entry 60. Volumes 3-8, index in back of each volume. 1859-1915, handwritten; 1916—, typed. Volumes 6-8 contains several photostats. Volumes average 650 pages. 18 x 12 x 2.5. County Courthouse, Room 217.

60. MISCELLANEOUS RECORD INDEX
1844—. 1 volume.

Index to church records (entry 54), cemetery records (entry 23), mortgage releases (entries 29 and 59), partnership records, (entry 53), soldiers' discharges (entry 57), railroad records (entry 37); also wills, certificates, apprenticeships, patent deeds, money receipts, bond affidavits, and agreements (entry 59). Alphabetically arranged by names of subjects. No index. Handwritten. 400 pages. 18 x 12 x 2.5. County Courthouse, Room 217.

Chattel Mortgage Division

The chattel mortgage division of the recorder's office was instituted by the recorder as a result of an act of the Ohio General Assembly, passed April 30, 1877, which required that "all chattel mortgages shall be filed by either the township clerk or the county recorder." (R. S. 4151; G. C. 8561.) A later act, effective August 30, 1935, provided that "Six years after the time for refiling mortgages has expired the county recorder may destroy such mortgages." (R. S. 4155; G. C. 8565.) The present policy in Hamilton County is to retain such mortgages six years from date; some, however, being retained longer.

61. CHATTEL MORTGAGES AND CONDITIONAL BILLS OF SALE
1914—. 628 file boxes. Prior records destroyed.
Original chattel mortgages, conditional bills of sale, wage assessments, cancellation orders, and attested accounts. Numerically arranged by instrument numbers. For index C entries 62 and 63. Handwritten and typed on printed forms. 138 file boxes, 5 x 10.5 x 4; 490 file boxes, 10.5 x 20 x 4. County Courthouse,1914-1931, 138 file boxes, Recorder's storeroom, basement; 1932—, 490 file boxes, Room 217.

62. MORTGAGOR INDEX (Direct) OF CHATTEL MORTGAGES AND FILED BILLS OF SALE
1895—. 84 volumes. (labeled chronologically, 2 volumes to each year).
Index listing names of mortgagor and mortgagee, date of filing, amount of mortgage, cancellation, and file box number. Alphabetically arranged by names of mortgagor. Handwritten on printed forms. Volumes average 370 pages. 19 x 17 x 3. County Courthouse,1895-1931, 74 volumes, Recorder's storeroom, basement; 1932—, 10 volumes, Room 217.

63. MORTGAGEE INDEX (Reverse) OF CHATTEL MORTGAGES AND FILED BILLS OF SALE
1895—. 84 volumes. (labeled chronologically, 2 volumes to each year).
Index listing names of mortgagee and mortgagor, date of filing, and file box number. Alphabetically arranged by names of mortgagees. Handwritten on printed forms. Volumes average 370 pages. 19 x 17 x 3. County Courthouse, 1895-1931, 74 volumes, Recorder's storeroom basement; 1932—, 10 volumes, Room 217.

Land Registration Division

This division was established by the county recorder to execute certain powers conferred on his office by statute. (G. C. sec. 8572-12.)

64. REGISTERED LAND TITLES
1914—. 24 volumes. (1-24).
Record showing separate plats for each title recorded and certificate title, also voluntary and involuntary liens against registered land. Alphabetically arranged and by names of property owners. Typed. Volumes average 400 pages. 18 x 16 x 4. County Courthouse, Room 217.

65. INDEX, REGISTERED LAND TITLES
1914—. 1 volume.
Index showing names of property owner and subdivision; also volume, page, lot, and certificate numbers. Alphabetically arranged by names of property owners. Handwritten. 400 pages. 20 x 17.5 x 2. County Courthouse, Room 217.

The office of clerk of courts, an ancient English institution originating before the time of Edward I, (Sir Frederick Pollock and Frederic William Maitland, *The History of English Law Before the Time of Edward I.* 2 volumes. Cambridge, 1895, I, 1884) was transplanted to America during the colonial period. The American Revolution made no radical change in the political heritage derived from England, and the office was continued by the states. The duties of the office were modified, however because of a separation of administrative and judicial functions in the newer states, which under the English system had been combined.

The sections of the Ohio constitution of 1802 creating the judicial system for the state provided for the appointment of a clerk of courts by the judges of the court of common pleas. He was to serve a seven-year term, but was subject to removal by the appointing power for a breach of good behavior. (*Ohio Const. 1802,* Art. III, sec. 9.) When, in 1851, a new constitution was adopted, the instrument made the office of clerk an elective one with a three-year term. (*Ohio Const. 1851,* Art. IV, sec. 6.) A constitutional amendment in 1905 provided that the terms of all elective offices should be for an even number of years, not exceeding four. In compliance with the amendment, the general assembly passed an act fixing the term of office of the clerk at two years. (98 O. L, 273.) The term remained two years until 1935 when it was extended to four years. (116 O. L. pt. ii, 184.) The remuneration of the office was by fees until 1906 when the legislature prescribed a definite salary. (98 O. L. 94, 117.)

The duties of the clerk of courts, like those of other officers, were prescribed by statute. The code of civil procedure, adopted in 1853, summarized the earlier duties and laid the basis for the present duties of the clerk. The duties as prescribed under this code were similar, in most respects, to those prescribed during the earlier years of the office. The clerk of courts was directed to issue all writs and orders for provisional remedies; endorse the date upon all papers filed in his office, and keep the journal, record books, and papers appertaining to the court and record its proceedings. Although the clerk had kept records during the earlier period, he was directed to keep at least five books to be called the appearance docket, the trial docket, and a printed duplicate of the trial docket, the journal, the record, and the execution docket. (51 O. L. 158-159; 78 O. L. 108; 79 O. L. 115; 86 O. L. 174.) The present practice of keeping an index, direct and reverse, to judgments began in 1866. (63 O. L. 10; 75 O. L. 103; 78 O. L. 88; 82 O. L. 39; 86 O. L. 26.) Eight years later, in 1871, the clerk was made official custodian of the law reports and books furnished by the state for the use of the court and bar, and was made liable for their destruction. (68 O. L. 109.)

While the duties of the clerk as defined by the civil code of 1853 are still effective, others have been added by subsequent legislation. Thus, for example, in 1858 the clerk was directed to receive notary commissions for record. (55 O. L. 13; 93 O. L. 406; 115 O. L. 117.) He was required, also, to receive for record special police commissions (1867), timber trademarks (1883), partnership agreements (1894), index to judgments of federal courts (1898), marks of ownerships [trademarks] (1911), bills of sales of motor vehicles (1921), and certificates of judgments to operate as a lien (1935) (64 O. L. 60; 80 O. L. 195; 91 O. L. 357; 92 O. L. 25; 93 O. L. 285; 102 O. L. 513-514; 109 O. L. 333; 116 O. L. 274.) On the other hand, many of the earlier duties of the clerk have been transferred to other departments of local government or have been abolished. The clerk issued marriage licenses and ministers' licenses until 1851, after that date they were issued by the probate court. Moreover the clerk issued peddlers' licenses until the decade of the sixties, since that time they have been issued by the auditor. The practice of recording in the office of the clerk, the names of black or mulatto persons to be used as certificates of freedom was, of course, discontinued following the War between the States.

In 1856 the clerk was directed by the legislature to preserve a list of births, marriages, and deaths as returned to his office by the assessors. Moreover, he was required to transmit a copy of such statistics to the secretary of state on or before the first day of June annually. From the lists, return to him from the various clerks of courts, the secretary of state prepared tabular statements showing the vital statistics in each county. The clerk received ten copies of the report, one of which he was required to preserve in his office. (53 O. L. 73-75.) The clerk was relieved of the task of collecting and preserving vital statistics, when, in 1867, such powers and duties were vested in the probate judge. (64 O. L. 63-64.)

The clerk of courts was given other duties in addition to those of serving the court of common pleas and receiving documents for record. Since 1850 he has been required to report each year to the county commissioners all fines assessed by the court in criminal cases, together with the names of the parties to each case, and the amount of money he has paid to the treasurer. (48 O. L. 66; 58 O. L. 69; 86 O. L. 239.) Moreover, since 1867 he has been required to report annually to the secretary of state on the number of crimes committed in his county, the number of pending cases, and the amount of fines collected. (64 O. L. 17.) An act of 1927, amending the act of 1867, directed the clerk to report on any matters which the secretary of state might require, and to forward a duplicate copy of his report on crime in his county to the state board of clemency. (112 O. L. 203.) (The state board of clemency was abolished in 1931.)

The county clerk of courts, like the county prosecuting attorney, is one of the important persons in the judicial system. His significance and influence, however, was not recognized until recent years. The clerk of courts of Hamilton County is, by statute, clerk of the municipal court of the city of Cincinnati, and clerk of the court of appeals.

General Office Division

The general office division was established by clerk of courts for the convenient locating of miscellaneous records.

Commissions and Licenses

66. NOTARY COMMISSIONS
1884—. 62 volumes. (10-71). Prior records destroyed in courthouse fire of 1884

Record of notary public commissions showing name of notary, date of issue, and date of expiration of commission. Chronologically arranged. Alphabetical index by names of notaries in back of each volume. Handwritten on printed forms. Condition fair. Volumes average 200 pages. 15 x 8 x 2. County Courthouse, Room 329, vault.

67. JUSTICE OF PEACE COMMISSIONS
1884—. 2 volumes

Exact duplicates of original commissions of all justices of peace with original letters of those who have resigned. Chronologically arranged. Alphabetical index by names of individuals in front of each volume. Handwritten. Volumes average 383 pages. 13 x 9 x 2. County Courthouse, 1884-1909, 1volume, Room 328; 1910—, 1 volume, Room 329.

68. OPTOMETRY LICENSES
1920—. 2 volumes

Register of persons who were granted licenses by state board of optometry to practice in Hamilton County. Chronologically arranged. Alphabetical index by names of licensees in back of each volume. Handwritten on printed forms. Volumes average 500 pages. 14 x 10 x 3.County Courthouse, Clerk of courts' office.

69. HUNTING LICENSES
1935—1 file box, prior records missing.
Records name, address, and description of applicant, date of issuance, amount paid, date of expiration, and signature of clerk. Numerically arranged by licensed numbers. No index. Handwritten on printed forms. 20 x 14 x 8. County Courthouse, Clerk of courts' office.

70. FISHING LICENSES
1934—. 1 file box. Prior records missing.
Records name, address, and description of applicant, date of issuance, amount paid, date of expiration, and signature of clerk. Numerically arranged by license numbers. No index. Handwritten on printed forms. 20 x 14 x 8. County Courthouse, Clerk of courts' office.

Miscellaneous

71. JURY BOOK
1900—. 3 volumes. (1-3).
Records names and addresses of jurors called to common pleas and municipal court cases. Alphabetically arranged by names of jurors. No index. Handwritten. Volumes average 200 pages. 18 x 10 x 1. County Courthouse, Clerk of courts' storeroom, basement.

72. CLERK'S REPORT OF FINES IN CRIMINAL CASES
1930—. 1 file box. Prior records missing.
Reports of fines and criminal cases which were made by the clerk of courts to county commissioners giving case number, name of defendant, amount of fine assessed, and amount of fine suspended. Numerically arranged by case numbers. No index. Typed. 16 x 12 x 4. County Courthouse, Auditor's office.

73. REAL ESTATE MAPS
1798-1853. 1 volume.

Land tenure maps of real estate in Hamilton County with restored records and decrees. Prepared by Hamilton County clerk, Cincinnati, Ohio, alphabetical index by names of maps in front of volume. Pen and ink sketch with handwritten description of locations and all data pertaining to survey. No scale. 168 pages. (1 map to each page.) 24 x 25 x 4. County Courthouse, Room 329.

Automobile Division

74. BILLS OF SALE, NEW AND USED AUTOMOBILES
1921—. 2103 file boxes.

Duplicate bills of sale showing names of grantor, grantee, and manufacturer, date of sale, vendor's license number and address, make of car, factory number, engine number, model, price, and signatures of grantor and grantee; and also sworn statement of ownership and registration date. Numerically arranged by bills of sale numbers. No index. 4 x 12 x 15. County Courthouse, 1921-1922, 67 file boxes, room 328; 1923—. 2036 file boxes, Room 329.

75. CASH BOOKS
1921—. 58 volumes (1921-March 31, 1935, 55 volumes, 1-55; April 1, 1935—. 3 loose-leaf volumes).

Records of bills of sale showing affidavit of ownership, certified copy of sworn statements, and cash receipts. Chronologically arranged. No index. Handwritten on printed forms. Volumes average 300 pages. 16.5 x 9 x 3. County Courthouse, Room 329.

The court of common pleas, like many other county institutions, originated in England during the reign of Henry II. (George Burton Adams, *Constitutional History of England,* New York, 1921, 109,134.) Established in America during the colonial period, the office was continued by the states following the War of American Independence. The territorial act of 1788, establishing in the newer west the American colonial policy in respect to the judiciary, contained sections authorizing the establishment of a common pleas court to be composed of not less than three nor more than five members, who, appointed and commissioned by the territorial governor, were given jurisdiction in all civil matters. (Pease, *op. cit.,* 7.)

When a constitution was drafted for Ohio in 1802 preparatory to the entrance of the state into the Union, provision was made for a continuation of the territorial court. (*Ohio Const. 1802,* Art. III, sec. 1.) The articles of the constitution, regarding the judiciary, provided for a court of common pleas to be composed of a president and associate judges. The members of the court, appointed by joint ballot of both houses of the general assembly, were to hold court in three judicial districts into which the state was to be divided by legislative action. (*Ibid.,* Art. III, sec. 8.). The court was assigned common law and chancery jurisdiction in all cases and should be provided by law. (*Ibid.,* Art. III, sec. 3.) To the court was assigned jurisdiction in probate and testamentary matters and in the appointment of guardians. Moreover the court of common pleas and supreme court were assigned original cognizance of criminal cases as might be provided by law. (*Ibid.,* Art. III, sec. 4.) Appeals in civil cases might be made from the county commissioners, justices of the peace, and other inferior courts to the court of common pleas. (*Ibid.,* Art. III, sec. 3.) Finally, the court was authorized to appoint a clerk. (*Ibid.,* Art. III, sec. 9.)

Since the constitution called for legislative action, an act interpreting the constitutional provisions was passed in 1803. Under this act the court was given original jurisdiction in all cases in law and equity, when the matter in dispute exceeded the jurisdiction of the justices of the peace. The court was to take original cognizance of all probate, testamentary, and guardianship matters, and in all criminal matters exceeding the jurisdiction of the justices of the peace, except in cases where the punishment of the crime was capital. (1. O. L. 39-40.) A year later the jurisdiction of the court of chancery was restricted to cases for the sum involved was more than $500. (2. O. L. 261.) In 1807 this restriction was removed, and the court was given original jurisdiction in all cases cognizable by a court of chancery, subject to an appeal to the supreme court. (5 O. L. 117.)

Meantime, the court was assigned cognizance of criminal cases wherein the punishment was capital if the accused elected to be so tried. (4 O. L. 57.) In 1805 the court was authorized to appoint a county prosecuting attorney. (3 O. L. 47.) The Chancery Act, adopted in 1824, conferred general chancery powers on the court. (22 O. L. 75) In 1843 the court was given jurisdiction concurrent with the supreme court in cases of divorce and alimony. (41 O. L. 94.)

Significant changes were made in the composition of the court and its jurisdiction during the middle of the nineteenth century. Under the constitution of 1851, the judges of the court of common pleas were made elective for a seven-year term. For the purpose of electing judges the state was divided into nine districts. The districts, of which Hamilton County constituted one, were to be composed of three or more counties. Each district, in turn, was to be subdivided into three parts, in each of which one common pleas judge was to be elected. Court was to be held in every district or county with such jurisdiction as should be fixed by law. (*Ohio Const. 1851*. Art. IV, secs. 3, 4.) Provision was made for the removal of judges by a concurrent resolution of two-thirds of the members elected to each house of the legislature. (*Ibid.,* Art. IV, sec. 17.)

Interpreting the constitutional provisions, the legislature made provisions for judicial districts, but left the jurisdiction of the court much the same as it had been in the earlier years of its existence. (50 O. L. 78.) However, with the reestablishment of the probate court by constitutional provision, the court of common pleas was denied jurisdiction in cases of probate, testamentary, and guardianship matters. However the judgments and final decrees of the probate court could be "reversed, vacated, or modified" on error proceedings by the court of common pleas. (51 O. L. 145.) A year later, in 1852, the court of common pleas was given original jurisdiction of all crimes and offenses, except minor criminal cases, the exclusive jurisdiction of which was invested in the justices of the peace or other minor courts. (G. C. sec. 13422-5; 51 O. L. 474; 52 O. L. 73.) In the same year the court of common pleas was invested with exclusive jurisdiction in divorce cases. (51 O. L. 377.)

During this period, the jurisdiction of the court, in certain counties, underwent a marked change. Thus, in 1852, the criminal court of Hamilton County was reestablished and to it was transferred the criminal jurisdiction formerly exercised by the court of common pleas, which was given original cognizance of civil matters. (50 O. L. 90.) Shortly afterward the superior courts were reestablished in Cincinnati, and in Franklin and Montgomery Counties. (52 O. L. 34; 53 O. L. 38;

54 O. L. 37.) Except in divorce, alimony, and bastardy cases, the courts had the same jurisdiction in civil cases as the court of common pleas. (See page 170.)

Since 1906 the court of common pleas has had jurisdiction in naturalization proceedings. In that year the federal statute was amended to limit jurisdiction, in the granting of naturalization, to the United States district courts and state courts having a clerk, a seal, and jurisdiction in matters of law and equity in which the amount in controversy is unlimited. (*U. S. Statutes at Large*, XXXIV, pt. ii, 596.) Although the statute did not specifically designate a state or federal court to exercise such jurisdiction, the federal courts have exclusively exercised such authority in Hamilton County since that date.

At the opening of the twentieth century changes in the organization of the courts were again made. By the constitutional amendment of 1912, the divisions and subdivisions as provided by the constitution of 1851 were abolished. Provision was made for the election of one or more common pleas judges in each county. (*Ohio Const.*, Art. IV, sec. 3.) Ten years later, the selection of a chief justice of the court of common pleas was authorized. Under an act of March 13, 1923, in counties where there were two or more common pleas judges, they were authorized to delegate one of their number as chief justice. The justice so designated by his colleagues was to serve in such capacity until the expiration of his term, after which time the office of chief justice was to be an elective one. The elective section of the act was nullified by the supreme court on the grounds that the creation of a new elective official was unconstitutional. Accordingly, in 1927, an amendment was passed eliminating the elective provision of the act.

With the increased number of issues presented to the court of common pleas, the problems of judicial administration have become greater. This problem was solved in part by the creation of a chief justice of the court of common pleas, who has been given the duties of superintendent the business of the court, clarifying it, and distributing it among the judges. Besides the duties enumerated, the chief justice annually makes a report to the clerk of courts showing the work performed by the court and by each judge in the preceding calendar year. Moreover, he reports such other data as the chief justice of the supreme court may require. (G. C. 1558.)

In recent years attempts have been made to improve the efficiency of the court by imposing stricter qualifications upon those who seek election to the bench. In 1917, there was passed an act providing that a common pleas judge shall have been admitted to practice as an attorney and counselor-at-law for period of six years preceding his election. (107 O. L. 164.)

During the first three decades of Ohio history, the movement for the extension of the popular election of public officers deprived the court of common pleas of the privilege of appointing the county recorder (1829), county surveyor (1831), and county prosecuting attorney (1833). (27 O. L. 65; 29 O. L. 399; Salmon P. Chase, *The Statutes of Ohio and of the Northwest Territory,* 3 volumes, Cincinnati, 1833-1835, III, 1935.) The court continued to appoint a clerk of courts until 1851. In recent years, however, as new functions have been added to county government, the court has again been given a limited point of power. Successive acts in 1886, 1891, 1914, and 1925 authorized the court to appoint a soldiers' and sailors' relief commission, a jury commission, and assignment commission, and a probation officer. (83 O. L. 232; 88 O. L. 200; 104 O. L. 13-64; 111 O. L. 423.) Other appointments, authorized during the development of the office, are a court interpreter and a criminal bailiff. Since 1929, the court, in counties having a population in excess of 300,000, has been empowered to appoint one or more psychiatrists, psychologist, or other examiners or investigators who shall hold their offices at the will of the court, and receive such compensation as the judge may determine, not exceeding the amount as maybe appropriated by the county commissioners. (G. C. 1541; 113 O. L. 467.)

The records of the court of common pleas are deposited for safekeeping with the clerk of courts, who is made liable for the destruction of all law reports and books furnished by the state for use of the court and the bar. (68 O. L. 109.)

Dockets and Clerk's Entries

76. INDEX TO APPEARANCE AND JUDGMENT DOCKET
1853—. 193 volumes (1-23, 1-50 and A-Z, 1-120).
Index of common pleas court cases showing case, docket, volume and page numbers. Numerically arranged by case numbers. Handwritten. Volumes average 200 pages. 14 x 8.5 x 3. County Courthouse, Room 329.

77. DIRECT INDEX TO GENERAL JUDGMENTS
1884—. 106 volumes. (104 volumes in 4 series 1-4, labeled A-Z; 1 volume, A-K; 1 volume, L-Z).
Index showing names of creditors to common pleas judgments; also name of debtor, date, amount, and docket, volume, and page numbers. Alphabetically arranged by

names of judgment creditors. Handwritten. Volumes average 200 pages. 20 x 14 x 3. County Courthouse, Room 329.

78. REVERSE INDEX TO GENERAL JUDGMENTS
1884—. 106 volumes. (104 volumes in 4 series 1-4, labeled A-Z; 1 volume, A-K; 1 volume, L-Z).
Index giving name of debtors to common pleas judgment; also name of creditor, date, amount, and docket, volume, and page numbers. Alphabetically arranged by name of debtors. Handwritten. Volumes average 200 pages. 20 x 14 x 3. County Courthouse, Room 329.

79. APPEARANCE DOCKET
1853—. 419 volumes. (1-419).
Record showing names of plaintiff, defendant, and attorneys; also statement of proceedings on suits pending, living judgments, and executions. Chronologically arranged. For index see entry 76. 1853-1910 handwritten on printed forms; 1911—, typed on printed forms. Volumes average 400 pages. 22 x 14 x 4. County Courthouse, Room 329.

80. JUDGMENT DOCKET
1930—. 1 volume.
Copy of judgment as decreed showing amount of judgment, amount of costs, and case number. Chronologically arranged. Alphabetical index by names of judgment creditors. For separate index see entry 76. Typed on printed forms. 300 pages. 20 x 12 x 3. County Courthouse, Room 329.
For prior records see entry 79.

Record of Trials

81. RECORDS OF PROCEEDINGS
1867—. 809 volumes. (1-809). Records from 1932 to date are now being bound and the numbering should continue from 809.
Record of proceedings of court of common pleas showing suits pending, living judgments, and executions. Chronologically arranged. Alphabetical index by name of plaintiffs in back of each volume.1867-1918, handwritten; 1919–1927, typed;

1928-1931, photostats. Volumes average 600 pages. 26 x 18 x 14. County Courthouse, Room 329, rack number 1.

82. COMMON PLEAS COURT SUITS
1906—. 390 file boxes (1906-1927, 335 file boxes, 136000-202200; 128—. 55 file boxes, A1-A54600).

Mortgage foreclosures, liens, executions, *habeas corpus*, suits to contest wills, injunction petition files, and copies of summonses; also domestic relations cases filed prior to 1909. Numerically arranged by case numbers. No index. Handwritten and typed. 24 x 12 x 12. County Courthouse, 1906-1920, 309 file boxes, Clerk of courts' storeroom, basement, west corridor; 1921—, 81 file boxes, Room 329.

For prior records of injunction petitions and copies of summonses see entry 83.

For subsequent divorce records see entries 98, 99, and 136.

83. MISCELLANEOUS PAPERS
1838—. 1,114 file boxes (1838-1927, 979 file boxes, 1-202200; 1928—, 135 file boxes, A1-A546000). 1883-1884, incomplete as some were destroyed in courthouse fire of 1884.

Petitions, copies of summonses, all office returns, all papers filed in common pleas court pertaining to pending suits, living judgments, and executions. Numerically arranged by case numbers. No index. Handwritten and typed. File boxes average 15 x 15 x 8. County Courthouse, 1838-1916, 550 file boxes, Clerk of courts' storeroom, basement; 1917—, 364 file boxes, Room 329.

84. UNDERTAKINGS IN STAY OF EXECUTIONS
1853-1898. 2 volumes. (1-2).

Undertakings to stay executions of judgments rendered before justices of peace pending appeal to court of common pleas. Chronologically arranged; also numerically arranged by case numbers. No index. Handwritten. Condition poor. Volumes average 180 pages. 14 x 10 x 1.5. County Courthouse, Clerk of courts' storeroom, basement.

85. ELEANOR C. W. ALMS ESTATE
1921—. 4 file boxes.

Record of last will and testament of Eleanor C. W. Alms, Case number 178,195 of court of common pleas including endowment and sales of personal properties; also records and disposition of property. Chronologically arranged; also numerically arranged by serial numbers of court orders. No index. Handwritten and typed. 24 x 18 x 13. County Courthouse, Room 329 in separate sealed filing cabinet, owned by heirs of Eleanor C. W. Alms.

86. CRIMINAL COURT RECORD
1885—. 36 volumes. (1-36).
Record of indictments and disposition of cases in criminal court chronologically arranged. Alphabetical index by names of defendants in back of each volume. 1885-1921, handwritten; 1922—, typed. Volumes average 600 pages. 18 x 14 x 2. County Courthouse, Room 329.

87. MUTILATED RECORDS, COMMON PLEAS
1845-1884. 45 volumes (1-45). Records are incomplete.
Mutilated records of common pleas court proceedings salvaged from the courthouse fire of 1884. Chronologically arranged. For index see entry 113. Handwritten. Condition poor. Volumes average 550 pages. 18 x 14 x 2. County Courthouse, Room 329.

Bonds

88. APPEAL BONDS, COMMON PLEAS COURT
1864-1898. 21 volumes. (1, 5, 8, 10-12, 14, 16, 18, 20-22, 24-25, 27-28, 30, 32-34, 35). 1864-1866, 1868-1869, 1871-1872, 1874-1875, 1878-1879, 1881-1882, 1884-1885, 1887-1888, 1890-1898, 16 volumes; 1 volume unnumbered and volumes 3-4, 6-7, 9, 13, 15, 17, 19, 23, 26, 29, 31, 35, 37, missing. Missing volumes prior to 1884, destroyed in courthouse fire of 1884.
Bonds posted by appellants to guarantee payment of costs in event cases are decided against appellants. Numerically arranged by case numbers. Numerical index by case numbers in back of each volume. Handwritten. Volumes average 157 pages. 14 x 10 x 1.5. County Courthouse, Clerk of courts' storeroom, basement.
For subsequent records see entry 89.

89. GENERAL BOND BOOK, CIVIL CASES.
1853—. 13 volumes (1-13).

Bonds to guarantee payment of court costs in appealed cases. Numerically arranged by case numbers. Numerical index by case numbers in back of each volume. Handwritten on printed forms. Volumes average 300 pages. 12 x 8 x 1.5. County Courthouse, Room 329.

90. APPEAL BONDS
1873—. 18 volumes. (1-3, 13-27). 1874-1878, volumes 4-12, destroyed in courthouse fire of 1884.

Record of bonds posted to carry cases to court of appeals showing names of plaintiff and defendant, case number, and amount of surety. Numerically arranged by case numbers. Numerical index by case numbers in back of each volume. 1873-1905, handwritten; 1906—, typed on printed forms. Volumes average 200 pages. 15 x 8 x 2. County Courthouse, 1873, 1879-1884, 3 volumes, Clerk of courts' storeroom, basement, west corridor; 1885—, 15 volumes, Room 329, vault.

91. INJUNCTION CASES
1884—. 16 volumes (13-28). Prior records, volumes 1-12, destroyed in courthouse fire of 1884.

Record of bonds signed in injunction cases showing suit, amount of bond, names of sureties and date. Numerically arranged by case numbers. No index. Handwritten. Volumes average 200 pages. 18 x 15 x 2. County Courthouse, Room 329.

92. UNDERTAKINGS FOR INJUNCTIONS
1885—. 29 volumes. (1-29).

Undertakings by plaintiffs for injunctions and indemnity bonds to insure defendants against loss. Numerically arranged by case numbers. Numerical index by case numbers in back of each volume. Handwritten. Volumes average 150 pages. 12 x 8 x 1. County Courthouse, 1885-1923, 26 volumes, Clerk of courts' storeroom, basement; 1924—. 3 volumes, Room 329.

Business Administration of Office

93. COST ITEM BOOKS
1884-1930. 269 volumes (90-358). Prior records destroyed in courthouse
fire of 1884.
Record of court costs and payment of common pleas and domestic relations courts
numerically arranged by case numbers no index. Handwritten. Volumes average 800
pages. 15 x 12 x 2. County Courthouse, Room 328.
For subsequent records see entry 94.

94. COST ITEM CARDS.
1931—. 92 file boxes (1-54971).
Record giving case number, date, miscellaneous entries in civil and criminal cases
of common pleas and domestic relations courts. Numerically arranged by case
numbers. No index. Handwritten. 16 x 9 x 4.5. County Courthouse, Room 329.
For prior records see entry 93.

Miscellaneous

95. MINUTES
1844—. 695 volumes. (1-695).
Daily record of proceedings of common pleas court. Chronologically arranged. No
index. 1844-1921, handwritten; 1922—, typed. Volumes average 700 pages. 18 x
14 x 2.5. County Courthouse, Room 329.

96. JUDGES' OATHS
1908—. 2 volumes. Prior records missing.
Copies of governor's commissions and common pleas judges' oaths of office.
Chronologically arranged. Alphabetical index by names of judges in front of each
volume. Handwritten and typed on printed forms. Volumes average 180 pages. 16
x 14 x 2, County Courthouse, 1908-1912, 1 volume, Clerk of courts' storeroom,
basement; 1913—, 1 volume, Room 329.

97. STENOGRAPHERS' NOTES
1887-1914. 65 bundles (1-103890). Subsequent records were filed with
original cases.

Transcripts of stenographers' notes of common pleas court. Numerically arranged
by case numbers. No index. Condition fair. 4 x 8 x 7. County Courthouse, Clerk of
courts' storeroom, basement, west corridor.

Prior to 1914, family matters in Hamilton County had been handled by several courts. Divorce and alimony cases had been successively handled by the supreme court (1803-1842), the common pleas court (1843-1908), and the insolvency court (1909-1914); while the probate judge, following the enactment of the juvenile court law of 1904, was assigned original jurisdiction in children's cases. (See pages 50, 31, 56.) The recognition that such a system, with divided administration and responsibility, was unsatisfactory led to a movement for the establishment of a court of domestic relations. Accordingly, in 1914, the legislature by amending the juvenile court law, made provision for the court of domestic relations in Hamilton County. Since that date successive acts have created such Courts in Montgomery (1915), Mahoning (1917), Lucas (1923), Franklin (1927), Stark (1927), and Summit (1927) Counties. (G. C. secs. 1532-1, 1532-4, 1532-6, 1532-7, 1532-8, 1832-2.) Except in Cuyahoga County, where the court began operation under the authority of the chief justice of the court of common pleas to redistribute the business of the court, the acts creating such courts simply provided for the election of an additional judge to be designated the judge of the court of common pleas, division of domestic relations. (110 O. L. 52.)

The Hamilton County division of domestic relations, patterned after similar courts established in the cities of Buffalo and Chicago in 1910, had exclusive original cognizance in divorce and alimony cases, and those concerning delinquent, neglected, and dependent children as defined by the Ohio juvenile court laws. Moreover the court has original jurisdiction in determining the paternity of illegitimate children, in charging adults with contributing to the delinquency of minors, and in cases of desertion or failure to provide for minor children. (G. C. secs. 12110, 121185, 13008, 1654, 1655. For additional jurisdiction of the court see G. C. secs. 6344, 6345, 12666, 12787, 13041, 13048.)

In order to carry on the work of the court, the domestic relations judge is authorized to appoint a referee in juvenile matters and to fix his salary. The referee, having the usual powers of masters in chancery, hears all cases and certifies to the judge of the domestic relations court his findings, together with his recommendations. The court may accept or reject the findings of the referee. (G. C. sec. (1662-1.)

The court is authorized, also, to appoint a probation officer. This official, like the referee, receives such compensation as it designated by the court, not to exceed the amount appropriated by the county commissioners. (G. C. sec. 1662.) It is the duty of the probation officer or his assistants, after a complaint has been filed against a minor, to investigate the facts and circumstances surrounding the alleged delinquency, neglect, or dependency. It is the duty of this official, or his assistants, to investigate the habits of the child, his school record, and other facts which might tend to throw light on his life and character. The probation officer represents the interest of the child in court, furnishes information to the judge during the proceedings, and takes charge of a child before, during, and after the trial. He has the same powers and authority as the county sheriff to serve warrants within or outside the county. (G. C. sec. 1663.) The probation department enables the court to carry into execution its decision and to discover what provisions should be made for the welfare of each child coming before the court.

The broad discretionary powers conferred upon the court enables the judge to departmentalize the work of the court by creating divisions corresponding to its statutory jurisdiction. There are, among others, the boys' and girls' delinquency divisions, the contributing division, family adjustment and conciliation division, and non-support and bastardy divisions. As a result of the Ohio legislature accepting the provisions of the federal social security act (requirements of title IV), the judge is authorized, unless other special boards are created, to administer aid to dependent and to crippled children. The legislature, when accepting the provisions of the national social security act relative to dependent and crippled children, repealed the Ohio statutes regarding mothers' pensions, which, since their enactment in 1913, had been administered by the domestic relations judge. (See page 243.) The creation of special departments, each under the direction of a specialist in juvenile matters, has done much in correcting some of the defects of judicial administration of family matters which existed prior to 1914.

Realizing the need of special treatment of children's cases, the members of the Ohio legislature made provision for the segregation of juvenile from adult offenders. To make this segregation as complete as possible, the judge is directed, by statute, to hear the trial cases of juvenile and adult offenders in separate rooms. (G. C. sec. 1649.) Then, too, upon the recommendation of the judge exercising jurisdiction, the county commissioners are required to provide by purchase or lease a place to be known as the "detention home," to be located a convenient distance from the courthouse. (G. C. sec. 1670.) Here a delinquent, dependent, or neglected child may be detained until after the final disposition of his case. (G. C. sec. 1670.) Here, too, dependent children may be separated from delinquents, and first offenders from recidivists. The judge is authorized to appoint a matron to manage such a detention home.

Besides empowering the judge to classify juvenile offenders, the legislature has made provision whereby children coming before the court may be subjected to physical and mental tests. (G. C. sec. 1652-1.) The results of these tests, which are made by experienced physicians and psychiatrists, enable support and its attaches to determine the disposition of each offender. Conflict in the home or in the school maybe the result of placing a superior or inferior child in the improper mental group.

The clerk of the court of common pleas serves as the clerk of the division of domestic relations. The records of the court include, among others, an appearance docket, a journal, case cards, and case studies. Although it returns statistical reports to the secretary of state and to the United States Children's Bureau, the court publishes no annual report.

The court of domestic relations, aside from administering justice and adjudicating controversies, attempts to solve social problems which have steadily increased in the postwar years. An immense amount of work, the object of which is crime prevention and placing the maladjusted child in normal society, is done by nonlegal agencies in cooperation with the court. Thousands of cases are dealt with informally by the Humane Society, the Council of Social Agencies, and municipal and county clinics. Protestant, Roman Catholic, and Jewish institutions throughout the county assist the court in its efforts to make social readjustments.

Divorce Records

98 DIVORCE DOCKETS
1915—. 25 volumes. (1-25).
Records names of plaintiff and defendant, case number, and complete record and disposition of case. Numerically arranged by case numbers. Alphabetical index by names of plaintiffs and defendants in back of each volume. Handwritten and typed. Volumes average 700 pages. 18.5 x 14.5 x 4. County Courthouse, Room 219.
For prior records see entries 82 and 136.

99. MINUTES, COURT OF DOMESTIC RELATIONS
1915—. 22 volumes. (1-22).
Record of court proceedings giving names of plaintiff and defendant; also disposition of case. Chronologically arranged. No index. Handwritten and typed.

Volumes average 780 pages. 18.5 x 13.5 x 3. County Courthouse, Room 329.
For prior records see entry 82.

100. ORIGINAL PAPERS, DIVORCE AND JUVENILE CASES
1915—. 550 file boxes.
Original papers and general correspondence. Numerically arranged by case numbers. No index. Typed. 20 x 21 x 1. County Courthouse, Room 228.

Juvenile Court

101. APPEARANCE DOCKET, JUVENILE COURT
1915—. 25 volumes. (1-25).
Record of all juveniles under custody of court advisor with records and disposition of cases. Chronologically arranged. Handwritten and typed. Volumes average $780 pages. 18.5 x 13.5 x 3. County Courthouse, Room 329.

102. INDEX TO APPEARANCE DOCKET, JUVENILE COURT
1915—. 7 volumes. (1-7).
Index recording case, docket, and page numbers. Alphabetically arranged by names of plaintiffs. Handwritten. Volumes average 250 pages. 18 x 12 x 3. County Courthouse, Room 219.

103. JUVENILE COURT MINUTES
1915—. 39 volumes. (1-39).
Record of proceedings referring to care and support of children and showing disposition of delinquent cases. Alphabetically arranged by names of juveniles. No index. Handwritten and typed. Volumes average 580 pages. 18 x 12 x 2.5. County Courthouse, Room 219.

In order to secure an even distribution of work among judges the legislature, in 1913, authorized the court of common pleas to designate the members of the jury commission to serve in the capacity of assignment commissioners. It was their duty, when serving in this capacity, to assign cases for trial and to perform such other duties as the court might require. (103 O. L. 512; 106 O. L. pt. ii, 1114; 109 O. L. 281.) Eight years later, in 1821, the court of common pleas in any county having not more than one common pleas judge and having a population of 8,000 or more with the consent of the county commissioners, was authorized to appoint such assignment commissioners. (109 O. L. 152.)

In 1931 the legislature passed an act relieving the jury commissioners of such tasks by making provision for a separate and distinct body of assignment commissioners. Under this act, the provisions of which are still in force, the judges of the court of common pleas in any county, where two or more judges held court at the same time, were authorized to appoint assignment commissioners. These officials, serving at the pleasure of the court or to receive such compensation as the court might direct, not to exceed $4,900 for each commissioner per year. In the event such appointments were made, the names of the appointees, together with their names and their salaries, were to be recorded in the court journal. (G. C. sec. 3007; 114 O. L. 22.) At the same time, the court of common pleas in any county was authorized, when the business of the court required it, to appoint an assignment commissioner. (G. C. sec. 3007-1; 114 O. L. 213.) This official, serving at the pleasure of the court, could also be appointed court constable.

All records are located in County Courthouse, Room 414.

104. ASSIGNED CIVIL SUITS
1923—. 31 file boxes.
Record of civil suits showing names of plaintiff, defendant, and attorneys; dates of filing, of service of summons, and of assignment; cause of action and trial court. Numerically arranged by case numbers. No index. Typed. 6. x 6. x 14.

105. UNASSIGNED CIVIL SUITS
1926—. 19 file boxes.

Record of all new civil suits for which trial date has not been set showing names of plaintiff, defendant, and attorneys, date filed, date of service of summons, and cause of action. Numerically arranged by case numbers. No index. Typed. 12 x 12 x 20.

106. RECORD OF CIVIL SUITS
1906—. 8 volumes (1-8).

Record of all civil suits showing names of plaintiff, defendant, and attorneys, date filed, trial date, cause of action, and court to which assigned. Numerically arranged by case numbers. No index. Handwritten. Volumes average 300 pages. 16 x 12 x 3.

Although the probation of prisoners had met with success in some eastern states in the latter part of the nineteenth century, it was not until 1908 that the first statute was passed in Ohio providing for the probation of convicted offenders. (For an interesting discussion of the development of probation, see Louis N. Robinson, *Penology in the United States.* Philadelphia, 1922, 194-217.) The act authorized the courts to place on probation convicted offenders who, in the opinion of the judge, were not likely to again engage in crime or offensive conduct. This did not include, however, persons convicted of murder, arson, burglary, incest, sodomy, rape without consent, or the administration of poison. (99 O. L. 339.)

The plan met with immediate success. As a result of the success the legislature, in 1925, passed an act extending the system of probation. The act provides that the judge of the court of common pleas of a county or judges of such court in joint session, if they deem it advisable, may, with the concurrence of the county commissioners, establish a county department of probation. The department consists of a chief probation officer, and such other employees, clerks, and stenographers as maybe fixed by the judges. The judge or judges of the court of common pleas appoint all officers in the department, fix the salaries of the appointees, and supervise their work. The person appointed as probation officer must possess such training, experience, and qualifications as may be prescribed by the department of public welfare. All positions within the department are in the classified service of the civil service of the county. (111 O. L. 423.)

The department has legal control and supervision of persons placed on probation in the county wherein the department is located and of any person resident within the county who may have been placed upon probation by any other court exercising criminal jurisdiction in the state whether within or outside the county. Moreover, upon the request of the court, the probation department receives into legal custody any person remaining or residing in the county who has been paroled or conditionally pardoned from the penal, reformatory, or correctional institution. The period of probation is determined by the court and may be extended, but not beyond a period of 5 years. (G. C. 13453-5; 113 O. L. 201-2.)

The department is required to furnish to each person on probation or parole under its supervision or custody, a written statement of the conditions of probation and parole and instruct him in his obligations to society. Moreover, the department is directed by law "to use all suitable methods, not inconsistent with the conditions of probation or parole, to aid and encourage such persons and bring about improvements in their conduct and condition." (111 O. L. 425.) The department is required, also, to keep informed concerning the conduct and conditions of each person in its custody. Persons on parole must report periodically to the county department and are visited regularly by members of the division.

Besides supervising and instructing probationers, the county department has the duty of keeping a detailed record of its work, and accurate and complete account of all moneys collected from persons under its supervision or in its custody; and to make such reports to the state department of public welfare as it may require.

In counties where no county probation department has been established or where the trial court has no regular probation officer, the trial judge may designate some suitable person to act as a probation officer. This probation official is required to make reports at designated periods not less than once a month, concerning the conduct of the probationers in his charge. This officer is given the same power and is subject to the same rules as provided for regularly constituted officers. (113 O. L. 202-3.)

In the event the probationer absconds during the period of his probation or is confined in any institution, the period of probation ceases until he is returned before the court. (G. C. sec. 13452-5; 113 O. L. 123.) During the period of probation, any field officer or probation officer may arrest the defendant without warrant and bring him before the judge before whom the case is pending. (111 O. L. 423; 113 O. L. 202.) The judge or magistrate may inquire into the conduct of the defendant, and approve the sentence originally imposed, or continue the probation. At the end of the probation period, the jurisdiction of the judge or magistrate ceases, the defendant is discharged, and the judge may restore his citizenship.

Since the probation department is relatively new, there is, to be sure, some inefficiency in its administration. The argument has been advanced, that probationers need no supervision. But authorities on criminal administration generally agree that suspension of sentences without supervision is not probation. Since modification of the offenders' behavior, rather than punishment, is the logic of probation, it is important that trained men be employed to supervise the activities of probationers–preferably not former policemen because of their earlier training, are not always careful to make a distinction between the principles of supervision and discipline. There is likewise a need for scientific diagnosis by specialists in order to determine not only which individuals should be placed on probation, but also the policies that should be used by the department in dealing with various classes of offenders. Finally, organization and centralization of records are becoming increasingly important. The entire record of previous crimes, as well as an educational and home record, should be carefully compiled, filed, and preserved for future reference.

In spite of its few defects, probation offers a solution for stamping out crime. Through such a system society learns what is needed to prevent men and women from becoming criminals and the steps necessary to lead them back into normal society, after they have started a criminal career. (Robinson, *op. cit.,* 216.)

107. PROBATION FILE
1928—. 28 file boxes (1-2500).
Records name and address of probationer, case history, brief social history, nature of offense, date of appearance before judge, name of judge, and duration of probation. Numerically arranged by case numbers. Typed. 25 x 13 x 11. County Courthouse, Room 409.

18. CARD INDEX
1928—. 48 file boxes.
Index to probation files. Alphabetically arranged by names of probationers. Typed. 23 x 6.25 x 4. County Courthouse, Room 409.

The constitution under which the state of Ohio operated for the first half century of its existence made provision for a supreme court. Consisting of three judges appointed by a joint ballot of the legislature for a seven-year term, this court was required to hold sessions at least once a year in each county. (*Ohio Const. 1802*. Art. III, sec. 2.) The number of judges, according to constitutional provisions, might be increased to four after a period of five years, in which case the judges were permitted to divide the state into two circuits. Accordingly, in 1808, the membership of the court was increased to four and the state was divided into the requisite number of circuits. (6 O. L. 32.) Two years later, in 1810, the membership of the court was reduced to three.

By constitutional provision, this court was given original and appellate jurisdiction in "both common law and chancery" cases, and in such cases it should be provided by law. Accordingly, by statutory provision, the court was assigned exclusive cognizance of all cases of divorce and alimony and concurrent jurisdiction of all civil cases, both of law and equity, where the title to land, or the matter in dispute exceeded $1,000, and appellate jurisdiction from the court of common pleas "in all cases respecting the title of lands, or where the matter in controversy exceeds the value of one-thousand dollars, and all cases where the proof of validity of wills or the right of administration shall be in question." (During the first half century of Ohio history the legislature granted decrees of divorce. Although the constitution of 1802 did not prohibit the legislature from exercising such jurisdiction, the supreme court prohibited the practice in 1848. *Bingham* v. *Miller*. 17 O. S. 455. The constitution of 1851, Art. II, sec. 32, contained a prohibiting clause.) Moreover, the court was given original cognizance in the trial of capital offenses. (1 O.L. 36-37.) All cases where the title to land or freehold was in question were to be tried in the county where the land was situated. Furthermore the court was given appellate jurisdiction from the court of common pleas in all cases in which the court of common pleas had original jurisdiction. (14 O. L. 310-354.)

In 1808 the membership of the court was increased to five, and again the state was divided into two circuits. (6 O. L. 32.) This arrangement, abrogated in 1810, when the membership of the court was reduced to three, was reestablished in 1823 when the number of judges was again increased to four. Then, in 1831, the supreme court was directed to meet annually in the town of Columbus for the final adjudication of all such questions of law as may have been reserved in any county for decision. This session of the court, known as the court in bank, was required to have its decisions, in each case, reduced to writing, and transmitted to the clerk of the supreme court in each county in which such question was reserved. (29 O. L. 93-94.) The clerk was directed to enter such decisions "on the journal of the said court" and such proceedings were to be taken, as if such decisions had been made in the county. (*Ibid.*) Six years later, in 1837, an act was passed providing that the final judgments in the supreme court, held within any county within the state, could be reexamined and revised or affirmed in the court in bank upon a writ of error. (35 O. L. 60-62.)

This judicial arrangement continued until the adoption of the constitution of 1851, which provided a judicial system modeled upon the federal system existing at the time. The supreme court, as established in 1851, became for the first time in Ohio history, a reviewing court of last resort. At the same time, the jurisdiction of the supreme court was restricted. In 1852 the court of common pleas, rather than the supreme court, was given original cognizance of all crimes and offenses, except minor criminal cases, the exclusive jurisdiction of which was infested in the justices of the peace and other minor courts. (G. C. sec. 13422-5; 51 O. L. 474; 52 O. L. 72.) The supreme court, which, between the years 1803 and 1843, had had original cognizance in divorce and alimony cases and after 1843 concurrent jurisdiction with the court of common pleas at such cases, was denied such jurisdiction in 1852. (41 O. L. 49; 51 O. L. 377.)

The opinions of the supreme court on circuit and the decisions of the court in bank, as transmitted to the clerk of the supreme court in each county, are in the offices of the respective clerks of courts.

(*Records of this court were probably destroyed in the courthouse fire of 1884.*)

On March 15, 1838, the legislature made provision for a superior court in Cincinnati. This court, consisting of a single judge appointed in the same manner and having the same tenure as the president of the court of common pleas, was given concurrent jurisdiction with the court of common pleas and Hamilton County of all "civil causes at common law in chancery." The court was authorized to hear and determine causes, punish contempt, and appoint and remove officers. The judgments and decrees of the court, according to the statute, "shall be liens upon the property of the judgment debtor, in the same manner and to the extent, that judgments and decrees are in the court of common pleas." The supreme court was given a pellet jurisdiction from the superior court, and cases might be removed to that court by appeal, writ of error, or other process. Sheriffs, coroners, and constables were bound to attend the court, preserve order, and return its processes. (36 O. L. 95-97.) After being in operation for thirteen years, the court was abolished in 1851 by constitutional provision, but it was to continue to operate until the second Monday in February 1852. All business not disposed of within the time limit for its continuance, was transferred to the court of common pleas. (*Ohio Const. 1851. Schedule.* sec. 6.)

In 1854 the superior court Cincinnati was reestablished. The court, composed of three judges chosen by the electorate of Cincinnati, was given original cognizance in civil cases when the sum or matter and dispute exceeded the jurisdiction of the justice of the peace it was authorized to hear, try, and determine action for the recovery of real property, performance of the contract for the sale of real estate, action for the recovery of fines, actions brought against companies(other than those included in sections 45-47 of the Ohio Code), action against a railroad company or owner of a mail stage or other coaches passing through Cincinnati, actions against turnpike companies (other than those included in sections 45-47 of the Ohio Code), actions brought against a nonresident of the state, or a foreign corporation, the property of which or debts owed to the defendant, were to be found in Cincinnati. (52 O. L. 34-36.) Any parties to any suit at common law, or in chancery, or to a civil action originally commenced in the court of common pleas of Hamilton County might, upon the written consent of the parties or their attorneys, remove the cause to the superior court. (52 O. L. 39.)

The terms of court, held at the courthouse in Cincinnati, commenced on the first Monday of each month, except the months of July, August, and September. A general term of court could be held by any two of the judges and a special term by any one of them. (52 O. L. 35.) At special term, the court had the same power to vacate or modify its own judgments or orders, rendered at a special term, and to enter judgment by confession, as was vested in the court of common pleas. Moreover, for errors appearing in the record, a decree rendered by the court at a special term, could be reversed, vacated, or modified by the court at the general term.

The court was given full power to classify and distribute its business, to make rules and regulations, and to appoint masters and other officers necessary to facilitate its business. The judges of the court, in the exercise of the jurisdiction conferred upon the court, and in granting remedial writs and orders, in the recess of the court, had the same powers and authority as the judges of the court of common pleas. (52 O. L. 39.)

This court, together with the insolvency court, was abolished by the legislature in 1921, and its power and jurisdiction were vested in the court of common pleas of Hamilton County. (109 O. L. 354.) However, the court continued to operate until the expiration of the term of office of the incumbents.

Dockets and Records of Trial

109. RECORDS OF SUPERIOR COURT
1882-1925. 114 volumes (1-114).
Records of proceedings of superior court, minutes, petitions, summonses, praecipes, and judgments. Chronologically arranged. Alphabetical index by names of plaintiffs in back of each volume. Handwritten. Volumes average 550 pages. 18 x 14 x 2. County Courthouse, Room 329.

110. CASE RECORDS
1911-1925 566 file boxes (2000-54099). Prior records missing.
Miscellaneous case papers on actions brought before superior court. Numerically arranged by case numbers. No index. Handwritten and typed. Condition poor. 14 x 10 x 5. County Courthouse, Clerk of courts' storeroom, basement.

111. CASES APPEALED
1857-1925. 800 file boxes. 1867-1884, missing; destroyed in courthouse fire of 1884.
Original case papers on appeals to superior court from lower courts. Numerically arranged by case numbers. No index. Handwritten. Condition poor. 10 x 5.5 x 4.5.

County Courthouse, 1857-1866, 216 file boxes, Clerk of courts' storeroom, basement, west wall; 1885-1925, 584 file boxes, Room 329.

112. MUTILATED SUPERIOR COURT RECORDS
1848-1884. 20 volumes (1-20).

Salvaged mutilated records, which are incomplete, of superior court proceedings prior to courthouse fire at 1884. Chronologically arranged; also numerically arranged by case numbers. Handwritten. Condition poor. Volumes average 550 pages. 18 x 14 x 2. County Courthouse, Room 329.

113. INDEX TO MUTILATED SUPERIOR COURT RECORDS
1848-1884. 1 volume.

Index giving names of plaintiffs and defendants; also case numbers on suits pending, live in judgments, and executions. Alphabetically arranged by names of plaintiffs. Handwritten on printed forms. 300 pages. 20 x 12 x 3. Upstairs, County Courthouse, Room 329.

114. APPEARANCE DOCKET
1853-1925. 98 volumes. (1-98).

Records names of plaintiff and defendant, petition, case, and form numbers, disposition of case; living judgments and suits pending. Chronologically arranged; also numerically arranged by case numbers. Handwritten on printed forms. Volumes average 300 pages. 20 x 12 x 3. County Courthouse, Room 329.

115. INDEX TO APPEARANCE DOCKET
1853-1925. 18 volumes. (1-18). 1853-1873 missing.

Index giving names of plaintiffs and defendants; also case numbers. Alphabetically arranged by names of plaintiffs. Handwritten. Volumes average 300 pages. 20 x 12 x 3, County Courthouse, Room 329.

116. DIRECT INDEX TO JUDGMENTS
1884-1925. 20 volumes. (A-Z). Prior records destroyed in courthouse fire of 1884.

Records name of plaintiff, case, docket, and page numbers. Numerically arranged by case numbers. Alphabetical index by names of plaintiffs in front of each volume.

Handwritten on printed forms. Volumes average 500 pages. 18 x 14 x 2. County Courthouse, Room 329.

117. REVERSE INDEX TO JUDGMENTS
1884-1925. 20 volumes. (A-Z). Prior records destroyed in courthouse fire of 1884.

Records name of defendant; also case, docket, and page numbers. Alphabetically arranged by names of defendants. Handwritten. Volumes average 500 pages. 18 x 16 x 2. County Courthouse, Room 329.

118. UNDERTAKING FOR ATTACHMENT
1868-1869. 1 volume. (5). 1866-1867, volumes 1-4, missing; destroyed in courthouse fire at 1884. Subsequent records kept by common pleas court.

Records undertakings for attachments to indemnify defendants against loss in event action was brought in error. Numerically arranged by case numbers. No index. Handwritten on printed forms. Condition poor. 200 pages. 14 x 10 x 2. County Courthouse, Room 329.

119. MINUTES
1884-1925. 155 volumes. (87-241). Prior records destroyed in courthouse fire of 1884.

Record of daily proceedings of superior court. Volume 241 (pages 134-158) contains a brief history of superior court which was discontinued November 30, 1925. Chronologically arranged. Chronological index and back of each volume. Handwritten. Volumes average 550 pages. 18 x 14 x 2. County Courthouse, Room 329.

Business Administration of Office

120. ITEM BOOKS
1884-1925. 45 volumes. (55-99). Prior records destroyed in courthouse fire of 1884.

Record of payments of superior court costs. Numerically arranged by case numbers. No index. Handwritten on printed forms. Volumes average 600 pages. 15 x 12 x 2. County Courthouse, Room 328.

In May 1894, the legislature made provision for a court of record in Hamilton County styled "the court of insolvency." Consisting of a single judge elected for a five-year term, this court was created to relieve the probate court of its ever-increasing volume of business. The judge was required to give bond in the sum of $5,000; was authorized to make rules and regulations, and appoint a deputy clerk or clerks, masters, and referees and other officers necessary to facilitate the business of the court. He was instructed to serve as clerk of his court. In the event the office became vacant, the probate judge was designated to fill the vacancy. Sheriffs, coroners, and constables were bound to attend the court, preserve order, and execute the return of processes as they were required to do in the probate court. (91 O. L. 845.)

The court was given original cognizance in all cases relating to and arising under the laws "regulating the mode of administering assignments in trust for the benefit of creditors." The probate judge was authorized to transfer to the court of insolvency any and all cases pending in the probate court in reference to assignments in trust. In the event the cases were transferred, the clerk of the probate court was directed to enter each transfer in his docket. Furthermore, if the business of the probate court required it, the probate judge was permitted to certify and transfer to the court any other case or cases pending in the probate court. (91 O. L. 846.) The court of insolvency was authorized to "vacate and modify its own judgments" or orders during or after the term.

The judge of the newly created court was given the care and custody of all "files, papers, books and records belonging to the court of insolvency." (91 O. L. 845.) In 1909, the insolvency court was given a concurrent jurisdiction with the court of common pleas in such matters as allowing and issuing writs of *habeas corpus* and determining the "validity of the detention of the persons brought before it on such writs," all actions to dissolve co-partnerships, and all actions to compel the specific performance of a contract for the sale of real estate. From the orders, decrees, and judgments in such cases, appeals might be taken in such cases to the circuit court. (100 O. L. 98-100; 101 O. L. 219-220.) In the same year, the court was given concurrent jurisdiction with the court of common pleas in divorce and alimony cases. This jurisdiction was abolished five years later. (104 O. L. 179.)

In 1921, after being in operation twenty-seven years, the court was abolished by the legislature. However, it continued to operate until the expiration of the term of the incumbent. All causes pending in the court were transferred to the court of common pleas in Hamilton County, which was given power to hear and determine them. (109 O. L. 357.)

Dockets, Clerk's Entries, and Records of Trials

121. CIVIL CASES
1898-1923. 452 file boxes. (1-5387, 1-9538).
Records summonses, affidavits, correspondence, and all case papers on divorce, civil, and injunction actions. Numerically arranged by case numbers. No index. Handwritten and typed. Filed boxes average 13.5 x 10.5 x 4 County Courthouse,1898-1914, 80 file boxes, Clerk of courts' storeroom, 5th floor; 1898-1923, 372 file boxes, Room 328.

122. CIVIL DOCKET
1898-1923. 22 volumes. (1-22).
Record of civil cases in insolvency court showing names of plaintiff and defendant, cause of action, and final disposition of case. Chronologically arranged. Alphabetical index by names of defendants in back of each volume. Handwritten on printed forms. Volumes average 600 pages. 18 x 14 x 3. County Courthouse, Room 328.

123. INDEX TO CIVIL DOCKET
1898-1923. 4 volumes. (1-4).
Index listing name of plaintiff, case number, also docket and page reference to insolvency court cases. Alphabetically arranged by names of plaintiffs. Handwritten on printed forms. Volumes average 300 pages. 20 x 12 x 3. County Courthouse, Room 328.

124. PROCEEDINGS, CIVIL CASES
1898-1923. 22 volumes. (1-22).
Record of civil cases in insolvency court covering suits pending, living judgments, and executions. Chronologically arranged. Alphabetical index by names of plaintiffs in back of each volume. Handwritten on printed forms. Volumes average 600 pages. 18 x 14 x 3. County Courthouse, Room 328.

125. ASSIGNMENT DOCKET
1883-1916. 10 volumes (1-10). Subsequent records kept by federal courts. Records name of assignee and complete record of each case chronologically arranged. Alphabetical index by names of assignees in back of each volume. Handwritten. Volumes average 200 pages. 15 x 8 x 2. County Courthouse, Room 328.

126. INDEX TO ASSIGNMENT DOCKET8
1883-1916. 2 volumes (1-2).
Records names of debtor and of case; also docket and page numbers. Alphabetically arranged by names of debtors. Handwritten. Volumes average 200 pages. 20 x 12 x 2. County Courthouse, Room 328.

127. ASSIGNMENT CASES
1878-1923. 314 file boxes (1-4635).
All papers in bankruptcy cases; summonses, affidavits, correspondence, and authority to sell real estate. Numerically arranged by case numbers. No index. Handwritten and typed. 15 x 12 x 4. County Courthouse, Room 328.

128. ASSIGNMENT RECORDS
1884-1916. 43 volumes. (1-43). Subsequent records kept by federal courts. Minutes of insolvency court giving complete record of court proceedings. Numerically arranged by case numbers. No index. Handwritten. Volumes average 600 pages. 18 x 14 x 3. County Courthouse, Room 328.

129. COURT OF INSOLVENCY DOCKET
1909-1915. 12 volumes. (1-14). 1910-1913. volumes. 8, 12, missing.
Docket entries of insolvency court giving names of litigants and attorneys, case numbers, and final disposition of cases. No index. Handwritten. Volumes average 300 pages. 8.5 x 10.5 x 1. County Courthouse, Superintendent of buildings storeroom, basement.

130. COURT RECORDS
1902-1923. 17 volumes. (1-17). Prior records missing.
Record of proceedings of insolvency court. Numerically arranged by case numbers. No index. Handwritten. Volumes average 600 pages. 18 x 14 x 3. County Courthouse, Room 328.

131. JOURNAL
1894-1923. 5 volumes. (1-5).
Complete record of court proceedings. Chronologically arranged. Numerical index by case numbers in back of each volume. Handwritten. Volumes average 600 pages. 18 x 14 x 3. County Courthouse, Room 328.

132. SALE CASES
1898-1910. 43 file boxes (1-456). Subsequent records kept by probate court. Summonses, affidavits, and correspondence pertaining to sale of real estate. Numerically arranged by case numbers. No index. Handwritten and typed. 15 x 12 x 4. County Courthouse, Room 328.

133. PROCEEDINGS TO SELL REAL ESTATE
1896-1915. 43 file boxes (1-457). Subsequent records kept by federal courts.
All papers in proceedings to sell real estate through insolvency court in bankruptcy cases. Numerically arranged by case numbers. No index. Handwritten and typed. 12 x 9 x 4.5. County Courthouse, Room 328.

134. ASSIGNEES' BONDS
1895-1915. 2 volumes. (1-2). Subsequent records kept by federal courts.
Record of assignees' bonds posted in insolvency court cases showing date, case number, amount of bond, names of sureties, and parties to suit. Alphabetically indexed by names of assignees in back of each volume. Handwritten. Volumes average 1,000 pages. 14 x 9 x 3. County Courthouse, Room 328.

135. CIVIL ACTION BONDS
1898-1909. 4 volumes. (1-4).

Record of bonds posted in insolvency civil cases giving title of case, amount of bond, names of plaintiff and defendant, and names of sureties. Numerically arranged by case numbers. No index. Handwritten. Volumes average 250 pages. 14 x 9 x 2. County Courthouse, Room 328.

> For subsequent records see entry 89.

136. DIVORCE RECORDS
1909-1915. 23 volumes. (1-23).

Record of petitions giving names of plaintiffs and defendants; also disposition of divorce cases heard in insolvency court. Chronologically arranged. Alphabetical index by names of plaintiffs and defendants in back of each volume. Handwritten. Volumes average 600 pages. 18 x 14 x 3. County Courthouse, Room 328.

> For subsequent records see entry 89.

137. INDEX TO DIVORCE RECORDS
1909-1915. 3 volumes. (1-3).

Index giving names of plaintiff and defendant; also case, docket, and page numbers. Alphabetically arranged by names plaintiffs. Handwritten. Condition fair. Volumes average 300 pages. 20 x 12 x 3. County Courthouse, Room 328.

Business Administration of Office

138. COST ITEMS
1910-1915. 12 volumes (6-17). Prior records and 1915-1923 missing.

Record of costs on individual cases of insolvency court. Numerically arranged by case numbers (3001-10200). No index. Handwritten. Volumes average 500 pages. 18 x 4 x 3. County Courthouse, Room 328.

139. JURY VOUCHER CHECK STUBS
1898-1923. 3 volumes. 1909-1922, missing.

Records names of jurors, insolvency court service, amount paid, and date. Numerically arranged by voucher numbers. No index. Handwritten. Volumes average 125 pages. 20 x 18 x 2. County Courthouse, Room 328.

140. CASH BOOKS
January 1910-July 1923. 60 volumes. (1, 1-59).
Record of cash for advance costs, Sundries, and fees in insolvency court cases. Chronologically arranged; also numerically arranged by voucher numbers. No index. Handwritten. Volumes average 500 pages. 18 x 15 x 2. County Courthouse, Clerk of courts' storeroom, basement.

Until 1851 the judicial power of the state of Ohio, in both matters of law and equity, was vested in the supreme court, court of common pleas, and justices' courts. The supreme court, during the first fifty years of Ohio history, served as a court of appeals, holding court in each county annually. When, in 1851, a new constitution was adopted, the judicial system was extended by the creation of district courts. Composed of one supreme court justice and several common pleas judges in the district, these courts were assigned original jurisdiction in the same matters as the supreme court, and such "appellate jurisdiction" as might be provided by law. (*Ohio Const. 1851.* Art. IV, secs. 5-6.) Thus, by constitutional provision the courts were assigned original cognizance in *quo warranto, mandamus, habeas corpus* and *procedendo.* (*Ibid.,* Art. IV, sec. 2.) In addition to this, the legislature, in 1852, authorized the courts to issue writs of error, *certiorari, supersedeas, ne exeat,* and all other writs not specially provided by statute, whenever such writs were necessary for the exercise of its jurisdiction. The same act gave the courts appellate jurisdiction from the court of common pleas in civil cases wherein the court of common pleas had original jurisdiction. (50 O. L. 69.)

For the purposes of the district courts, the nine common pleas districts were apportioned into five judicial districts. At the sessions of the district courts, a judge of the supreme court was designated to preside; in case no judge of the supreme court were present, as was often the case, the judge of the court of common pleas in whose subdivision court was being held was directed to preside. (50 O. L. 69.)

The district courts failed to function properly. Evidence seems to indicate that the increasing numbers of cases coming before the supreme court made it difficult for the justices to attend the meetings of the district courts. Indeed, six years before the creation of the district courts, the supreme court dockets were overcrowded. In 1845 the legislature found it necessary to afford relief, temporarily, by prohibiting appeals from the courts of common pleas to the supreme court. (43 O. L. 80.) A similar condition of overcrowding existed in the sixties; so that, in 1865, the supreme court justices were relieved of the duty of attending the meetings of the district courts for that particular year. (62 O. L. 72.) The judicial system had become slow and cumbersome. The courts declined rapidly after 1865 and were finally abolished in 1885. (82 O. L. 19-20.)

141. APPEARANCE DOCKET

1881-1912. 17 volumes. (1-7, 1-10). 1881-1884, 7 volumes, salvaged from courthouse fire of 1884 and are incomplete. Prior records missing.

Record of proceedings, suits pending, living judgments, and executions of district and circuit courts. Chronologically arranged; also numerically arranged by case numbers. Handwritten. Condition fair. Volumes average 600 pages. 18 x 12 x 3. County Courthouse, Room 328.

This is the same record as entry 143.

142. INDEX TO APPEARANCE DOCKET

1881-1912. 2 volumes.

Index giving names of plaintiff and defendant, cause of action, and court decision in cases tried in district court from 1881 to 1885; also of cases tried and circuit court from 1886 to 1912. Alphabetically arranged by names of plaintiffs. Handwritten. Volumes average 300 pages. 18 x 12 x 2. County Courthouse, Room 328.

This is the same record as entry 144.

Following the complete collapse of the district courts an amendment to the constitution, adopted in 1883, made provision for circuit courts. "The circuit courts," stated the amendment, "shall be the successors of the district courts, in all cases, judgments, records, and proceedings pending in said district courts, in the several counties, of any district, shall be transferred to the circuit courts." (*Ohio Const.*, Art. IV, sec. 6.) The courts were assigned the same "original jurisdiction with the supreme court, and such appellate jurisdiction as may be provided by law." The composition of the courts and the number of circuits was left to the discretion of the legislature. Accordingly, in 1884, an act was passed dividing the state into seven circuits, and provision was made for the election of three judges in each circuit. (81 O. L. 170.)

The circuit courts, in addition to the jurisdiction conferred upon them by the constitution (Art. IV, sec. 6), were authorized by the legislature to issue writs of *supersedeas* in any case, and all other writs not specially provided by statute when they were necessary for the exercise of its jurisdiction. (81 O. L. 170.) Moreover, the courts were authorized, as they deemed expedient, to make and publish rules of procedure in their respective circuits, not in conflict with the law or rules of the supreme court. (81 O. L. 170.) On the other hand, the legislature directed that all cases taken to the circuit courts were to be entered on the docket in the order in which they were commenced, received, or filed, and they shall, stated in law, "be taken up and disposed of in the same order." However, cases in which persons were seeking relief from imprisonment or persons who are convicted of a felony; cases involving the validity of any tax levy or assessment; cases involving the constitutionality of a statute; and cases involving public right and proceedings in *quo warranto, mandamus, procedendo,* or *habeas corpus*, could be taken up in advance of their assignment or order on the docket. (*Ibid.*) In 1913 the circuit courts were superseded by the courts of appeals.

143. APPEARANCE DOCKET
1881-1912. 17 volumes. (1-7, 1-10). 1881-1884, 7 volumes, salvaged from courthouse fire of 1884 and are incomplete.
Record of proceedings, suits pending, living judgments, and executions of district and circuit courts. Chronologically arranged; also numerically arranged by case numbers. Handwritten. Conditioned fair. Volumes average 600 pages. 18 x 12 x 3. County Courthouse, Room 329.
This is the same record as entry 141.

144. INDEX TO APPEARANCE DOCKET
1881-1912. 2 volumes.
Index giving names of plaintiff and defendant, cause of action, and court decision in cases tried in district court from 1881 to 1885; also of cases tried and circuit court from 1886 to 1912. Alphabetically arranged by names of plaintiffs. Handwritten. Volumes average 300 pages. 18 x 12 x 2. County Courthouse, Room 328.
This is the same record as entry 142.

145. CIRCUIT COURT PROCEEDINGS
1885-1912. 10 volumes (1-10).
Record of proceedings of all cases in circuit court. Chronologically arranged. Alphabetical index by names of plaintiffs in back of each volume. Handwritten. Volumes average 450 pages. 18 x 14 x 2. County Courthouse, Room 329.

146. CIRCUIT COURT RECORDS
1885-1912. 250 file boxes (1-15751).
Affirmation of judgments, cases appealed, and cases dismissed. Numerically arranged by case numbers. No index. Handwritten. 14 x 10 x 5. County Courthouse, Clerk of courts' storeroom, basement, east corridor.

147. CIRCUIT COURT ITEM BOOKS
1885-1912. 10 volumes (1-10). Discontinued.
Record of court costs and payments of circuit court. Numerically arranged by case numbers. No index. Handwritten. Volumes average 600 pages. 15 x 12 x 2. County Courthouse, Room 328.

148. RECORDS OF CIRCUIT COURT AND COURT OF APPEALS
1883—. 7 volumes. (1-7).
Record of proceedings of circuit court and court of appeals. Alphabetical index by names of plaintiffs in back of each volume. Handwritten. Volumes average 450 pages. 18 x 14 x 2. County Courthouse, Room 329.
This is the same record as entry 150.

149. MINUTES OF CIRCUIT COURT AND COURT OF APPEALS
1885—. 24 volumes. (1-24).
Record of minutes of circuit court and court of appeals. Chronologically arranged. Alphabetical index by names of plaintiffs in back of each volume. 1881-1921, handwritten; 1922—, typed. Volumes average 600 pages. 18 x 14 x 2. County Courthouse, Room 329.
This is the same record as entry 151.

The judicial system of Ohio was again slightly changed in 1912. By an amendment to the constitution in that year, the current courts were renamed courts of appeals. "The courts of appeals," stated the amendment, "shall continue the work of the respective circuit courts and all pending cases and proceedings in the circuit courts shall proceed to judgment and be determined by the respective courts of appeals." (*Ohio Const.*, Art. IV, sec. 6.) The judges of the several circuit courts were designated as the judges of the courts of appeals, and were directed to perform the duties thereof until the expiration of their terms of office. Vacancies caused by the expiration of terms of office of the judges were to be filled by the electors of the respective appellate districts. The term of office was fixed at six years.

The jurisdiction of the court remained much the same as it had been in 1851. However, the court was assigned original cognizance in writs of prohibition (*Ibid.*, Art. IV, sec. 6), an appellate jurisdiction in the trial of chancery cases. (*Ibid.*, Art. IV, sec. 6.) But certain restrictions were imposed upon the court: "No judgment of a court of common pleas, a superior court or other court of record shall be reversed except by the concurrence of all the judges of the court of appeals." (*Ibid.*, Art. IV, sec. 6.)

At present the court consists of three judges in each of the nine districts into which the state is divided, each of whom shall have been admitted to practice as an attorney at law in the state for a period of six years immediately preceding his election. One court of appeals judge is chosen every two years, and he holds office for six years beginning on the ninth day of February next after his election. The salary of the court of appeals judge, fixed at $6,000 per year in 1913, was increased to $8,000 in 1920 and so continues. (103 O. L. 418; 108 O. L. pt. ii, 1301.) The judges hold at least one session of court annually in each county in the district. (G. C. sec. 1514.)

150. RECORDS OF CIRCUIT COURT AND COURT OF APPEALS
1883—. 7 volumes. (1-7).

Record of proceedings of circuit court and court of appeals. Alphabetical index by names of plaintiffs in back of each volume. Handwritten. Volumes average 450 pages. 18 x 14 x 2. County Courthouse, Room 329.

This is the same record as entry 148.

151. MINUTES OF CIRCUIT COURT AND COURT OF APPEALS
1885—. 24 volumes. (1-24).

Record of minutes of circuit court and court of appeals. Chronologically arranged. Alphabetical index by names of plaintiffs in back of each volume. 1881-1921, handwritten; 1922—, typed. Volumes average 600 pages. 18 x 14 x 2. County Courthouse, Room 329.

This is the same record as entry 149.

152. APPEARANCE DOCKETS
1913—. 9 volumes (1-9). (Records 1932—, held by clerk of courts to be bound.)

Records of court of appeals pending suits, living judgments, and executions. Chronologically arranged; also numerically arranged by case numbers. No index. Handwritten. Volumes average 500 pages. 18 x 12 x 3. County Courthouse, Room 329 on rack in center of room.

153. PROCEEDINGS DOCKET
1914—. 10 volumes (1-10).

Record of case proceedings and decisions a court of appeals. Chronologically arranged. Alphabetical and numerical index by names of plaintiffs and case numbers in front of each volume. Handwritten. Volumes average 450 pages. 17 x 11 x 2. County Courthouse, Room 511, vault.

154. OPINIONS
1913-1918. 15 bundles (1248-61884).

Records of opinions written by judges of court of appeals. Numerically arranged by case numbers. No index. Handwritten. 5 bundles, 24 x 16 x 2; 10 bundles, 14 x 11 x 5.

For subsequent records see entry 83.

The probate court, established by an act of the Northwest Territory on August 30, 1788, consisted of a probate judge with jurisdiction in probate and testamentary and guardianship matters, and two judges of the court of common pleas, who sat with him and ruled on contested points, defective sentences, and final judgments. (Pease, *op. cit.*, 9.)

The judicial system established under the first constitution of Ohio in 1802 made no provision for a probate court, but invested in the court of common pleas such powers as had been exercised by the court in the territorial period. The constitution of 1851 recreated the probate court and gave it original jurisdiction in "probate and testamentary matters, the appointment of administrators and guardians, the settlement of the accounts of executors, administrators and guardians, and such jurisdiction in *habeas corpus*. . .and for the sale of land by executors, administrators and guardians, and such other jurisdiction . . .as may be provided by law." (*Ohio Const. 1851* Art. IV, sec. 8.) An amendment to the constitution, adopted in 1912, authorized the common pleas judge, when petitioned by ten percent of the qualified voters in the counties having a population less than 60,000, to submit to the voters at any general election the question of combining the probate court and the court of common pleas. (*Ohio Const.*, Art. IV, sec. 7.)

One of the primary functions of the court then, since its inception has been the settlement of estates. By the civil code, adopted in 1853, the court was given original jurisdiction in taking proof of wills, in granting letters testamentary, and in settling accounts of executors and administrators. (51 O. L. 167.) Until 1854 the court had jurisdiction in the matter of enforcing the payment of debts and legacies of deceased persons. While the court retains the original jurisdiction regarding estates, new duties have been added in recent years. With the development of inheritance tax laws as a new means of taxation the probate court has been required to determine and assess the tax after the county auditor has appraised the decedent's estate. (108 O. L. pt. i, 561.)

By constitutional provision the probate court has original jurisdiction in granting marriage licenses. The court also issues licenses to ministers to solemnize marriages. The former provision was modified by an act adopted in 1931, which requires an elapse of at least five days between the time of application and that of the issuance of marriage licenses. However, power to suspend the operation of the act is vested in the probate judge, by whose order it is not operative in Hamilton County. (114 O. L. 93.) The probate courts in certain counties were given concurrent jurisdiction with the court of common pleas in "divorce, foreclosure, and partition cases." Thus, in 1894, the legislature conferred such jurisdiction upon the probate courts in Allen, Richland, Perry, Defiance, and Wood Counties. (91 O. L. 799-800.) The original act, subject to amendments in 1896, 1900, and 1904, which granted and denied such jurisdiction to the probate courts in certain counties, was repealed in 1911. (92 O. L. 643; 94 O. L. 137-138; 97 O. L. 113-114; 102 O. L. 100.) In 1919 concurrent jurisdiction was reestablished in Pickaway, Licking, Perry, Defiance, Henry, and Ashland Counties, and established in Fayette County (108 O. L. pt. i, 625.) This jurisdiction was abolished in 1931. (114 O. L. 320.)

The jurisdiction of the court extends to the state's unfortunate. The constitution of 1851 gave the court jurisdiction in making inquests respecting lunatics, insane persons, and idiots. The constitutional provision in this respect was interpreted by the civil code of 1853. Since 1855 the court has been granted jurisdiction in the appointment of guardians for minors, idiots, imbeciles, lunatics, and those incompetent by reason of advanced age. A year later, the court was authorized to commit persons who were mentally incompetent to state institutions maintained for such purpose. (53 O. L. 81.) In recent years the court has been given jurisdiction in trial cases involving neglected, dependent, and delinquent children. In Hamilton County, however, this jurisdiction has been transferred to the court of domestic relations. (See page 41.)

Since the middle of the nineteenth century the probate judge has been required to keep a record of vital statistics. In 1867 the duty of keeping a permanent record of births and deaths, which, in 1856, had been conferred upon the clerk of courts, was transferred to the probate judge. (64 O. L. 63-64.) When, in 1908, a bureau of vital statistics under the direction of the secretary of state was created, the probate judge was relieved temporarily of this task. (99 O. L. 296-307.) Then, in 1921, the act of 1908 was amended so as to require the local registrars to transmit to the district health commissioner, who was directed to serve as the state deputy registrar of vital statistics, all certificates of births and deaths received during the preceding month, and a copy of all such certificates to the probate court. Although the General Code still required the probate judge to keep a permanent record of births and deaths and an index to such records, none has been kept since 1908. (G. C. sec. 10501-15.)

Until 1906 the probate court had jurisdiction in naturalization proceedings. In that year the federal statute was amended and exclusive jurisdiction in naturalization matters was vested in the United States district courts and all state courts of record having a seal, a clerk, and jurisdiction in actions at law and equity.

in which the amount in controversy was unlimited. (*U. S. Statutes at Large*, XXXIV, pt. ii, 596. See also *State of Ohio*, v. *George Metzger and Albert L. Irish*, 10 N. P., N. S., 97 ff.) Although the General Code still requires the probate judge to keep a naturalization record and an index to the records, such jurisdiction was transferred to the courts of common pleas. In Hamilton County the state courts, since 1906, ceased to exercise any further jurisdiction in naturalization matters.

During the early years of its existence the court was given limited criminal jurisdiction in cases in which the sentence did not impose capital punishment or punishment by imprisonment. By the code of civil procedure (1853) the judgments and final decrees of the probate court could be reviewed by the court of common pleas on error. (51 O. L. 146.) In 1857 the criminal jurisdiction of the probate court was transferred to the court of common pleas (54 O. L. 97), but later acts retained it in certain counties only. The last vestige of criminal jurisdiction disappeared with the adoption of the probate code in 1931. (114 O. L. 475.)

Miscellaneous duties, remotely related to probate and testamentary matters, have been added by legislative action. Since 1888 the court has been required to file a certified list of all unknown depositors as furnished by institutions or persons engaged in lending money for profit. (85 O. L. 65.) In 1896 the probate court was given concurrent jurisdiction with the court of common pleas in the matter of changing the names of persons who desired it. (92. O. L. 28.) To this time (between the years 1842-1896), the court of common pleas had had exclusive cognizance in such matters. (40 O. L. 28-29.) Since 1896 the probate court has been required to file certificates of doctors and surgeons, and since 1916 the certificates of registered nurses which authorizes them to practice their professions in the county. (92 O. L. 46; 99 O. L. 499; 106 O. L. 193.) Since 1913 the court has been invested with the power to grant injunctions (103 O. L. 427), and since 1915 has had concurrent jurisdiction with the court of common pleas in condemnation proceedings for roads. (105 O. L. 583.)

The probate judge, aside from his authority to appoint guardians and administrators, has enjoyed an additional appointing power which was conferred upon him by a legislative act of 1861. Under the provisions of this act he was, and is authorized to appoint one gauger and inspector of spirits, linseed, lard, and coal oil; one inspector of flour and meal; one inspector of beef, pork, lard, and butter; one inspector of sawyer lumber and shingles; and one inspector of salt. (58 O. L. 105.) Then, too, from 1908 to 1913 the probate judge was authorized to appoint a county blind relief commission (see page 235) comprised of three members, each of whom served a three-year term. (99 O. L. 57; 103 O. L. 60.) Since 1913 he has had a party to appoint members of the county board of visitors, and since 1917 the district boards of park commissioners. (103 O. L. 173-174, 888; 107 O. L. 65. See also page 277.)

The probate judge, like other county officials, has been required by Statute to keep a record of the business of his office. The present system of records, originating for the most part in 1853 and continued by the probate code of 1931, includes a criminal record, and administrative docket, a guardian's docket, a marriage record, a record of bonds, a naturalization record, and a permanent record of births and deaths. (51 O. L. 167; 52 O. L. 103; 72 O. L. 9; 114 O. L. 324.)

The probate judge has the care and custody of the files, papers, books, and records belonging to the probate office and is ex-officio clerk of the court. The probate code, adopted in 1931, directed the probate judge to preserve for future reference and examination all pleadings, accounts, vouchers, and other papers in each estate, trust, assignment, guardianship, or other proceedings. Such papers are to be properly jacketed and tied together. Moreover, he is required to make proper entries and indexes omitted by his predecessors. Certificates of marriages, reports of birth, and similar papers not a part of a case or proceeding are to be arranged and preserved separately in the order of dates in which they are filed. (114 O. L. 321-322.)

At present the probate judge is elected for a four-year term. (*Ibid.*, 320.) In recent years there has been an attempt to raise the qualifications of those seeking election to this office. Accordingly, in 1935 the probate code of 1931 was amended and eligibility to the office was restricted to a practicing attorney or to a person who "*shall have previously served as a probate judge immediately prior to his election.*" (116 O. L. 481.)

Recording Division

Dockets and Clerk's Entries

155. PROBATE ENTRIES
1791-1837. 4 volumes. (1, 3-4, a1). 1826-1829 missing.
Miscellaneous entries of territorial and early state courts. Chronologically arranged. Alphabetical index by names of cases in back of volumes 1, 3-4, and in front of

volume A1. Handwritten. Volumes average 600 pages. 12.5 x 7.5 x2. County Courthouse, Room 501, cashier's vault.

156. PROBATE INDEX
1791-1852, 1 volume (A-G). 1791-1852, 1 volume, H-Z missing.
General index to original records listing name of deceased or minor, executor or administrator, and date of court term. Records to which this volume is an index are missing; apparently destroyed in courthouse fire of 1884. Alphabetically arranged by names of decedents. Handwritten. 400 pages. 17 x 11 x 2. County Courthouse, Room 541, Annex A.

157. ASSIGNMENT PAPERS
1860—. 23 bundles, 15 file boxes (A1-A273). 1880-1912, missing
Assignment of cases for appearance, hearing, or trial. Numerically arranged by case numbers. No index. Bundles average 12 x 8.5 x 2. File boxes, 17 x 10 x 4.5. County Courthouse, 1860-1879, 23 bundles, Probate court storeroom, basement; 1913—, 15 file boxes, Room 501.

158. APPEARANCE DOCKET
1852—. 32 volumes (1-32).
Records estate numbers, names of parties to actions, dates of filing petitions, orders, answers, and final decrees. Chronologically arranged. Alphabetical index by names of plaintiffs and defendants in back of each volume. Handwritten. Volumes average 600 pages. 18 x 11 x 2. County Courthouse, Room 536

159. ADMINISTRATION DOCKET
1852—. 107 volumes. (1-107).
Docket entries of administration proceedings. Chronologically arranged. Alphabetical index by names of decedents in back of each volume. Handwritten. Volumes average 600 pages. 18 x 10 x 3. County Courthouse, Room 501.

160. INDEX TO ADMINISTRATION DOCKET
1852—. 11 volumes.
Index showing number of estate, date, and volume and page numbers of entry in docket book. Numerically arranged by case numbers. Handwritten on printed forms. Volumes average 300 pages. 18 x 10 x 3. County Courthouse, Room 501.

161. GUARDIAN DOCKET
1791—. 31 volumes. (1-31). 1852-1884, restored.
Entries of guardianship proceedings. Chronologically arranged. Alphabetical index by names of wards in back of each volume. Handwritten. Volumes average 600 pages. 22 x 15 x 3. County Courthouse, Room 501.

162. INDEX TO GUARDIAN DOCKET
1791—. 11 volumes. (1-5, 2 volumes. A-Z, 1-4).
Index showing estate number, name of ward, and date; also volume and page numbers of docket. Two volumes, A-Z are an index to the restored volumes.1791-1851, 1885—, alphabetically arranged by names of guardians; 1852-1884, by names of wards. Handwritten. Volumes average 600 pages. 22 x 15 x 2. County Courthouse, 1791-1884, 7 volumes, Room 546; 1885—, 4 volumes, Room 536.

163. CITATION DOCKET
1884-1890. 1 volume. Discontinued.
Court issues of citations against administrators and executors listing dates citation was issued, returned, and filed. Numerically arranged by case numbers. Alphabetical index by names of individuals cited in back of volume. Handwritten. 640 pages. 16 x 13 x 2.5. County Courthouse, Room 541.

164. RESTORATION DOCKET
1884-1934. 4 volumes. Discontinued.
Restoration of records through court procedure listing date of application, type of record, dates citation was issued and returned, date application was filed, order of entry, and costs. Numerically arranged by case numbers. Alphabetical index by names of applicants in back of volume. Handwritten. Volumes average 590 pages. 18 x 13 x 2.5. County Courthouse, Room 541.

165. MISCELLANEOUS DOCKET
1896—. 2 volumes. (1-2).
Docket entries of miscellaneous records. Numerically arranged by case numbers. Alphabetical index by names of plaintiffs in back of each volume. Handwritten. Volumes average 600 pages. 17 x 10 x 3. County Courthouse, Room 501.

166. DETERMINATION OF HEIRS AND CONSTRUCTION OF WILLS DOCKET

1932—. 1 volume. Initiated 1932 to comply with probate code.
Record showing names of plaintiff and defendant involved in petition to determine heirship and docket entries of proceedings on action. Numerically arranged by case numbers. Alphabetical index by names of decedents in front of each volume. Handwritten. Volumes average 600 pages. 22 x 15 x 3. County Courthouse, Room 536.

167. ASSIGNMENT DOCKET

1858-1877, 1923—. 41 volumes. (1-40, A1).
Records number and name of estate, date of appearance, and date of filing account. Numerically arranged by case numbers. Alphabetical index by names of decedents in back of each volume. Volumes average 300 pages. 15 x 10 x 1.5. County Courthouse, 1858-1877, 40 volumes, Room 550; 1923—, 1 volume, Room 501.
For records 1878-1923, see entry 127.

168. ASSIGNMENT RECORDS

1858-1894. 42 volumes. (1-42).
Record showing assignments for benefit of creditors. Numerically arranged by case numbers. Alphabetical index by names of assigners in back of each volume. Handwritten. Volumes average 600 pages. 18 x 14 x 3. County Courthouse, Room 328.

169. ASSIGNMENT FOR BENEFIT OF CREDITORS

1924—. 6 volumes. (A1-A3, 4-6).
Records name of assigner (individual or firm), date of acceptance, bond approval, appraisers' inventory of assets, inventory of liabilities, amendments (if any), authorization to assignee, records of account and claims, date approved, sworn statement, assignee's final account, and court confirmation. Numerically arranged by case numbers. Alphabetical index by names of assigners in back of each volume. Typed. Volumes average 650 pages. 17 x 12 x 2. County Courthouse, Room 550.

170. *HABEAS CORPUS*
1861-1865. 3 volumes. (1-2, 4). 1863-1864, missing.
Records petition, names of parties, date, writ, return, final entry, seal, and signature
of probate judge. These are records of cases arising during the Civil War, in which
parents or guardians sought custody of minors who enlisted in army or navy; also
a few cases involving the custody of slaves. Numerically arranged by case numbers.
Alphabetical index by names of petitioners in back of each volume. Handwritten.
Volumes average 600 pages. 17 x 11 x 2. County Courthouse, Room 541, Annex
A.

171. PROCEEDINGS IN AID
1922-1932. 1 file box. Discontinued.
Proceedings to recover judgments listing estate file number, name of decedent, date,
and names of witnesses. Numerically arranged by case numbers. No index.
Handwritten. 20 x 11 x 5. County Courthouse, Room 501.

Wills

172. WILLS
1791—. 412 file boxes (A-Z, 24-129823).
Original wills showing estate number, names are decided, beneficiaries, witnesses,
administrator or executor, and attorney; also property valuation and seal. These
records, with the exception of one will, are the only complete records saved in the
courthouse fire of 1884. Chronologically arranged. Handwritten and typed. 17 x 10
x 4.5. County Courthouse, Room 535.

173. INDEX TO WILLS
1791—. 9 volumes. (1 volume unnumbered, 1-8).
Index recording name of decedent, estate number, name of testator, date of
recording, and admission to probate. Alphabetically arranged by names of
decedents. Handwritten and typed. Volumes average 500 pages. 17 x 12 x 2. County
Courthouse, Room 501.

174. RECORDS OF WILLS
1791—. 222 volumes, 1 file box. (Volumes 1-222).
Records name of decedent, preamble, date of probate, copy of will proper.

signatures of testator and witnesses, and date of admission to probate. File box contains copies of original wills sent to foreign counties. Alphabetically arranged by names of testators. Alphabetical index by name of decedents in front of each volume. Handwritten. Volumes average 600 pages. 18 x 11 x 2. File box, 15 x 10 x 4.5. County Courthouse, 1791—. 222 volumes, Room 538; 1791—, 1 file box, Room 535.

175. WILLS DEPOSITED BY LIVING
1852—. 6 file boxes (1-2871).
Original wills with names of testators and witnesses, disposition of properties, dates, and seals. Alphabetically arranged by names of testators. No index. Handwritten and typed. 15 x 10 x 4.5. County Courthouse, Room 535.

176. OLD WILLS, NOT PROBATED.
1852—. 8 file boxes, 2 bundles.
Original wills not probated listing disposition of property, names of decedent, administrator or executor, and witnesses, value of property, and date. Alphabetically arranged by names of testators. No index. Handwritten and typed. Boxes average 15 x 12 x 6. Bundles, 15 x 12 x 3. County Courthouse, Room 535.

177. ELECTIONS UNDER WILLS
1884—. 23 volumes. (1-23).
Records number of estate, names of widow or widower and decedent, declaration of satisfaction, signatures of applicant and witnesses; also date and attestation. Chronologically arranged by date of election. Alphabetical index by names of decedents in back of each volume. Handwritten on printed forms. Volumes average 600 pages. 15 x 11 x 3. County Courthouse, 1884-1913, 9 volumes, Room 537; 1914—. 14 volumes. Room 535.

178. DETERMINATION OF HEIRSHIP AND WILL CONSTRUCTION.
1932—. 388 file boxes (1-388). Initiated 1932 to comply with probate code. Petitions listing name of decedent, heirship determination, and construction of will. Numerically arranged by case numbers. No index. Handwritten and typed. 17 x 10 x 4.5. County Courthouse, Room 501.

Appointments, Bonds, and Letters of Fiduciaries

179. LETTERS TESTAMENTARY
1904——. 18 volumes.

Record of wills duly proven and admitted to probate; listing name of testator, date of appointment of executor by court, bond and signature of probate judge. Chronologically arranged by time of court term. Alphabetical index by names of testators in back of each volume. Handwritten on printed forms. Volumes average 500 pages. 15 x 11 x 2. County Courthouse, Room 541.

180. ADMINISTRATION AND GUARDIAN APPOINTMENTS
1791-1852. 4 VOLUMES. 1852-1884, destroyed in courthouse fire of 1884.

Record showing name of minor or incompetent person, name of guardian appointed and date of appointment, amount of bond, names of sureties, and reference to volume and number of private entries. Chronologically arranged. Alphabetical index by names of minors or incompetent persons in back of each volume. Handwritten. Volumes average 600 pages. 22 x 15 x 3. County Courthouse, Room 536.

For subsequent records see entries 181 and 182.

181. APPLICATION FOR GUARDIANSHIP
1884——. 116 volumes. (1-116).

Record showing application of petitioner for guardianship of minor or incompetent person and approximate value of real and personal property to be administered by guardian; also record of appointments of guardians. Alphabetical index by names of minors or incompetent persons in back of each volume. Handwritten on printed forms. Volumes average 225 pages. 15 x 9 x 1.5. County Courthouse, Room 536.

For prior records see entry 180.

182. ADMINISTRATION APPLICATIONS
1884——. 448 volumes. (1-448).

Petitions listing name of decedent, date of death, value and nature of estate, relationship of petitioner to deceased, amount of bond, appraiser's place of business, petitioner's residence, name of attorney, date of appearance, and signatures of petitioners and probate judge; also record of administrators' appointments. Alphabetical index by names of decedents in back of each volume.

Handwritten on printed forms. Volumes average 250 pages. 12 x 8 x 1.5. County Courthouse, 1884-1934, 412 volumes, Room 537; 1935—, 36 volumes, Room 536. For prior records see entry 180.

183. ADMINISTRATION BONDS
1852—. 45 volumes. (1-2, 1-21, A1-A23). 1919, volume A12, missing.
Records of bonds listing estate number, names of administrator and decedent, amount of bond, signatures of witnesses, date, and attestation. Alphabetical index by names of administrators in front of volume 1, 1852-1902, and in back of each of the other volumes. Handwritten on printed forms. Volumes average 1,000 pages.15 x 9 x 3. County Courthouse,1852-1902, 2 volumes, Room 537; 1880-1918, 32 volumes, Probate court storage, basement; 1920—, 11 volumes, Room 538.

184. ADMINISTRATION BONDS WITH WILL ANNEXED
1916—. 5 volumes. (A2-A6). Volume A1, missing.
Records names of principals and bonding company, amount of bond, date, seal, names of decedents and witnesses. Chronologically arranged. Alphabetical index by names of principals in back of each volume. Handwritten and typed. Volumes average 1,000 pages. 14 x 9 x 4. County Courthouse, 1916-1934, 3 volumes, Room 541, Annex A; 1935—, 2 volumes, Room 533.

185. ADMINISTRATORS' BONDS
1791—. 174 file boxes (1-129754).
Original bonds listing name of administrator, date, amount, name of estate, and names of sureties for bond. Numerically arranged by case numbers. No index. Handwritten and typed. 15 x 10 x 4.5. County Courthouse, Room 535.

186. EXECUTORS' BONDS
1918—. 3 volumes. (A2, A8, A9). Volumes A1, A3-A7, missing.
Records names of sureties, amount of bond, date issued, names of executor, decedent, and witnesses, signatures, and seal. Alphabetical index by names of executors in back of each volume. Handwritten on printed forms. Volumes average 1,000 pages. 14 x 9 x 3. County Courthouse,1918-1934, 2 volumes, Room 541, Annex A; 1935—, 1 volume, Room 537.

187. GUARDIANS' BONDS (Preserved)
1912—. 12 volumes (A1-A12).

Records bond number, amount, seal, and date of bond; also names of probate judge, council, guardian, and bonding company. Alphabetical index by names of guardians in back of each volume. Handwritten and typed. Volumes average 1,000 pages. 14 x 8.5 x 2. County Courthouse, Room 541.

188. TRUSTEE BONDS
1909—. 1 volume.

Records names of principals, sureties, trustee, and decedent; also amount of bond, signatures of witnesses, and attestation. Alphabetical index by names of trustees in back of volume. Handwritten on printed forms. 1000 pages. 14 x 9 x 3. County Courthouse, Room 537.

189. LETTERS OF ADMINISTRATION
1852—. 79 volumes, 4 bundles. 1884-1903, volumes missing.

Records estate number, names of decedent and administrator, proceedings, confirmation of sale, final decree, and signature appropriate judge. Contents of the four bundles have been transcribed into the 79 volumes. Numerically arranged by case numbers. Alphabetical index by names of decedents in back of each volume. For separate index, 1852-1884, see entry 191. Handwritten on printed forms. Volumes average 500 pages. 14.5 x 9 x 2. Bundles, 8 x 6 x 2. County Courthouse, 1852-1883, 1904—, 79 volumes, Room 537; 1866-1882, 4 bundles, Probate court storage, basement.

190. RESTORED ADMINISTRATION RECORD
1872-1884. 1 volume.

Record of administration proceedings. Alphabetically arranged by names of decedents. Handwritten. 600 pages. 22 x 15 x 3. County Courthouse, Room 501.

191. INDEX TO RESTORED ADMINISTRATION RECORD
1852-1884. 14 volumes. (1-12, A-K, L-Z). Discontinued

Index to letters of administration listing number of estate, name of decedent, date, and volume and page numbers of record. Alphabetically arranged by names of decedents. Handwritten. Volumes average 300 pages. 17 x 12 x 2. County Courthouse, Room 537.

192. LETTERS OF ADMINISTRATION DE BONIS NON WITH WILL
1904-1932. 4 volumes (1-2, 4-5). Volume 3 missing. Discontinued.
Records names of decedent and administrator; also attestation of probate judge.
Alphabetical index by names of decedents in back of each volume. Handwritten and
typed. Volumes average 600 pages. 14 x 9 x 2.5. County Courthouse, Room 541.

193. LETTERS OF GUARDIANSHIP
1852—. 34 volumes (1-8, 1-26). 1885-1903, missing. Volumes 1-8,
restored.
Records estate number, names of the decedent, minor, and guardian; also account,
final order, date, and attestation of probate judge. Numerically arranged by case
numbers. Alphabetical index by names of guardians in back of each volume.
Handwritten. Volumes average 500 pages. 15 x 10 x 2. County Courthouse, Room
550.

194. AFFIDAVITS OF PUBLICATION OF APPOINTMENT
1917—. 37 volumes.
Records names of decedent, appointee, and councel; also date of publication and
affidavit and signature of notary. Chronologically arranged. Alphabetical index by
name of decedents in back of each volume. Handwritten and typed. Volumes
average 600 pages. 17 x 13 x 2.5. County Courthouse, 1917-1925, 15 volumes,
Room 546; 1926—, 22 volumes, Room 501.

Inventories and Schedules of Debts

195. APPLICATIONS TO EXAMINE CONTENTS OF SAFETY BOXES
1922—. 10 bundles.
Records estate number, name of decedent, name of bank, safety box number, date,
and signature of administrator or executor. Numerically arranged by estate numbers.
No index. Handwritten. 12 x 9 x 2. County Courthouse, Room 538, vault.

196. INVENTORY RECORD
1809—. 166 volumes. (1-203). 1842-1853, 37 volumes, missing. 1814-
1815, 1827-1829, 1836-1842, 1858-1865, 10 volumes, restored.
Records number, name of decedent, inventories, names of appraisers, sales record,
affidavit, signature of administrator, and date. Numerically arranged by case

numbers. Alphabetical index by names of estates in back of each volume. Handwritten. Volumes average 600 pages. 18 x 12 x 2, County Courthouse, Room 541.

197. MISCELLANEOUS INVENTORY RECORDS AND ACCOUNTS
1854-1882. 3 volumes. (1, 1-2). Restored.
Administrators' or executors' accounts and inventories listing estate number, name of decedent, and schedule of debts paid. Numerically arranged by case numbers. Alphabetical index by names of estates in front of each volume. Handwritten. Volumes average 600 pages. 16 x 10 x 2. County Courthouse, Room 541, Annex A.

For prior and subsequent records see entry 196.

198. EXCEPTIONS TO INVENTORIES AND SCHEDULE
1903—. 5 file boxes (118372-12882).
Inventory and schedule of assets, claims, and debts; also waivers of notice. Alphabetically arranged by names of states. No index. Handwritten. 10 x 4.5 x 17. County Courthouse, Room 501.

199. SCHEDULE OF DEBTS
1932—. 12 volumes.
Records name of decedent, claims allowed, date of submission, name of executor or administrator, affidavit, and date of filing. Numerically arranged by case numbers. Alphabetical index by names of decedents in back of each volume. Typed. Volumes average 650 pages. 16 x 12 x 2. County Courthouse, 1932-1935, 8 volumes, Room 545; 1936—, 4 volumes.

200. CONFIRMATION OF SCHEDULE OF ACCOUNTS AND DEBTS
1905—. 5 file boxes (44520-450158).
Records allowances and confirmations of accounts; also debts filed and advertised. Numerically arranged by case numbers. No index. Handwritten. 4.5 x 10 x 17. County Courthouse, Room 501.

Cost Bills and Sales Records

201. COST BILLS
1853—. 81 volumes. (4 series; 1-24, 1-15, 1-28, 1-14). 1853-1919, 67 volumes. 1-24, 1–15, 1-28, restored.
Records number of estate, name of decedent or ward, bills, date of filing final record and order, and attestation of judge. Numerically arranged by case numbers. Alphabetical index by names of estates in back of each volume. Handwritten and typed. Volumes average 600 pages. 13 x 9 x 2.5. County Courthouse, 1853-1882, 24 volumes, Room 550; 1853-1919, 43 volumes, Probate court storage, basement, west wall; 1920—, 14 volumes, Room 541, Annex A.

202. CERTIFICATE OF DEPOSIT
1852-1902. 2 volumes. (1-2). Discontinued.
Record of certificates of deposit of funds belonging to estates. Alphabetical index by name of estates in front of volume 1 and in back of volume 2. Handwritten. Volumes average 200 pages. 13 x 10 x 1. County Courthouse, Room 537.

203. SALES RECORDS
1852—. 207 volumes. (1-29, 1-2, 68-242). 1852-1883, volumes 1-29, 1-3, restored.
Records case number, names of decedent and administrator, description of property, schedule of debts, appraisal, order of sale, date of final entry and attestation of judge. 1852-1883, 32 volumes have been restored but do not include all records destroyed in fire of 1884. Numerically arranged by case numbers. Alphabetical index by names of estates in back of each volume. For separate index, 1852-1884, see entry 204. Handwritten and typed. Volumes average 600 pages. 18 x 14 x 3. County Courthouse, Room 550.

204. INDEX TO SALES RECORDS
1852-1884, 4 volumes. (1, 1-3). Restored. Discontinued.
Records case number, names of parties, date, and volume and page numbers of record. Alphabetically arranged by names of estates. Handwritten. Volumes average 300 pages. 16 x 11 x 1.5. County Courthouse, Room 550.

205. ESTATE PAPERS
1854—. 74 bundles, 4,528 file boxes (479-129479).
Miscellaneous estate papers including administrators' and executors' inventories of accounts, schedules of debts, guardianships, journals, sale bills, and all correspondence pertaining to estates. Numerically arranged by estate numbers. No index. Handwritten and typed. Bundles 12 x 8.5 x 2. File boxes, 20 x 11 x 5. County Courthouse, 1854-1865, 74 bundles, Probate court storage, basement; 1866-1933, 2,845 file boxes, Room 537; 1934—, 1,683 file boxes, Room 501.

206. COURT PAPERS OF ESTATES
1883—. 306 file boxes (1208-11654).
Official court papers listing estate number, names of administrator and parties to action, cost accounts, date, and volume and page numbers of estate record. Numerically arranged by estate numbers. No index. Handwritten and typed. 17 x 10 x 4.5. County Courthouse, Room 501, vault.

Settlement of Estates

207. VOUCHERS IN SETTLEMENT OF ESTATES
1893—. 5 file boxes (1-126327).
Vouchers showing expenditures in settlement of estates, recording name, date, and amount paid. Numerically arranged by voucher numbers. No index. Handwritten on printed forms. 20 x 11 x 5. County Courthouse, Room 501.

208. MISSING VOUCHERS
1905—. 12 file boxes.
Estate accounts not allowed because of missing vouchers, recording estate number, name of decedent, schedule of accounts, and name of executor or administrator. Numerically arranged by voucher numbers. No index. Handwritten on printed forms. 17 x 10 x 4.5. County Courthouse, Room 501.

209. RECORD OF ACCOUNTS
1846—. 403 volumes. (1-441). 1878-1884, 38 volumes missing.
Records partial and final accounts of administrators, executors, trustees, and guardians. Alphabetical index by names of estates and back of each volume.

Handwritten and typed. Volumes average 650 pages. 17 x 10 x 2. County Courthouse, Room 550.

Records of Dependents

210. ADOPTION PETITIONS
1856—. 12 volumes. (1-11). 1856-1881, 1 volume restored.
Records date of application, name of applicant, place of residence, name of minor, change of name if any, age of minor, date of consent, names of parents or institution giving consent, signatures of witnesses, court authorization, and signature of judge or deputy. Chronologically arranged. Alphabetical index by names of petitioners in back of each volume. Typed. Volumes average 500 pages. 16 x 12 x 2.County Courthouse, Room 538.

211. ADOPTION DOCKET
1884—. 3 volumes (1-3).
Docket entries of adoption proceedings from filing a petition to decree of court. Chronologically arranged. Alphabetical index by names of petitioners in back of each volume. Handwritten. Volumes average 500 pages. 18 x 10 x 3. County Courthouse, Room 501.

212. ADOPTION RECORDS
1885—. 10 volumes, 17 file boxes (volumes 1-10; file boxes 1-2836).
Records of adoption including original petitions, consent of parents or court, name of minor, signature of judge, date, seal, and entry of court authorizing adoption. Volumes chronologically arranged. File boxes, numerically arranged by case numbers. Alphabetical index by names of children in back of each volume. File boxes, no index. Handwritten and typed. Volumes average 570 pages. 16 x 13 x 2.5. File boxes, 5 x 11 x 20. County Courthouse, 1885—, 10 volumes, Room 537; 1885—, 17 file boxes, Room 501.

213. RESTORED ADOPTION RECORD
1860-1902. 1 volume.
Restored records of adoption of children listing petition, consent, and decree of adoption. Chronologically arranged. Alphabetical index by names of children in back of volume. 690 pages. 16 x 13 x 2.5. County Courthouse, Room 537.

Naturalization Records

All naturalization records for Hamilton County have been kept by federal courts since 1906.

214. ALIENS DECLARATIONS OF INTENTION
1848-1906. 49 volumes, 1 bundle. (Volumes 1-17, 1-6, 1, 7, 14, 17, 18, 22-45). 3 volumes, 1-3, restored.
Records date, name of person forswearing sovereignty, declaration of allegiance, and signatures of applicant and probate judge. Chronologically arranged. Alphabetical index by names of applicants in back of each volume. Handwritten on printed forms. Volumes average 600 pages. 16 x 10 x 2. Bundle, 12 x 8.5 x 2. County Courthouse, 1848-1881, 17 volumes, 1 bundle, Probate court storage, basement; 1856-1906, 32 volumes, Room 537.

215. RESTORED NATURALIZATION RECORDS
1884. 13 volumes. Originals destroyed in courthouse fire of 1884.
Restored records prior to 1884 showing application, exhibits, affidavits, entries, and final entries of probate court. Chronologically arranged. Alphabetical index by names of applicants in back of each volume. Handwritten and typed. Volumes average 600 pages. 22 x 15 x 3. County Courthouse, Room 541.

216. NATURALIZATION RECORD
1880-1906. 65 volumes. (3-24, 6-48).
Record showing duplicates of certificates of naturalization. Chronologically arranged. Alphabetical index by names of applicants in back of each volume. Handwritten on printed forms. Volumes average 500 pages. 20 x 15 x 2.520. County Courthouse, Room 538.

217. INDEX TO NATURALIZATION RECORDS
1864-1908. 1 volume.
Index to naturalization records showing name of applicant, date of naturalization, and volume and page numbers of records. Alphabetically arranged by names of applicants. Handwritten. 200 pages. 20 x 12 x1. County Courthouse, Room 538.

218. APPLICATIONS FOR NATURALIZATION OF MINORS
1903-1905. 2 volumes (1-2).
Records name, address, and age of applicant; also names of parents or guardian.
Chronologically arranged. Alphabetical index by names of applicants in front of
each volume. Handwritten on printed forms. Volumes average 600 pages. 20 x 15
x 2.5. County Courthouse, Room 541.

219. RECORD OF MINORS NATURALIZED
1903-1906. 2 volumes.
Records names and addresses of applicants and names of parents or guardians, oaths
of allegiance, and testimonies of witnesses. Chronologically arranged. Alphabetical
index by names of applicants in front of each volume. Handwritten on printed
forms. Volumes average 600 pages. 22 x 15 x 2.5. County Courthouse, Room 541.

220. RECORD OF SOLDIERS NATURALIZED
1903-1906. 2 volumes.
Record showing names, addresses, and ages of aliens honorably discharged from
United States army who made applications for citizenship. Chronologically
arranged. Alphabetical index by names of applicants in back of each volume.
Volumes average 600 pages. 20 x 15 x 2.5. County Courthouse, Room 541.

Vital Statistics

221. CERTIFICATES OF BIRTH RECORDS BY PHYSICIANS AND
MIDWIVES
1863—. 4 volumes. (1-2, 1-2).
Records name of child, date and place of birth, color, names of parents, residence,
and name of person reporting birth. Chronologically arranged. Alphabetical index
by names of parents in back of each volume. Handwritten on printed forms.
Volumes average 500 pages. 16 x 10 x 23. County Courthouse, Room 537.

222. RECORD OF DEATHS

1882-1899. 5 volumes. 1867-1881, missing. Records for 1900-1919 kept by the bureau of vital statistics, city of Cincinnati, Courthouse, room 242. Records since 1920 kept by state bureau of vital statistics.

Reports giving full name, date and place of death, marital status, age, place of birth, occupation, names of parents, cause of death, color, and last place of residence. Chronologically arranged. Alphabetical index by names of decedents. Handwritten. Volumes average 500 pages. 15 x 12 x 3. County Courthouse, Room 537.

Certificates and Grants of Authority

223. PHYSICIANS' CERTIFICATES OF DIPLOMA

1896—. 5 volumes (1-5).

Certificates of state medical board listing name of applicant and county, degree and medical college, location of college, date of graduation, seals and signatures of president and secretary of state medical board, date of record, and signature and seal of probate judge or deputy. Chronologically arranged. Alphabetical index by names of physicians in front of each volume. Handwritten and typed on printed forms. Volumes average 620 pages. 16 x 11 x 2. County Courthouse, Room 537.

224. RECORDS OF MIDWIVES' CERTIFICATES

1896-1925. 1 volume. Discontinued.

Records certificates issued upon recommendation of state medical board listing applicants name and residence, date, signatures of president and secretary of state board, date of record, and signature probate judge. Chronologically arranged. Alphabetical index by names of midwives in front of volume. Handwritten on printed forms. 620 pages. 16 x 11 x 2 County Courthouse, Room 538.

225. REGISTRATION OF NURSES

1915—. 4 volumes. (1-4).

Record of certificates of registered nurses listing applicant's name, county, date of graduation, diploma, name of school, location, date of issuance, signatures of chief examiner and secretary, and date of record; also signature of probate judge or deputy. Chronologically arranged. Alphabetical index by names of nurses in back of each volume. Handwritten and typed on printed forms. Volumes average 625 pages.17 x 12 x 2. County Courthouse, Room 537.

226. LIMITED PRACTITIONERS' CERTIFICATES
1916—. 1 volume.
Records name of applicant authorized to practice, data issuance, signatures of President and Secretary of State Medical Board, date of record, signature of probate judge or deputy, and seal. Chronologically arranged. Alphabetical index by names of practitioners in back of volume. Handwritten and typed on printed forms. 620 pages. 17 x 12 x 2. County Courthouse, Room 537.

227. POWERS OF ATTORNEY
1905—. 3 file boxes.
Powers of attorney granted to individuals, bonding companies, and banks. Alphabetically arranged by names of persons or firms empowered. No index. Handwritten and typed. 15 x 10 x 4. County Courthouse, Room 535, vault.

228. CLERGYMEN'S LICENSES
1870—. 15 volumes.
Records name of clergyman licensed to perform marriage ceremonies, church denomination, date license issued, seal, attestation, and signature of probate judge or deputy. Chronologically arranged. Alphabetical index by names of clergy men in back of each volume. Handwritten and typed on printed forms. Volumes average 500 pages. 13 x 8 x 2. County Courthouse, 1870-1895, 7 volumes, Room 546; 1896—, 8 volumes, Room 537.

Business Administration of Office

229. MISCELLANEOUS LEDGER AND CASH BOOK.
1870-1900. 1 volume. Discontinued.
Records miscellaneous accounts for office supplies, stationery, stamps, ledgers, blanks, and printing. Chronologically arranged. Alphabetical index by names of payers in back of volume. Handwritten. 450 pages. 17 x 12 x 3. County Courthouse, Probate court storage, basement.

230. DAILY JOURNAL
1884—. 388 volumes. (1-449). 1886-1890, 1894-1908, 61 volumes, missing.
Daily record of all business of probate court. Chronologically arranged. Alphabetical index by names of litigants in back of each volume. Handwritten and typed. Volumes average 600 pages.15 x 10 x 2. County Courthouse, Room 537.

231. WITNESS BOOK
1895-1906. 1 volume. Discontinued.
Records estate number, names of decedent and witnesses, number of days served, and amount of fees. Numerically arranged by a state number. Alphabetical index by names of witnesses. Handwritten. 310 pages. 12 x 10 x 1. County Courthouse, Room 550.

232. UNKNOWN DEPOSITORS
1870-1931. 6 volumes (1-6). Discontinued
Affidavits by banks and loan companies, turning over to state, moneys deposited and not withdrawn. Chronologically arranged. Alphabetical index by names of depositors in back of each volume. Handwritten and typed. Volumes average 600 pages. 17 x 12 x 2. County Courthouse, Room 550.

Maps

233. GREATER CINCINNATI MAP.
1930. 1 map.
Political map showing boundaries of Cincinnati, suburbs, and adjacent municipalities; also streets, roads, and inter-urban, bus, and street railway lines. Published by National Map Company, Indianapolis, Indiana. Printed. No scale. 60 x 40. County Courthouse, Room 535.

234. NEW OFFICIAL SURVEY MAP OF OHIO
1930. 1 map.
Political map showing congressional districts, counties, roads, and city boundaries. Published by the National Map Company, Indianapolis, Indiana. Printed. No scale. 40 x 40. County Courthouse, Room 535.

Miscellaneous

235. MISCELLANEOUS CORRESPONDENCE
1910—. 5 volumes. 29 file boxes (volumes 1-5).
Miscellaneous correspondence to court from persons regarding estates, guardians, claims, debts, and accounts. Volumes, chronologically arranged. File boxes, alphabetically arranged by names of correspondents. Alphabetical index by names of correspondents in front of each volume. File boxes, no index. Handwritten and typed. Volumes average 200 pages. 12x 10 x 1. File boxes, 13 x 11 x 5. County Courthouse, 1910—. 5 volumes, Room 550; 1917—, 29 file boxes, Room 535, vault.

236. MISCELLANEOUS RECORDS
1851—. 16 bundles, 29 file boxes.
Petitions and certificates listing change of name, naturalization application, proof of publication, stock certification, and account records. Chronologically arranged. No index. Handwritten and typed. Bundles, 12 x 8.5 x 2. File boxes, 11 x 5 x 20. County Courthouse, 1851-1895, 16 bundles, Probate court storage, basement; 1896—. 29 file boxes, Room 501.

237. MISCELLANEOUS RECORDS
1884—. 6 volumes (1-6).
Miscellaneous records, not provided for by regular forms, including those of guardians, leases, letters, court orders, judgments, widows' elections, and accounts. Numerically arranged by case numbers. Numerical index by case numbers in back of each volume. Handwritten and typed. Volumes average 600 pages. 17 x 12 x 2. County Courthouse, Room 538.

238. INDEX TO MISCELLANEOUS RECORDS
1884—. 4 volumes. (1-4).
Index showing case number, names of parties to action and volume and page numbers of Miscellaneous Records (entry 237). Numerically arranged by case numbers. Handwritten on printed forms. Volumes average 600 pages. 17 x 11.5 x 2. County Courthouse, Room 541.

Inheritance Tax Division

This division was not created by statute but was established by the probate court to handle inheritance taxes.

239. INHERITANCE TAX (Form A)
1919—. 22 volumes. (1-22).
Record of docket giving residence of decedent, date and place of death, name of administrator or executor, estimated and appraised value of estate, names of heirs and legatees, exemptions, and amount of inheritance tax. Numerically arranged by case numbers. Alphabetical index by names of decedents in front of each volume. Typed on printed forms. Volumes average 500 pages. 18 x 13 x 2. County Courthouse, Room 537.

240. COLLATERAL INHERITANCE TAX
1916—. 6 volumes. (1-6).
Records name of decedent, order of court to appraise realty, name of appraiser, description of property, date of death, seal, signature of probate judge or deputy, and notarial affidavit of appraisal. Numerically arranged by case numbers. Alphabetical index by names of decedents in back of each volume. Typed. Volumes average 500 pages. 17 x 14 x 2.5. County Courthouse, Room 550.

241. DIRECT INHERITANCE TAX
1919—. 218 volumes, 35 boxes (volumes 1-218; file boxes 1-9000).
Records estate number, name of decedent, application for determination, inventory appraisal, schedule of real property and cash, determination of taxes, attestations of county treasurer and state auditor, valuation fixed by court, and signature of probate judge. The file boxes are confidential records and are not available for public use. Complete information refused by department. Volumes numerically arranged by case numbers. File boxes, alphabetically arranged by names of decedents. Alphabetical index by names of decedents in back of each volume. File boxes, no index. Handwritten and typed. Volumes average 600 pages. 17 x 13 x 2. File boxes, 14 x 10 x 5. County Courthouse, 1919—, 218 volumes, Room 550; n. d. 30 file boxes, Probate court storage, basement.

Marriage License Division

Division was not created by Statute but was established to facilitate certain duties of the probate court offices. The division issues marriage licenses and grants authority to ministers and other proper officials to perform marriages.

242. GENERAL MARRIAGE INDEX
1808-1931. 20 volumes (A-Z). 1808-1884, 10 volumes, restored. Discontinued.
Index showing names of contracting parties, date by years, and volume and page numbers of record. Alphabetically arranged by names of contracting parties. 1808-1909, handwritten; 1910-1931, typed. Volumes average 500 pages. 13 x 9 x 2. 9 County Courthouse, 1808-1889, 12 volumes, Room 541, Annex A; 1890-1909, 2 volumes, Probate court storage, basement, west wall; 1910-1931, 6 volumes, Room 501.

243. MARRIAGE RECORDS, APPLICATIONS AND RETURNS
1808—. 877 volumes. (10 series numbered consecutively by separate series).
Records names, ages, residences, occupations, dates, attestations, dates of consummation, names of persons officiating, and dates of returns. Chronologically arranged. Alphabetical index by names of contracting parties in back of each volume. Handwritten on printed forms. Volumes average 500 pages. 18 x 12 x 2. County Courthouse, Room 541.

244. MARRIAGE APPLICATIONS AND RETURNS
1815—. 373 bundles, 26 file boxes.
Records name of person, date, file book and page numbers, and name of authority solemnizing marriage. Overlapping dates in different locations are due to applications for restoration being made at different times as original records were destroyed. Alphabetically arranged by names of contracting parties. No index. Handwritten. Bundles average 12 x 8.5 x 2. File boxes 9 x 8 x 4. County Courthouse, 1815-1921, 280 bundles, Room 537, vault; 1899-1901, 15 bundles, Probate court storage, basement; 1922-1931, 78 bundles, Room 541, Annex A; 1922—. 26 file boxes, Room 536.

245. RESTORED MARRIAGE RECORD
1808-1933. 40 volumes (1-11, 1-29). 1876-1884, missing.
Petition for restoration of marriage records listing application, name of petitioner, testimony and report, copy of license, and final entry. Numerically arranged by case numbers. Alphabetical index by names of petitioners in back of each volume. Handwritten and typed. Volumes average 600 pages. 18 x 13 x 3. County Courthouse, Room 541.

246. MARRIAGE BANS
1893—. 16 volumes, 11 bundles (volumes 1-16, bundles 10-183).
Records names of contracting persons, name of church, and date of returns. Volumes chronologically arranged. Bundles, alphabetically arranged by names of contracting persons. Alphabetical index by names of contracting persons in back of each volume. Bundles, no index. Handwritten on printed forms. Volumes average 500 pages.14 x 8 x 2. Bundles, 12 x 18.5 x 2. County Courthouse, 1883-1901, 11 bundles, Probate court storage, basement; 1902—. 16 volumes, Room 541, Annex A.

247. CLERGYMEN'S APPLICATIONS FOR LICENSES
1884—. 2 bundles, 1 file box (bundles 180-317). 1889-1924, missing.
Applications for licenses to perform marriage ceremonies. Alphabetically arranged by names of clergy men. No index. Handwritten on printed forms. Bundles average 2 x 8.5 x 12. File boxes, 8 x 4 x 12. County Courthouse, 1884-1888. 2 bundles, Probate court storage, basement; 1925, 1 file box, Room 501.

Lunacy Division

This division was not created by statute but was established by the court to handle lunacy cases.

248. INSANE DOCKETS
1884—. 25 volumes (6-30). Prior records destroyed in courthouse fire of 1884.
Records case number, date of filing, name of patient, amount of fees, date of inquest, and date committed to asylum. 1884-1889, alphabetical index by names of patients in back of each volume. For separate index, 1900-1932, see entry 289.

1932—, alphabetical index by names of patients in back of each volume. Handwritten. Volumes average 600 pages. 18 x 13 x2. County Courthouse, Room 537.

249. INDEX TO INSANE DOCKETS
1900-1932. 1 volume (A-Z). Discontinued.
Records date, name, and volume and page numbers. Alphabetically arranged by names of patients. Typed. 250 pages. 18 x 12 x 1. County Courthouse, Room 537.

250. AFFIDAVITS ON INSANITY
1884—. 59 file boxes (A1-83100).
Affidavits of affiants charging insanity. Numerically arranged by numbers of affidavits. No index. Handwritten on printed forms. 17 x 12 x 4.5. County Courthouse, Room 536.

251. FEEBLE-MINDED AND EPILEPTIC CASES
1908—. 19 bundles (368-2482). Record initiated 1908.
All papers pertaining to feeble-minded and epileptic cases. Alphabetically arranged by names of patients. No index. Handwritten. 4 x 9 x 12. County Courthouse, Room 538, vault.

252. EPILEPTIC AND FEEBLE-MINDED RECORD
1922—. 6 volumes (5-10). 1922-1928, volumes 1-4, missing.
Applications for admission to institutions for epileptic and feeble-minded, listing name, institution, residence, age, nativity, religion, affidavit and certificate of doctor, notification from hospital, warrant of conveyance, and amount of fees. Chronologically arranged. Alphabetical index by names of patients in back of each volume. Handwritten. Volumes average 300 pages 15 x 12 x 2, County Courthouse, Room 537.

253. GUARDIANSHIP OF FEEBLE-MINDED
1893—. 9 volumes (1-9).

Records name of feeble-minded person, hospital or institution, residents, age, nationality, religion, occupation, color, name of medical examiner, certified copy of application and medical certificate, also liability for support. Chronologically arranged. Alphabetical index by names of guardians in back of each volume. Handwritten on printed forms. Volumes average 300 pages. 16 x 11 x 2. County Courthouse, Room 537.

254. MEDICAL CERTIFICATES
1893—. 28 file boxes (1-2667).

Reports of medical witnesses concerning cases of epilepsy and insanity listing names of medical witnesses, name of examinee, report, certification by probate judge, and seal. Numerically arranged by serial numbers; also chronologically arranged. No index. 22 x 11 x 5. County Courthouse, Room 541.

In 1891 the judges of the court of common pleas, in counties having a population of not less than 33,000 nor more than 50,000, were authorized to appoint four residents of the county to serve as a jury commission for a term of one year. It was the duty of this commission to determine the qualifications and fitness of persons to be selected as jurors. (88 O. L. 200.) Three years later, in 1894, the provisions of the act were extended to all counties in the state. (91 I. L. 176; 96 O. L. 3.) In 1913 the number of jury commissioners in each county was reduced to two. (103 O. L. 513; 105 O. L. 106.)

The jury code, which became effective August 2, 1931, provided for a jury commission of the same number and same qualifications previously enjoined, to hold office at the pleasure of the court, and to meet and select, from a list provided by the board of elections, prospective jurors, both grand and petit, for the ensuing year. (114 O. L. 193-213.) Annually, at the beginning of each jury year, the commissioners are required to make up a new and complete jury list. The names are entered in a book or record, known as the annual jury list, and are arranged alphabetically by precincts, districts, and townships. With each name is listed the occupation, place of business, and place of residence. The commissioners are required to prepare an index to this list. A duplicate of the annual jury list is certified by the commissioners and filed in the office of the clerk of the court of common pleas. (*Ibid.*, 205.)

The jury commissioners select prospective jurors for civil and criminal cases as well as for the grand jury. They select jurors for the probate, juvenile, and other minor courts.

All records are located in the jury commissioner's office, County Courthouse, Room 415.

255. JURY BOOKS
1934—. 336 volumes. (numbered by precincts). Prior records missing.
Records names of all qualified voters in Hamilton County from which jurors were selected. Alphabetically arranged by names of voters. No index. Printed. Volumes average 30 pages. 18 x 12 x .25.

256. RECORD OF QUALIFICATIONS
1930—. 1 volume. Prior records missing.
Records qualifications of prospective jurors, date of examination, and findings of

jury commission. Alphabetically arranged by names of voters. No index. Handwritten. 300 pages. 18 x 15 x 3.

257. SELECTED JURORS
1930——. 1 volume. Prior records missing.
Records names of all persons in Hamilton County qualified for jury service. Alphabetically arranged by names of voters. No index. Handwritten. 300 pages. 18 x 15 x 3.

258. JURY SUMMONS
1930——. 1 file box. Prior records missing.
Record of summonses served on yours, date, by whom served, and court term. Alphabetically arranged by names of jurors. No index. Handwritten and typed on printed forms. 6 x 6 x 14.

259. SUMMONED VENIRES
1933——. 1 file box. Prior records missing.
Records names of jurors summoned, date, name of court, and time to report for service. Alphabetically arranged by names of jurors. No index. Typed on printed forms. 6 x 6 x 14.

260. RESIDUE OF WHEEL
1932——. 1 file box. Prior records missing.
Includes all names taken from jury wheel when emptied by jury commission. Alphabetically arranged by names of jurors. No index. Typed. 6 x 6 x 14.

261. DISCHARGED JURORS
1930——. 1 file box. Prior records missing.
Records names, addresses, and telephone numbers of jurors discharged by court. Alphabetically arranged by names of jurors. No index. Handwritten. 6 x 6 x 14.

262. EXCUSED JURORS
1930——. 1 file box. Prior records missing.
Includes summonses, date served, date excuse from jury service, cause, and physicians' certificates. Alphabetically arranged by names of jurors. No index. Typed on printed forms. 6 x 6 x 14.

263. GRAND JURORS

1932—. 2 file boxes. Prior records missing.

Records names of grand jurors, date someone, time served, court term, and amount of fees received. Alphabetically arranged by names of jurors. No index. Handwritten and typed. 6 x 6 x 14.

264. TIME SHEETS

1932—. 1 volume. Prior records missing.

Records of all jurors serving and common pleas court and amount of fees paid. Alphabetically arranged by names of jurors. No index. Handwritten. 200 pages. 18 x 15 x 2.

265. OFFICIAL CORRESPONDENCE

1933—. 1 file box. Prior records missing.

Includes all correspondence of jury commission relative to their official duties. Alphabetically arranged by names of correspondents. No index. Hand written and typed. 6 x 6 x 14.

The grand jury, sometimes called the palladium of English liberty, has as its function the preliminary examination of persons charged with a capital or other infamous crime. The inherent right to an indictment by a grand jury, guaranteed by the federal constitution, found a place in the provisions of the Ohio constitution of 1802, 1851, and the amendments of 1912.

Under the present system, which does not differ in detail from the system inaugurated in the early days of the state's history, the grand jury is composed of fifteen members, resident electors of the county having "the qualifications of jurors." (G. C. sec. 13436-2.) It is the duty of the grand jury "to inquire of and present all offenses committed in the county in and for which it was empaneled and sworn." (G. C. sec. 13436-5.) The proceedings are secret and each juror is required to take an oath to preserve the secrecy of its proceedings. No grand juror may be required to reveal the way he or other grand jurors voted. (G. C. sec. 13436-16.)

In their investigations the grand jurors are aided by the county prosecuting attorney. Since 1869 he has been authorized, by statute, to present evidence before this body, and compel the attendance of witnesses, against whom he may institute contempt proceedings if they refuse to testify. (See page 102.) The prosecuting attorney must leave the room before the jurors begin their debating or before a poll is taken. However, the courts have decreed the mere presence of the prosecuting attorney in the room during the deliberation is "not sufficient to sustain a plea in abatement." (See *State* v. *Stichtenoth*, 8 N. P., n. s. 297-338.) Since 1902, the official court stenographer, at the request of the prosecuting attorney, may take shorthand notes of testimony, and furnish a transcript to the prosecuting attorney. This reporter, like the prosecuting attorney and his assistants, is required to retire from the jury room, before the grand jury begins its deliberations. (G. C. sec. 13436-8.)

At least twelve of the fifteen jurors must concur in finding and indictment. Indictments found by the grand jury are presented by the foreman to the court and are filed with the clerk of courts. (G. C. sec. 13436-21.) No grand juror or officer of the court is permitted to disclose that a person has been indicted before such indictment is filed in the case docketed. (G. C. sec. 13436-15.) Any incarcerated person charged with an indictable offense who has not been indicted during the term of court at which he is held to answer is discharged. (G. C. sec. 13436-23.)

Since 1869 it has been the duty of the grand jury, once in each term of court at which they may be in attendance, to visit the county jail, examine its state and condition and inquire into the discipline and treatment of prisoners. This report in writing, is returned to the court. (G. C. sec. 13436-20.)

The majority of contemporary opinion holds that the grand jury, although still defended as a safeguard against needless oppressive prosecution, seems to be a little usefulness in the administration of modern criminal justice. It is argued that the grand jury not only delays the prosecution of criminal offenses, but makes it impossible to place responsibility for neglect of duty, and, in many instances, is a rubber stamp for the opinions of the county prosecuting attorney.

266. INDICTMENTS
1883——. 56 volumes. (8-63). Volumes 1-7, destroyed in courthouse fire of 1884.
Indictments for felonies and misdemeanors were imprisonment in penitentiary is part of penalty listing name of defendant, date, and indictment returned. Numerically arranged by case numbers. Alphabetical index by names of defendants in back of each volume. Handwritten on printed forms. Volumes average 400 pages. 20 x 12 x 3. County Courthouse, Room 315.

267. INDICTMENTS
1910——. 309 file boxes (1-21600).
Record of indictments for larceny, burglary, robbery, and rape listing name of defendant, date, and indictment returned. Numerically arranged by case numbers. No index. Handwritten and typed. 12 x 12 x 6. County Courthouse, Clerk of court's storeroom, basement.

The county prosecuting attorney, unlike the sheriff and coroner, is relatively one of the newer agencies in the administration of criminal justice. This office, established in America by the English during the colonial period offers a striking difference in the development of American criminal procedure in contrast to the English where criminal prosecutions, in the main, we're instituted by private persons. As developed in recent years, the office of the prosecutor has become one of the state's most important agencies in its defense against modern crime.

The acts of the Northwest Territory place the responsibility for criminal prosecutions upon the attorney general, who, in turn, appointed and commissioned persons to prosecute cases in their respective counties.

While the acts of the Northwest Territory outlined the local institutions for the newer states, the constitution of Ohio contained no provision for a prosecutor leaving its creation to the discretion of the legislature. In 1803, during the first session of the legislature, and act was passed authorizing the supreme court to appoint in each county of the state an attorney to prosecute cases on behalf of the state. (1 O. L. 50.) Two years later, the appointing power was vested in the court of common pleas. (3 O. L. 260; 98 O. L. 271-272.)

Under the present system the prosecutor is elected for a four-year term. He is required to give bond of not less than one thousand dollars conditioned for the faithful performance of the duties of his office. In the event the office becomes vacant the court of common pleas is authorized to appoint of successor. (G. C. sec. 2912.)

The county prosecuting attorney is authorized to appoint clerks, assistants, and stenographers and fix their salaries subject to the approval of the county commissioners. Since 1911, he has been authorized to appoint a secret service agent or officer whose duty it is to aid him in the collection of evidence to be used in the trial of criminal cases and in matters of a criminal nature. The compensation of such an officer is determined by the court of common pleas. (G. C. secs. 2914, 2915-1.)

Most important among the duties of the prosecuting attorney are those connected with criminal prosecutions. Differing little from those of the early days of the office, these duties include the prosecution on behalf of the state of all complaints, suits, and controversies in which the state is a party, and such other suits, matters, and controversies as he is directed by law to prosecute within or without his county, in the probate court, court of common pleas, and court of appeals. In conjunction with the attorney general, he prosecutes cases in the supreme court which originated in his county. (G. C. sec. 2916.)

In felony cases, when a complaint is made to the prosecutor, he is required to examine the evidence and determine if it is sufficient for prosecution. If he decides in the affirmative, he prepares the evidence for presentation to the grand jury. (See page 100.) If this body returns an indictment the prosecutor prepares to present the evidence in trial court. The court of common pleas may appoint an attorney to assist the prosecutor in criminal cases. (G. C. sec. 2918.) In case of conviction, the prosecutor causes execution to be issued for the fines or cause and pays into the county treasury all moneys so received. (G. C. sec. 2916.) Without reference to the grand jury, the county prosecutor may initiate prosecutions in misdemeanor cases in the court of common pleas by information. (G. C. sec. 13437-34.) After prosecution is inaugurated, he may eliminate the case without trial by means of the *nolle prosequi.* Although he is prohibited from enlisting the *nolle prosequi* without leave of the court on good cause shown, his requests are usually granted. (G. C. sec. 13473-32.) After prosecution has begun, it remains with the prosecuting attorney whether the case shall be pressed and steps taken that will lead to conviction.

Besides prosecution and criminal cases, the prosecuting attorney also acts in civil matters. He may bring suit in the name of the state when he is convinced that public money is being misapplied or is being illegally withheld or withdrawn from the county treasury. Moreover, he may bring suit against persons violating the obligations of contracts of which the county is a party, or when county property is being used or occupied illegally. (G. C. sec. 2921.)

In addition to these, other duties have been prescribed by Statute. On the request of the judge having jurisdiction over juvenile cases, he must prosecute individuals for committing crimes against children. (G. C. sec. 1664.) Furthermore, when directed by the court of common pleas, he must prosecute persons for keeping a house of prostitution. (G. C. sec. 6212-5, 6212-7.) At the instigation of the secretary of state, he must prosecute any officer who refuses to furnish gratuitously statistical information for the use of that office. (G. C. sec. 174.)

The prosecuting attorney has also served in an advisory capacity since 1906. (98 O. L. 160-61.) He acts as an advisor to all county boards and officials and to township officers who may require his opinion in writing on matters connected with their official duties. (G. C. sec. 2917.) In addition to this, he prepares official bonds for all county officers. (G. C. sec. 2920.)

The prosecuting attorney to make annually a report to the County commissioners stating the number of criminal prosecutions completed, the name or names of the party or parties to each, and the amount collected in fines, and costs, and the amount forfeited. (G. C. sec. 2926.) Moreover, on the demand of the attorney general he must make an annual report on forms provided by the state on all criminal actions prosecuted by indictment in his county. (G. C. sec. 2925; 78 O. L. 120; 90 O. L. 225.)

All records prior to 1917 missing, see page xxvii.

Criminal Division

The criminal division was not created by statute but was established by the prosecuting attorney for convenience in handling criminal cases.

All records of this division are located in the County Courthouse, room 420.

268. CRIMINAL CASES, OPEN AND DORMANT
1917—. 30 file boxes.
Open and dormant criminal cases showing name of defendant, date, crime charged, and status of case. Numerically arranged by case numbers. No index. Handwritten and typed. 24 x 12 x 12,

269. DOCKET, CRIMINAL CASES
1917—. 15 volumes. (1-15).
Record showing name of defendant in criminal cases, court orders, date, and final disposition of case. Numerically arranged by case numbers. Alphabetical index by names of defendants in front of each volume. Handwritten. Volumes average 250 pages. 18 x 12 x 4.

270. RECORD OF DEFENDANTS
1917—. 8 volumes. (1-8).
Record listing name of defendant brought before the grand jury, crime charged, date, and disposition of case. Numerically arranged by case numbers. Alphabetical index by names of defendants in front of each volume. Volumes average 300 pages. 11 x 8 x 2.

271. WITNESS BOOKS, GRAND JURY RECORD
1917—. 54 volumes. (1-54).
Record listing names of all witnesses called before the grand jury, case in which called, days of attendance, miles traveled, and amount of fees received. Alphabetical index by names of case defendants in front of each volume. Handwritten. Volumes average 300 pages. 11 x 8 x 3.

272. CRIMINAL CASES, DOW-AIKEN LAW
1917-1928. 4 file boxes (A-Z).
Record of all prosecutions under the Dow-Aiken Law for whiskey violations showing name of defendant, case number, and judgment of court. Alphabetically arranged by names of defendants. No index. Handwritten and typed. 26 x 14 x 10.

273. CRIMINAL CASES, CLOSED
1917—. 130 folders.
Criminal cases for final dispositions have been made listing name of defendant, date, case number, and judgment of the court. Numerically arranged by case numbers. No index. Handwritten and typed. 13 x 8 x .5. Vault.

274. CORRESPONDENCE, CRIMINAL CASES
1917—. 5 file boxes.
All correspondence pertaining to criminal cases. Alphabetically arranged by names of correspondents. No index. Handwritten and typed. 24 x 14 x 12.

275. CRIMINAL CASES, IGNORED
1917—. 2 file boxes.
Criminal cases brought before the grand jury but ignored by them recording name of defendant, case number, and offense charge. Alphabetically arranged by names of defendants. No index. Typed. 24 x 14 x 12. Vault.

Civil Division

The civil division was not created by statute, but established by the prosecuting attorney for convenience in handling civil cases.

All records of this division are located in the County Courthouse, Room 419.

276. CIVIL SUITS, PENDING AND CLOSED
1917—. 32 file boxes.
All civil suits were in Hamilton County was plaintiff or defendant giving cause of action, date, number of case, court orders, and final decree. Numerically arranged by case numbers. No index. Typed. 26 x 14 x 10.

277. BONDS FORFEITED
1917—. 8 file boxes.
Record of bonds forfeited in criminal cases where suit was brought to enforce collection giving names of principal and sureties, date of forfeiture, amount of bond, case number, and judgment of court. Numerically arranged by case numbers. No index. Typed. 26 x 14 x 10.

278. REQUEST FOR OPINIONS
1917—. 10 volumes (1-10).
Request from public officials for opinions showing date, subject matter, and opinion rendered. Alphabetical index by names of persons seeking opinions in front of each volume. Handwritten. Volumes average 300 pages. 13 x 8 x 3.

279. OPINIONS
1916—. 20 volumes, 8 file boxes.
Opinions rendered by the prosecuting attorney on request of the public officials of Hamilton County. Chronologically arranged. Volumes, printed. Contents of file boxes, typed. Volumes average 150 pages. 10 x 8 x 1. File boxes, 26 x 14 x 10.

280. CARD INDEX, OPINIONS
1916—. 8 file boxes.
Record showing name of county official to whom opinion was rendered, date, number, volume and page reference. Alphabetically arranged by names of persons

to whom opinions were rendered. Typed. 18 x 5 x 3.

281. TAX CLAIMS, PENDING AND CLOSED
1917—. 4 file boxes.

Record of closed and pending tax claims brought before the county commissioners for adjustment showing date, case number, and final ruling made by commissioners. Alphabetically arranged by names of persons filing claims. No index. Handwritten and typed. 26 x 14 x 10.

282. CORRESPONDENCE, CIVIL CASES
1917—. 4 file boxes.

All correspondence pertaining to civil cases. Alphabetically arranged by names of correspondents. No index. Handwritten and typed. 26 x 14 x 10.

The office of coroner, next to the sheriff the oldest county office in America, had its Inception in England during the latter part of the twelfth century. The coroner kept a record of the activities in the county, especially regarding criminal justice. At the end of the thirteenth century, it was his duty to make inquest whenever there was a sudden death in the shire, and the results were recorded in the coroner's rolls, and were presented to the justices when they made their eyre. (Pollock and Maitland, *op. cit.,* I, 519, 571; II, 588, 641.)

This office, transplanted to America during the colonial period, was continued by the states following independence, and was adopted by the territory of which the state of Ohio was then a part. An ordinance of the Northwest Territory, published in 1788, authorized the governor to appoint a coroner in each county within the Territory. This act, together with a supplementary act of 1795 adopted from the Massachusetts code, fixed the power and duties of a coroner. He was empowered to do any act which, by previous legislation had been delegated to the sheriff; he was given the ancient English duty of coroners in holding preliminary investigations over the bodies of all persons found within his county who were believed to have died by violence or casualty. (Pease, *op. cit.,* I, 24-25, 272-275.)

The Ohio Constitution of 1802 continued the historic office, making it elective for a two-year term. (*Ohio Const. 1802*, Art. VI, sec. 1.) A statute of 1805 defined the duties and authority of the coroner which in the main, were comparable to those prescribed in the territorial code. He was, however, denied the privilege of concurrent jurisdiction with the sheriff. (3 O. L. 156-161.) The act further provided that the coroner should receive his remuneration from fees; that if the office of sheriff were to become vacant due to death, resignation, or otherwise, the coroner was to execute temporarily the duties of the sheriff. (3 O. L. 158-161.) The latter provision remained active until its abrogation in 1887. (84 O. L. 208-210.)

The constitution of 1851 and the constitutional amendments of 1912 left the duties of the coroner unchanged and not until recent years, when he became an aid in the scientific detection of crime, have any laws been passed which materially affected his office. By the legislative act of 1921 in all counties have a population of 100,000 or more only licensed physicians were eligible to the office and at the same time the coroner was made the official custodian of the morgue. (109 O. L. 43-44.) In 1927 and act was passed, apparently designed to attract more highly trained physicians, which set the salary of a coroner at $6,000 per year in all counties having a population of 400,000 or more inhabitants, and authorized him to appoint one stenographer, a secretary, and three assistant custodians of the morgue. (112 O.

L. 204-205.) Two years later the coroner, in counties having a population of 400,000 or more, was empowered to appoint a pathologist to serve as deputy coroner. The deputy was directed to make chemical tests and to conduct autopsies. (113 O. L. 497.) In 1936 the tenure of office was extended from two to four years. (G. C. sec. 2823.)

283. ORIGINAL PAPERS IN DEATH CASES
1890—. 1,408 file boxes. Prior records missing.
Certificates of death and inquest proceedings. Numerically arranged by case numbers. No index. Handwritten on printed forms. 16 x 4 x 4. County Courthouse, 1890-1929, 1,273 file boxes, Coroner's storeroom, basement; 1930—, 135 file boxes, Room 127.

284. DEATH RECORDS
1887—. 36 volumes. (7 volumes, 1-7; 29 volumes, unnumbered). Prior records missing.
Records name of decedent, date, case number, name of undertaker, and case history. Chronologically arranged. 1887-1909, alphabetical index by names of decedents in front of each volume. For separate index, 1893—, see entry 285. Handwritten. Volumes average 467 pages. 15 x 10 x 2. County Courthouse, 1887-1909, 24 volumes, Coroner's storeroom, basement, west wall; 1910—, 12 volumes, Room 127.

285. INDEX TO DEATH RECORDS
1893—. 17 volumes, Prior records missing.
General index to death records. Alphabetically arranged by names of decedents. Alphabetical thumb tab index attached to margins. Handwritten. Volumes average 64 pages. 19 x 10 x 1.25. County Courthouse, 1893-1904, 5 volumes, Coroner's storeroom, basement; 1910—, 12 volumes, Room 127.

286. RECORD OF EFFECTS
1897—. 14 volumes (1-14). Prior records missing.
Records name of decedent, inquest number, marital status, names and address of relatives or friends, effects found on body, and by whom. Numerically arranged by inquest numbers. Alphabetical index by names of decedents in front of each volume handwritten on printed forms. Volumes average 519 pages. 14 x 8.5 x 2. County

Courthouse, 1897-1916, 3 volumes, Coroner's storeroom, basement; 1917—, 11 volumes, Room 127.

287. CORONER'S DOCKET IN SHERIFF'S CASES
1895—. 2 volumes.

Records case number, summons, date received, date returnable, amount of bond, names of bondsman and appraisers, amount of expenses, date of writ, cost received, and amount paid into treasury. Numerically arranged by case numbers. Alphabetical index by names of persons summoned in front of each volume. Handwritten. Volumes average 500 pages.15 x 8 x 2.5. County Courthouse, 1895-1920, 1 volumes, Coroner's storeroom, basement, west wall; 1921—. 1 volume, Room 127.

288. RECORDS OF AUTOMOBILE ACCIDENTS, SUICIDES, HOMICIDES, AND ACCIDENTAL DEATHS
1917—. 2 volumes. Prior records missing.

Record of accidental deaths, suicides, and homicides. Alphabetically arranged by names of the seasons. No index. Handwritten on printed forms. Volumes average 400 pages. 16 x 10 x 3. County Courthouse, Room 127.

289. CORRESPONDENCE
1910—. 17 file boxes. Prior records missing.

General correspondence pertaining to deceased persons. Alphabetically arranged by names of correspondence. No index. Typed. 26 x 12 x 10. County Courthouse, 1910-1929, 14 file boxes, Coroner's storeroom, basement; 1930—, 3 file boxes, Room 127.

The office of county sheriff, one of the oldest elective offices in America, had its inception in the Anglo-Saxon period of English History. (Adams, *op. cit.,* 17-19; W. A. Morris, "The Office of Sheriff in the Anglo-Saxon Period," *English Historical Review*, XXXI, 19-40.)

The ancient institution was introduced in the American colonies in modified form and continued by the states created after independence. For a comparative study of the sheriff in England and the Chesapeake colonies, see Cyrus Harreld Kerraker, *The Seventeenth-Century Sheriff*, Chapel Hill, 1930.) The office assumed a new significance, when in the latter part of the eighteenth century, a flood of colonists swept across the Alleghenies to establish homes in the Northwest Territory, as organized by congress in 1787. In the remoter West the pioneers, far removed from the orderly legal processes and courts of the East, were subjected to the machinations of a lawless element, as evidence in every new community. In 1792 the governor and judges of the territory adopted an act which provided for the appointment by the governor of a sheriff in each county, and defined his duties. The sheriff was directed to keep and preserve the peace, and suppress, routs, riots, unlawful assemblies, and insurrections; he was bound to apprehend, and confine in jail all felons and traitors; he was to return persons who, after having committed a crime in his county, had taken refuge in another. In addition to this, he was directed to attend upon the court of common pleas and the court of appeals during their sessions, and, when directed, execute all warrants, writs, and processes directed to him by the proper and lawful authority. (Pease, *op. cit.,* I, 8.)

Ohio entered the union as a state in 1803. The office of sheriff was continued by constitutional provision, and was made elected for a two-year term. (*Ohio Const. 1802,* Art. V, sec. 1.) Although it did not specifically provide for the office, the constitution of 1851 stated that no person should be eligible to the office for more than four in any period of six years. (*Ohio Const. 1851,* Art. X, Sec. 3. This provision was repealed (1933) with the adoption of an amendment authorizing any county to adopt a charter form of government.) The term of office remained at two years until 1936, when it was extended to four years. (116 O. L. pt. ii, 1st sec. H. 603.) The sheriff received his remuneration from fees, and not until 1906 was the definite salary specified by the legislature. (3 O. L. 49-51; 33 O. L. 18; 35 O. L. 53; 52 O. L. 86; 98 O. L. 95.)

The duties of the sheriff were, and are, prescribed by statute. During the legislative session of 1805 the general assembly passed an act defining the duties of the sheriff, which, in all respects, with similar to the provisions inherited from the territorial code. (3 O. L. 156-158.) In the same year the sheriff was designated as the county's executioner, and was bound to carry out sentences of death as imposed by the courts upon those convicted of murder. Hanging was the legal method for the infliction of the death penalty. (Chase, *op. cit.*, I, 97-101, 109, 442-443.)

Public executions, the general rule during the earlier years, we're abolished in 1844. (42 O. L. 71.)

As in England the sheriff, during the earlier years of his office, was required to notify the electors of his county of the time and place of holding elections. He was required to furnish ballot boxes at the expense of the county, hold special elections when so directed by the governor, and deliver the poll books to the secretary of state. (2 O. L. 88-89; 3 O. L. 331-332.)

An act of 1831, repealing the act of 1805, redefined the duties of the sheriff as the conservator of the piece in his county and as an executive agent of the courts. (29 O. L. 112.) The present duties of the sheriff and disrespect are survivals from the provisions of this act. (*Ibid.*, 112-113; 82 O. L. 26.) In the execution of his duties, as prescribed by law, he was empowered again to summon to his aid such persons as he deemed necessary to perform his lawful duty in the apprehension of criminals. (29 O. L. 112-113.) Thus the *posse comitatus* was at his disposal as it is today. In 1818, the sheriff had been authorized to appoint, with a consent of the court of common pleas, one or more deputies, who, like himself, were required to give bond for the faithful performance of the duties of their office. The sheriff was made responsible for their neglect of duty or misconduct in office. (*Ibid.*, 410.)

Not only was the sheriff charged with the duty of apprehending law violators, but he was made responsible for their safe keeping. As early as 1803 he was made official custodian at the county jail. (3 O. L. 157.) Although the early statutes directed the county commissioners to provide dungeons for the incarceration of prisoners, the act of 1847 directed the sheriff to exercise reasonable care for the preservation of the life, health, and Welfare of those committed to his care. Indeed he was and is, authorized to transport prisoners to other counties for safe keeping. (*Ibid.*, 157; 29 O. L. 112-113; 93 O. L. 131.) In 1910 provision was made for the removal of the sheriff by the governor if he were proved guilty of negligence in not affording a prisoner adequate protection from mob violence. (101 O. L. 109.)

Although the sheriff is still regarded as the chief peace officer in the county, many of his earlier duties in this respect have been absorbed by the development of other agencies of law enforcement, notably the state highway patrol. On the other hand, the powers of the sheriff to suppress affrays, riots, and unlawful assemblies become especially important in times of strikes or threatened riots. The sheriff, too, may arrest on a properly issued warrant any person charged with the probability of doing injury to another person or the property of another. (G. C. sec. 13463.) Moreover, since 1921 the sheriff has forwarded to the bureau of criminal identification all fingerprints of persons arrested for a felony (110 O. L. 5; 109 O. L. 585), and since 1913 has been authorized to arrest any prisoner violating his parole. (103 O. L. 405.)

As an executive agent of the court the sheriff still executes all writs, warrants, and other processes directed to him by lawful authority; he attends the court of common pleas and court of appeals during their sessions, and, when required upon the probate court. (29 O. L. 112, 316; 82 O. L. 26.)

Other historical functions of the sheriff have been altered or abolished. His duties regarding the announcement of elections long since have been taken over by the county board of elections, and those regarding executions were delegated, in 1886, to the warden of the Ohio Penitentiary. (83 O. L. 145.) Although the jury commission has supplanted the clerk of courts in the matter of selecting names of prospective jurors from the jury wheel, the sheriff's duties in this respect remain much as they were in the earlier years of his office.

The sheriff was, and is, required by law to keep a record of the business of his office. The present practice of keeping a foreign execution docket began in 1838. (36 O. L. 18; 57 O. L. 6; 84 O. L. 208-209.) Since 1842 the sheriff has kept a cash book (40 O. L. 25; 65 O. L. 115; 84 O. L. 209; 86 O. L. 239.), and since 1843 a jail register. (41 O. L. 74.) In Texas, direct and reverse to the foreign execution docket, were prescribed by the legislature in 1925. (111 O. L. 31.) Since 1850 the sheriff has been required, on the first Monday of September in each year, to submit to the county commissioners a certified statement of all fines and costs collected during the year and the amount of fees collected and paid to the clerk of courts of common pleas. (G. C. sec. 2504; 48 O. L. 66.) Moreover, since 1843 he has been required annually to transmit the jail register, in certified copies, to the clerk of courts, the county auditor, and the secretary of state. (41 O. L. 74.)

The sheriff's records, public property and open to the inspection of the public, are transferred, together with all effects appertaining to the office, to his successor.

General Office Division

The general office division of the sheriff's bureau was not created by statute, but was established by the sheriff to facilitate the filing of miscellaneous records under his supervision.

Court Orders

290. ORDER OF DELIVERY
1884——. 17 volumes (labeled by names of sheriffs). Prior records missing. Record of court orders showing number of order, date, amount of appraiser's fee, mileage, date delivered to plaintiff, and signature of deputy. Numerically arranged by order numbers. Alphabetical index by names of plaintiffs in front of each volume. Handwritten on printed forms. Volumes average 160 pages. 14.5 x 9.5 x 1.25. County Courthouse, 1884-1934, 15 volumes, Room 222, vault; 1935——, 2 volumes, Room 222, safe.

291. BLOTTER
1885-1906, 7 volumes. (labeled by names of sheriffs). Discontinued. Record showing names of litigants; date of litigation number, and summary of judgment. Chronologically arranged. No index. Handwritten on printed forms. Volumes average 150 pages. 16 x 11.5 x 1. County Courthouse, Room 222, vault.

292. SUPERIOR COURT EXECUTIONS
1884-1925, 12 volumes. (labeled by names of sheriffs). Discontinued. Record showing execution number, names of litigants, date issued, amount of execution, and costs. Numerically arranged by execution numbers. Alphabetical index by names of litigants in front of each volume. Handwritten on printed forms. Volumes average 350 pages. 16 x 12 x 2. County Courthouse, Room 222, vault.

292. COMMON PLEAS COURT EXECUTIONS
1884——. 40 volumes. (labeled by names of sheriffs). Record showing execution number, names of litigants, date issued, amount of execution, and court costs. Numerically arranged by execution numbers. Alphabetical index by names of litigants in front of each volume. Handwritten on

printed forms. Volumes average 350 pages. 16 x 12 x 2. County Courthouse, 1884-1933, 37 volumes, Room 222, vault; 1934——, 3 volumes, Room 222, safe.

294. CRIMINAL EXECUTION DOCKET
1921——. 1 volume. System of recording initiated 1921.
Record showing names of litigants, case and execution numbers, and amounts of court and sheriff's fees. Chronologically arranged. No index. Handwritten on printed forms. Volumes average 400 pages. 17 x 10 x 1.5. County Courthouse, Room 222, safe.

295. FOREIGN EXECUTION DOCKET
1884——. 7 volumes. Prior records missing.
Record of executions, orders of sale, and other processes issuing from courts outside of Hamilton County listing date of writ, when received by sheriff, name of court and county, amount of judgment or decree, description of property levied upon or offered for sale, sheriff's return or writ, and bill of costs. Chronologically arranged. 1884-1925, alphabetical index by name of litigants in front of each volume. For separate index, 1926——, see entry 296. Handwritten on printed forms. Volumes average 346 pages. 13.5 x 8.5 x 1, County Courthouse, 1884-1903, 3 volumes, Room 222, vault; 1904——, 4 volumes, Room 222, safe.

296. INDEX TO FOREIGN EXECUTION DOCKET
1926——. 1 volume.
Direct and reverse index to Foreign Execution Docket. Alphabetically arranged by names of litigants. Handwritten on printed forms. 500 pages. 18 x 14 x 4. County Courthouse, Room 222, safe.

297. FOREIGN WRITS
1884——. 36 volumes. (labeled by names of sheriffs). Prior records missing.
Record listing writ number, names of litigants, directions of service, and date writ was received and served. Numerically arranged by writ numbers. Alphabetical index by name so litigants in front of each volume. Handwritten on printed forms. Volumes average 400 pages. 14.5 x 9.5 x 2.5. County Courthouse, 1884-1934, 34 volumes, Room 222, vault; 1935——, 2 volumes, Room 222, safe.

298. SUBPOENA SERVICE RECORD
1917—. 200 volumes.
Reports of deputies on service listing name of defendant, address, mileage, and time subpoena was received and served. Chronologically arranged. No index. Handwritten on printed forms. Volumes average 100 pages. 9 x 4 x 1.5. County Courthouse, Room 222, vault, in glass case.

299. DEPUTY'S DAILY REPORTS
1931—. 7 bundles (labeled chronologically).
Daily reports of radio and telephone calls received by deputy sheriffs and county police officers. This is not a permanent record, but is destroyed when so ordered by the sheriff. Chronologically arranged. No index. Handwritten on printed forms. 11 x 8.5 x 3. County Courthouse, Room 222, vault.

300. LUNACY, EPILEPTIC, AND FEEBLE-MINDED RECORD
1903—. 37 volumes. (1903-1920, 20 volumes labeled Lunacy, Epileptic and Feeble-minded Record; 1921—. 17 volumes labeled lunacy record).
Records listing costs of serving warrant, mileage, service and return of subpoena, mileage on subpoena, serving of each red, conveyance service, mileage for deputy, supporting patient, and conveying patient to institutions; also case number, signature of probate judge, name and address of patient, and signature of clerk or deputy. Chronologically arranged. Alphabetical index by names of patients in front of each volume. Handwritten on printed forms. Volumes average 400 pages. 15 x 9 x 1.5. County Courthouse, 1903-1934, 35 volumes, Room 222, vault; 1935—, 2 volumes, Room 222, safe.

Property Transfers

301. APPRAISEMENT CARDS
1933—. 24 file boxes (A-XYZ).
Cards listing names of property owners, locations and descriptions of properties, and amounts of appraisements. Alphabetically arranged by names of property owners. No index. Handwritten on printed forms. 12 x 10.5 x 5. County Courthouse, Room 222.

302. ORDER OF SALE

1884—. 59 volumes (labeled by names of sheriffs). Prior records missing. Record of order of court for sale of real estate listing date of order and signatures of judge, sheriff, and recorder. Chronologically arranged. Alphabetical index by names of property owners in front of each volume. Handwritten on printed forms. Volumes average 330 pages 18 x 12 x 2.5. County Courthouse, 1884-1934, 57 volumes, Room 222, vault; 1935—, 2 volumes, Room 222, safe.

303. ATTACHMENT BOOKS

1884—. 24 volumes (labeled by names of sheriffs). Prior records missing. Record of attachments on real and personal property listing value of property, names of like litigants, attachment number, and date of attachment. Numerically arranged by attachment numbers. Alphabetical index by names of litigants in front of each volume. Handwritten on printed forms. Volumes average 300 pages. 14 x 8.5 x 2. County Courthouse, 1884-1932, 20 volumes, Room 222, vault; 1933—, 4 volumes, Room 222, counter.

304. SHERIFF'S SALES

18898—. 48 volumes (labeled by names of sheriffs). Prior records missing. Record showing article sold, date of sale, docket number, price received, and newspaper clippings of notice of sale. Chronologically arranged. 1889-1932, Alphabetical index by names of property owners in front of each volume. For separate index, 1933—, see entry 305. Handwritten on printed forms. Volumes average 300 pages. 13.5 x 11.5 x 2. County Courthouse, 1889-1928, 40 volumes, Room 222, vault; 1929—, 8 volumes, Room 222, safe.

305. INDEX TO SHERIFF'S SALES

1933—. 1 revolving rack of 12 metal shutters. System of recording initiated 1933.
Index listing names of litigants, docket number, and amount of judgment. Alphabetically arranged by names of property owners. Typed on cards. 19.5 x 8.5. County Courthouse, Room 222, front counter.

Business Administration of Office

306. LEDGER
1884—. 17 volumes (labeled by names of sheriffs).
Records of sheriff's fees, court costs, judgments, and miscellaneous accounts. Chronologically arranged. No index. Handwritten on printed forms. Volumes average 350 pages. 16 x 12 x 1. County Courthouse, 1884-1933, 15 volumes, Room 222, vault; 1934—, 2 volumes, Room 222, safe.

307. CASH BOOK
1884—. 36 volumes (labeled by names of sheriffs). Prior records destroyed by fire.
Record showing case number, by whom paid, to whom due, amount, sheriff's fee, court costs, judgment, and sundry expenses. Lyrically arranged by case numbers. No index. Handwritten on printed forms. Volumes average 500 pages. 16.5 x 15 x 2.5. County Courthouse, 1884-1933, 31 volumes, Room 222, vault; 1934—, 5 volumes, Room 222, safe.

308. RECEIPTS
1893-1919. 5 volumes (labeled by names of sheriffs). Prior records missing. Discontinued.
Record listing sums paid by sheriff to county, to treasurer, and others; also date of payment. Chronologically arranged. No index. Handwritten on printed forms. Volumes average 200 pages. 12 x 8 x 2. County Courthouse, Room222, vault.

309. COST CARDS
1933—. 24 file boxes (1-24). Prior records destroyed.
Kardex system listing court, sheriff's, and miscellaneous fees. Numerically arranged by case numbers. No index. Handwritten.18 x 6 x 4.5. County Courthouse, Room 222, front wall.

3110. SHERIFF'S MISCELLANEOUS CORRESPONDENCE
1904—. 25 file boxes (A-Z). Prior records missing.
General correspondence pertaining to sheriff's office. Chronologically arranged. No index. Handwritten and typed. 12 x 11.5 x 3. County Courthouse, 1904-1934, 22 file boxes, Room 222, vault; 1935—, 3 file boxes, Room 222, safe.

County Jail Division

The county jail record division of the sheriff's office was not created by statute but was established by the sheriff to segregate the official jail records.

311. PRISONERS' RECORD CARDS
1933—. 4 file boxes (A-Z). Record initiated 1933.
Records name of prisoner, address, age, sex, color, occupation, crime, date committed, arresting officer, case number, sentence, date of discharge, date of final discharge from custody, and information pertaining to prisoners social and criminal record. Alphabetically arranged by names of prisoners. No index. Handwritten on printed forms. 27 x 6 x 5. County Jail, Clerk's office.

312. PRISONERS BOUND OVER TO GRAND JURY
1935—. 1 volume. Record initiated 1935.
Record listing names of prisoner, cell number, date bound over to grand jury, pleas of prisoner, time served in jail, facts found in probation investigation, date of discharge, and disposition of case. Chronologically arranged. No index. Handwritten. 200 pages. 9.5 x 8 x 1. County Jail, Clerk's office.

313. INVESTIGATION AND PROBATION RECORD
1935—. 1 volume. Record initiated 1935.
Record listing name of prisoner, cell number, crime, date bound over to grand jury, pleas of prisoner, time served in jail, facts found in probation investigation, date of sentence, date of discharge, and disposition of case. Chronologically arranged. No index. Handwritten. 200 pages. 9.5 x 8 x 1. County Jail, Clerk's office.

314. COMMITMENT FORM
1912—. 48 file boxes, 21 bundles (labeled chronologically). Record initiated 1912.
Register listing name of each prisoner, age, color, sex, height, weight, crime, sentence, date of commitment, court, name of judge, disposition of case, and date of discharge. Chronologically arranged. No index. Handwritten on printed forms. File boxes, 11.5 x 11 x 5. Bundles, 15 x 11 x 5. County Jail, 1912–1932, 21 bundles, office vault; 1933—, 48 file boxes, Clerk's office.

315. RELEASES ON PROBATION
1935——. 1 volume. System of recording initiated 1935.
Record listing names of prisoners, cell number, crime, date bound over to grand jury, pleas of prisoner, date of sentence, time served, facts found in probation investigation, date of discharge, condition and terms of probation, and disposition of case. Chronologically arranged. No index. Handwritten. 200 pages. 8.5 x 8 x 1. County Jail, Clerk's office.

316. JAIL REGISTER
1884——. 24 rolls, 5 volumes. Prior records missing.
Listing name of each prisoner, date of commitment, crime, date committed, age, sex, color, education, classification of offense, social condition, time served, date and disposition of case, and general remarks. This record is removed from the binder every 5 years, rolled, wrapped, stamped with year, and filed in the jail vault. Chronologically arranged. No index. Handwritten on printed forms. Rolls, 18 x 5.5. Volumes average 100 pages. 17.5 x 14.5 x 1.5. County Jail, 1884-1935, 24 rolls, 4 volumes, vault; 1936——. 1 volume, Clerk's office.

317. SENTENCES AND EXPIRATIONS
1935——. 1 volume. System of recording initiated 1935.
Record showing name of each prisoner, date of commitment, cell number, crime, date bound over to grand jury, plea of prisoner, time served, facts found in probation investigation, date of sentence, and disposition of case. Chronologically arranged. No index. Handwritten. 200 pages. 9.5 x6 x 1. County Jail, Clerk's office.

318. REFORMATORY SENTENCES
1935——. 1 volume. System of recording initiated 1935.
Record listing name of each prisoner, cell number, date bound over to grand jury, pleas of prisoner, time served, facts found in probation investigation, date of sentence, and disposition of case. Chronologically arranged. No index. Handwritten. 200 pages. 9.5 x 8 x 1. County Jail, Clerk's office.

319. OHIO PENITENTIARY SENTENCES

1935—. 1 volume. System of recording initiated 1935.

Record listing name of each prisoner, cell number, date bound over to grand jury, pleas of prisoner, time served, that's found in probation investigation, date of sentence, and disposition of case. Chronologically arranged. No index. Handwritten. 200 pages. 9.5 x 8 x 1. County Jail, Clerk's office.

320. MONTHLY STATEMENT, MEALS SERVED FEDERAL AND COUNTY PRISONERS

1912—. 302 sheets. Record initiated 1912.

Statement showing names of federal and county prisoners, date received, time served, date discharged, number of meals served each prisoner per day and month, cost of each meal, total number of meals, and total cost per day and month. Chronologically arranged. No index. Handwritten on printed forms. 17.5 x 17.5. County Jail, 1912-1935, 1 roll (208 sheets), vault; 1937—, 4 sheets, Clerk's office.

The office of county treasurer, established by an act of the Northwest Territory in 1792, was continued by the state of Ohio. (Pease, *op. cit.,* 68-69.) Although the constitution of 1802 made no provision for the office of county treasurer, it was created by a legislative act of 1803. (1 O. L. 98.) The treasurer, appointed by the associate judges in 1803 and by the county commissioners in 1804, was required to take an oath; and give bond for the faithful performance of the duties of his office; and he was subject to removal by the appointing power. (1 O. L. 98; 2 O. L. 154.) The treasurer remained an appointive official until 1827, and after that date an elective one by popular vote in the county. (25 O. L. 25-32.) Although it did not specifically create the office, the constitution of 1851 stated that no person should hold the office of treasurer for more than four years in any six. (*Ohio Const. 1851.* Art. X, sec. 3. With the adoption of an amendment authorizing any county to adopt a charter form of government this provision was repealed in 1933.) Interpreting the constitutional provision, the legislature fixed the term of office at two years in 1859. (56 O. L. 105.) The term of office continued at two years until 1935 when it was extended to four years. (116. O. L. pt. ii, 1st s. sess. H. 603.) Until 1906 the county treasurer received his remuneration from fees; since that date his salary has been determined by law according to the population of the county.

Although the duties of the treasurer were defined by statute in the earlier period, the act of 1827 and that of 1831, repealing the previous acts, to find his duties in detail. The provisions of the latter act, although subject to amendment and repeal, furnished the basis for subsequent legislation and laid the basis for the present duties of the treasurer, which, in the main, do not differ greatly from those prescribed in the earlier statutes.

In 1803 the treasurer was given his present duty of giving public notice of the tax duplicate. Upon receiving from the county auditor a duplicate of the taxes assessed upon the property of the county, the treasurer prepares notices to be posted in three places in each township—one, the place in which elections are held. Also, the notice is inserted for six consecutive weeks in the newspaper having the greatest circulation in the county. (1 O. L. 98; 29 O. L. 291; 52 O. L. 124.) He receives money in payment of taxes levied for the county, for the state, and for other purposes, and gives the payer a receipt. (G. C. sec. 2650; 29 O. L. 292; 76 O. L. 70; 85 O. L. 327.) In the earlier years of the office the treasurer was required to give announcement of the time he would be in the respective townships of the county and in his office at the seat of justice to receive tax collections. Since 1858 the

treasurer has been authorized to prescribe the semiannual payment of taxes or assessments levied upon real estate or upon delinquent real estate taxes or assignments. (55 O. L. 62; 56 O. L. 101.) Moreover, since 1908, the commissioners have been authorized to extend the time of paying taxes for not more than thirty days after the time fixed by law. (99 O. L. 435; 114 O. L. 730; 115 O. L. pt. ii, 226.)

After each semiannual collection of taxes, the treasurer is required to report to the auditor showing the amount of taxes received in each taxing district in the county since the last settlement. Since 1904 the semiannual settlements have been made under the heads of liquor, cigarette, inheritance, delinquent personal, road, and general taxes. The treasurer keeps his accounts in books which enables him to compile such reports. (G. C. sec. 2643; 29 O. L. 295; 97 O. L. 458.)

After the taxes are collected and immediately after each settlement with the county auditor, the county treasurer, upon the presentation of the proper warrant from the auditor, pays to the township treasurer, city or village treasurer, the treasurer of the school district, or treasurer of any "legally constituted board authorized by law to receive the funds or proceeds of any special tax levy," or other officer delegated with authority to receive such funds, all money in the county belonging to such boards and subdivisions. (G. C. sec.2689; R. S. 1122; 55 O. L. 101.) In addition, after the treasurer has made each settlement with the county auditor, he is required to pay to the state treasurer, on warrant from the state auditor, "the full amount of all sums" found by the state auditor to belong to the state. (56 O. L. 101; 114 O. L. 732.)

The treasurer is required to keep an account current with the county auditor–a practice which originated in 1831. Each day the treasurer makes a statement to the county auditor for the previous day's business showing the amount of taxes received on auditor's drafts, the amount received from other sources, together with the amount of money deposited in the depository, the total amount paid out by check and by cash, and the balance in the treasury. (G. C. sec. 2660; 56 O. L. 175; 99 O. L. 435.)

During the last decade provision has been made whereby delinquent taxes, assessments, and penalties charged on the tax duplicate against any entry of real estate may be paid in installments during the five consecutive semiannual tax paying periods, "whether such real estate has been certified as delinquent or not." (G. C. sec. 2672; 114 O. L. 827.) The Whittemore Act, passed as an emergency measure in 1933, provides for the collection by installments, without interest or penalty, of delinquent real estate taxes and assessments, personal property, and classified property taxes. (115 O. L. 161-164; 116 O. L. pt. ii, 14-21; *ibid.*, 261-267.) In some of the more populous counties the treasurers maintain a separate bureau for the collection of delinquent taxes.

The county treasurer has charge on the funds collected by taxes, and also of other funds belonging to the county. Although earlier acts made provision for storage vaults in the county treasury for county deposits, the commissioners have been authorized, since 1894, to receive sealed bids for the deposit of county funds; and the bank or trust companies offering the highest rate of interest are selected as the county depositories. (91 O. L. 403; 102 O. L. 60; 115 O. L. pt. ii, 215.)

The treasurer, as well as the sheriff, the prosecuting attorney, and the clerk, is required to report annually to the county commissioners. (G. C. sec. 2504.) Since 1874 the county auditor and county commissioners have been required to make a thorough examination of all books, vouchers, accounts, moneys, bonds, securities, and other property in the treasury at least every six months. (G. C. sec. 2699; R. S. 1129; 71 O. L. 137.) Besides being under the supervision of the county commissioners and county auditor, the treasurer is subject to the supervision of the state auditor. In 1902 and act was passed providing for a uniform system of accounting and auditing for all public offices in the state, under the direction of a bureau of inspection in the office of the state auditor. As the act provides, also, for the annual examination of the finances of all public offices. (G. C. sec. 2641; 114 O. L. 728; R. S. 1084.)

The treasurer, like other county officials, is required at the expiration of his term to turn over to a successor all books, papers, moneys, and records appertaining to his office. (G. C. sec. 2639.) Since the inception of the office the treasurer has been the official custodian of the bonds furnished to the state by the county auditor, county commissioners, and county sheriff. Since 1889, he has been required to record and preserve a record of the deputies appointed and removed by the county auditor. (G. C. sec. 2563; 66 O. L. 35.)

The treasurer is a member of the budget commission, the county board of revision (G. C. sec. 5825-10; G. C. sec. 5580), and serves as a trustee of the sinking fund. (See pages 170, 172, 181.)

General Tax Division

Tax Lists and Duplicates

321. REAL ESTATE PROOF TAPES
1932—. 6 cartons. Prior records destroyed as customary.
Proof tape showing listings of taxes. Chronologically arranged. No index. Typed.
16 x 13 x 5. County Courthouse, Auditor's storeroom, basement.

322. TAX DUPLICATES
1883—. 1,318 volumes. (A-Z). Prior records destroyed in courthouse fire
of 1884.
Duplicate record giving dates, name of property owner, description and location of
property. Alphabetically arranged by names of property owners. No index.
Handwritten on printed forms. Volumes average 400 pages. 19.5 x 18.5 x 3. County
Courthouse, Auditor's storeroom, basement.

323. FORFEITURE DUPLICATES
1918-1927. 19 volumes. (1-19).
Record listing number of duplicate, name of property owner, description and
location of property, amount of tax due, and record of suit. Alphabetically arranged
by names of property owners for city; also alphabetically arranged by names of
townships for county. No index. Typed on printed forms. Volumes average 150
pages. 19.5 x 15.75 x 1. County Courthouse, Auditor's storeroom, basement.
For subsequent records see entry 362.

324. ESTATE CERTIFICATES
1932—. 4 cartons, 1 bundle.
Real and personal property certificates showing certificate number, name of
property owner, amount of taxes, and date certificate was issued. Chronologically
arranged. No index. Handwritten on printed forms. Cartons, 18 x 15 x 6. Bundle,
22 x 12 x 2. County Courthouse, 1932, 1 bundle, Auditor's storeroom, basement;
1933—, 4 cartons, Room 114, vault.

325. PERSONAL TAX (City and County)
1918-1928. 140 volumes. Discontinued.
Lists city and county real and personal property, consecutive number of ward or subdivision, name of property owner, residents, description of property, date of tax payment, and amount. Numerically arranged by ward numbers; also alphabetically arranged by names of townships. No index. Typed on printed forms. Volumes average 125 pages. 27 x 18 x 3. County Courthouse, Auditor's storeroom, basement.

Delinquent Taxes

326. DISTRIBUTION OF DELINQUENT CERTIFIED LANDS
1918-1931. 2 volumes. Discontinued.
Lists of land certified for sale for unpaid taxes showing amount of sale and name of purchaser. Chronologically arranged. No index. Handwritten on printed forms. Volumes average 300 pages. 15 x 11 x 1.5. County Courthouse, Room 114, vault.

327. DELINQUENTS, CERTIFIED
1926-1930. 4 volumes. Discontinued.
Certified copy of quadrennial certificate of unredeemed delinquent tracts of land listing date of delinquency, name of property owner, description and location of property, value of property, and amount of taxes due. Numerically arranged by certificate numbers. No index. Typed on printed forms. Volumes average 400 pages. 17.5 x 15 x 2. County Courthouse, Room 114, vault.

328. RECORD OF FORECLOSURE ON REAL ESTATE
1914-1929. 1 volume. Discontinued.
Record of real estate foreclosure and bankrupts listing name of property owner, description and location of property, value of property, date of foreclosure, assessment due, and settlement made. Chronologically arranged. No index. Handwritten. Condition poor. 300 pages. 14.5 x 9 x 1.5. County Courthouse, Auditor's storeroom, basement.

329. DELINQUENT   TAXES,   DIRECTING   TREASURER   TO
FORECLOSE
1922—. 8 volumes.
Foreclosures on real estate listing date of foreclosure, names of property owners,
lot numbers, description of property, value of property, and amount of taxes.
Chronologically arranged. No index. Typed on printed forms. 4 volumes. 1000
pages. 12 x 9.5 x 6; 4 volumes, 300 pages 11.5 x 8 x 2. County Courthouse, Room
114, vault.

330. PERSONAL DELINQUENT TAX SETTLEMENT
1932-1934. 4 cartons. Prior receipts destroyed.
Cashier's memorandum listing name of delinquent property owner, address,
amount, and date of settlement. Chronologically arranged. No index. Typed on
printed forms. 16 x 13 x 5. County Courthouse, Room 114, vault.

331. DELINQUENT PERSONAL TAX RECORDS
1912—. 22 volumes. Prior records destroyed.
Record listing names and addresses of delinquent property owners, and a
description of their personal property. Chronologically arranged. Alphabetical index
by names of property owners in front of each volume. Handwritten on printed
forms. Volumes average 300 pages. 20 x 20 x 1.5. County Courthouse, Room 114,
vault.

332. DELINQUENT TAX LIST, MIAMI CONSERVANCY DISTRICT
1931—. 11 volumes.
Tax list showing township, name of property owner, description of property, and
amount of tax. Alphabetically arranged by names of townships. No index. Typed
on printed forms. Volumes average 100 pages. 25 x 20 x 1. County Courthouse,
Room 114, vault.

333. PERSONAL DELINQUENT TAX DUPLICATE
1925—. 8 file boxes.
List of paid cards, auditor's charge, and receipts on excise tax stamps.
Alphabetically arranged by names of taxpayers. No index. Typed on printed forms.
18 x 9 x 6. County Courthouse, Room 102.

334. GENERAL TAX RECEIPT BOOKS

1918—. 146 volumes. (A-Z). Prior records missing.

Record listing semiannual tax collections, name of city and county, property owner, residence, property value, date of tax payment and amount. Numerically arranged by receipt numbers. No index. Typed on printed forms. Volumes average 400 pages. 19.5 x 15.75 x 3. County Courthouse, 1918-1927, 54 volumes, Auditor's storeroom, basement; 1928—, 92 volumes, Room 114.

335. TAX RECEIPTS

1934—. 1,000 paper envelopes (A-Z). Destroyed after 1 year.

Uncalled for real estate tax receipts showing receipt number, name of property owner, date of tax payments, and amount paid. Numerically arranged by receipt numbers. No index. Typed on printed forms. 6 x 3. County Courthouse, Room 114, filed loose on steel shelves.

336. PERSONAL PROPERTY TAX COLLECTED

1927—. 18 volumes.

Record listing name of property owner, address, amount collected, and date of payment. Chronologically arranged. No index. Typed on printed forms. 2 volumes. 300 pages. 19 x 12 x 4; 16 volumes, 1000 pages. 21 x 10 x 8. County Courthouse, Room 114, vault.

337. TREASURER'S REMITS

1934—. 1 carton. Prior records destroyed.

Real estate refunds listing number, name of property owner, subdivision, lot number, book and item number, location and description of property, and amount of refund. No systematic arrangement. No index. Typed on printed forms. 18 x 16 x 8. County Courthouse, Auditor's storeroom, basement.

338. REDEMPTION ORDERS

1887-1908. 27 volumes. Discontinued.

Tax redemption receipts showing receipt number, date, name of property owner, lot number, township, and amount paid. Numerically arranged by receipt numbers. No index. Handwritten on printed forms. Volumes average 200 pages. * x 6 x 2. County Courthouse, Auditor's storeroom, basement.

339. DIRECT INHERITANCE TAX RECORD

1920—. 11 volumes.

Treasurer's record of inheritance tax assessed listing case number, date will filed, name of decedent, amount of tax, and name of administrator. Numerically arranged by case numbers under initial letters of names of decedents. Alphabetical thumb tab index attached to margins. Typed on printed forms. Volumes average 1,000 pages. 12 x 10 x 4. County Courthouse, Room 114, vault.

340. DIRECT INHERITANCE TAX, QUADRUPLICATE RECEIPTS

1919—. 17 volumes.

Receipts for inheritance tax listing name of executor, administrator or trustee, receipt number, case number, and amount of tax fixed by court. Chronologically arranged. No index. Typed on printed forms. Volumes average 500 pages. 10 x .4.5 x 3. County Courthouse, Room 114, vault.

Excise Tax Division

This division is not authorized by statute but was established by the county treasurer to facilitate the work of the treasurer's office. The division keeps all records pertaining to liquor and cigarette taxes.

341. LIQUOR TAX

1918-1927. 2 volumes. Discontinued.

Lists dealer's name, ward or township, amount of tax paid, and date of payment. Chronologically arranged. No index. Handwritten on printed forms. Volumes average 165 pages. 13 x 9.5 x 1. County Courthouse, 1918-1920, 1 volume, Auditor's storeroom, basement; 1921-1927, 1 volume, Room 114, vault.

342. CIGARETTE TAX RECEIPT STUBS

1927—. 33 volumes. Prior records missing.

List name of dealer, amount of tax paid, and date of payment. Numerically arranged by receipt numbers. No index. Typed on printed forms. 27 volumes, 1000 pages. 10 x 7 x 4; 6 volumes, 2,100 pages. 20 x 7 x 5. County Courthouse, 1927-1931, 27 volumes, Auditor's storeroom, basement; 1932—, 6 volumes, Room 114, vault.

Sales Tax Division

This division was not created by statute but was established in 1935 by the county treasurer to facilitate the work of the office. The division issues sales tax receipts to vendors. (See pages 208, 209.)

343. VENDORS' PURCHASE ORDERS
1935——. 3 file boxes.
Prepared sales tax receipts showing name of vendor, amount of tax receipts purchased, and date of purchase. Chronologically arranged. No index. Typed on printed forms. 15 x 15 x 7. County Courthouse, Room 114, vault.

Bookkeeping Division

344. TREASURER'S JOURNAL OF ACCOUNTS REDEEMED
1924——. 6 volumes. 1926-1930, missing.
List warrants covering road, bridge, and other county funds. Chronologically arranged. No index. Handwritten on printed forms. Volumes average 300 pages. 23 x 19 x 3. County Courthouse, 1924-1925, 1 volume, Auditor's storeroom, basement; 1931——, 5 volumes, Room 114.

345. WARRANTS, ENDORSED BUT UNPAID
1891-1896. 7 volumes. Discontinued
County warrants endorsed but unpaid for lack of funds, showing warrant number, date warrant issued, name of payee, amount due. Numerically arranged by warrant numbers. No index. Handwritten on printed forms. Condition poor. Volumes average 70 pages. 12 x 9.5 x 1. County Courthouse, Auditor's storeroom, basement.

346. OVERS ON RECEIPTED BILLS
1919——. 1 volume.
List name, date, and amount of refund. Alphabetically arranged by names of taxpayers. No index. Handwritten on printed forms. Condition poor. Volumes average 250 pages. 12.5 x 11.5 x 2. County Courthouse, Room 114, vault.

347. CLERK'S FINANCIAL LEDGER
1918—. 10 volumes. (2 sets, each 1-5).
Miscellaneous accounts showing cash received and disbursed by county treasurer, bank investment accounts, *ad valorem* taxes, warrants, bonds and judgments, appropriations, crippled children's fund, sinking fund, special courthouse and county highway fund, and bridge fund. Chronologically arranged. Alphabetical index in front of each volume. Handwritten on printed forms. Volumes average 550 pages. 17 x 12.5 x 2.5. County Courthouse, 1918-1926, 5 volumes, Auditor's storeroom, basement; 1930—, 5 volumes, Room 114, vault.

348. MISCELLANEOUS CORRESPONDENCE
1928—. 40 bundles, 2 file boxes. Prior correspondence destroyed.
Office correspondence of a general nature. Chronologically arranged. No index. Handwritten and typed. Bundles, 12 x 6 x 4. File boxes, 18 x 9 x 6. County Courthouse, Room 114.

Cashier's Division

This division is not authorized by statute but was established by the county treasurer to facilitate the work of the treasurer's office. The division keeps records of all cash received and disbursements by the county treasurer.

349. DAILY CASH RECORD
1896—. 19 volumes. Prior records missing.
Lists daily statements of receipts, disbursements, and balance applicable to general cash in the county treasury. Chronologically arranged. No index. Handwritten and typed. Volumes average 500 pages. 12 x 10 x 3. County Courthouse, 1896-1932, 17 volumes, Auditor's storeroom, basement; 1933—, 2 volumes, Room 114.

350. RECEIPTS FOR MONEY
1930—. 8 volumes. (1-8).
Receipts from Treasurer to auditor for money deposited in county treasury by auditor. Numerically arranged by receipt numbers. No index. Typed on printed forms. Volumes average 600 pages. 10.5 x 4.25 x 3.25. County Courthouse, Room 114, vault.

351. SECURITIES HELD BY COUNTY COMMISSIONERS
1933—. 1 volume, 1 file of 20 steel shutters.
Record of securities held by commissioners as county investments listing name of
bank issuing security, value of security, and date of maturity. Volume,
chronologically arranged. File, alphabetically arranged by names of securities. No
index. Handwritten and typed on printed forms. Volume 100 pages. 15 x 10 x 1.
Steel shutters, 18 x 8. County Courthouse, Room 114, vault.

352. TREASURER'S RECORD OF FEES
1907-1927. 1 volume. Subsequent records kept by office making payments.
Record of miscellaneous fees paid to county treasurer showing date of payment and
by whom paid. Chronologically arranged. No index. Handwritten. 200 pages. 15 x
10 x 2. County Courthouse, Room 114, vault.

353. CASHIER'S MISCELLANEOUS MEMORANDA
1932—. 147 cartons. Prior records destroyed.
Miscellaneous record of cigarette, real estate, and tangible and intangible tax
receipts listing name of taxpayer, amount of tax paid, and date of payment.
Numerically arranged by receipt numbers. No index. Handwritten on printed forms.
73 cartons, 36 x 11 x 6; 74 cartons, 16 x 13 x 5. County Courthouse, Room 114,
vault.

While the acts of the Northwest Territory outlined the local institutions of the newer states, the first constitution of Ohio contained no provision for the office of county auditor, leaving his creation to the discretion of the legislature. It was not, however, until 1820 that the general assembly by joint resolution appointed a county auditor in each county for a one-year term. (18 O. L. 70.) A year later the office became an elective one, and has so continued. (19 O. L. 116.) The term of office was fixed at one year in 1821, two years in 1831, and three years and 1877. (19 O. L. 116; 29 O. L. 280; 74 O. L. 381.) The term remained at three years until 1906 when it was reduced to two years. (98 O. L. 273.) In 1919 the term of office was extended to four years. (108 O. L. pt. ii, 1294.)

During the early years of his office the auditor was required, as he is today, to take an oath, give bond for the faithful performance of the duties of his office, and transfer to his successor all books, records, maps, and other papers at pertaining to his office. (19 O. L. 116; R. S. 1033; G. C. secs. 2559, 2582.) He was required, also, to preserve in his office all copies of entries, surveys, extracts, and other documents as may have been transmitted to his office from the auditor of state. (22 O. L. 270; Chase, *op. cit.*, II, 1378.) With the approval of the county commissioners, the auditor was authorized to appoint deputies to aid him in the performance of his duties. (55 O. L. 20.) He and his sureties were, and are, liable for the official acts of his subordinates. Since 1869 a record of such appointments has been filed with the county treasurer. (G. C. sec. 2563; 66 O. L. 35.) If the office were to become vacant the county commissioners were, and are, authorized to appoint some suitable person to fill the vacancy. (29 O. L. 280-291; 67 O. L. 103.)

The first auditor in each county was required to list all lands subject to taxation lying within his county. From this list and a list submitted to him by the county commissioners and the state auditor, he was directed to make out a tax duplicate to be kept in a book for that purpose. After completing the duplicate, he turned it over to the "tax collector," who, in turn, proceeded to demand payment. (18 O. L. 70.) Moreover, the auditor was directed to make, from the treasurer's duplicate a list of all lands on which taxes were delinquent. In the event such lands were sold for taxes the auditor was authorized to grant a deed to the purchaser. (18 O. L. 70; 19 O. L. 116.) Subsequent legislation expanded and itemized the duties of the auditor regarding taxation. During the forties the office of county assessors was abolished and provision was made for township assessors, whose duty it was to list all taxable property in the township and make a return to the auditor. (39 O. L. 22-25.) Since 1874 the auditor has been required, by statute, to keep a book in which he lists additions to and deductions from the amount of the tax assessment. (71 O. L. 30.) With modifications to meet modern requirements, the auditor's duties regarding taxation have continued much as they were during the earlier years of the office.

Along with the county treasurer and county prosecutor, the county auditor has served as a member of the county budget commission. (See page 170.) As secretary to this body he is required to keep full and accurate records of the proceedings of the board. For the purpose of adjusting the tax rates and fixing the amount to be levied each year, the commissioners are governed by the amount of taxable property as shown on the auditor's tax list for the current year. The auditor submits to the commissioners the annual tax budget submitted to him by each taxing authority of each subdivision, together with an estimate prepared by the auditor of state, of the amount of any state levy, and other information as the budget commission may request or the state tax commission may require. (G. C. sec. 5625-19; 112 O. L. 339.)

Another important function of the county auditor has been the examination and approval, before payment, of bills and other claims against the county. Since 1831 the auditor has been authorized to issue, upon the presentation of the proper voucher, all warrants on the county treasurer for moneys payable from the county treasury, and has been required to preserve all warrants showing the number, date of issue, amount for which drawn, in whose favor, and for what purpose and on what fund. (G. C. sec. 2570; R. S. 1024; 29 O. L. 280-291; 67 O. L. 103.) Money due to the state is paid on warrant of the auditor of state. Since 1904 a bill or voucher for payment from any fun controlled by the county commissioners or board of county infirmary directors has been filed with the county auditor and entered in a book for that purpose at least five days before its approval for payment by the commissioners. When approved the date thereof is entered in such a book opposite the claim. (97 O. L. 25; 108 O. L. pt. I, 272.)

Besides approving bills and claims against the county, the auditor was early given the duty of certifying all moneys, except collections on the tax duplicate, into the county treasury, specifying by whom paid and the fund to which such payment is credited. Such money he charges to the treasurer and keeps a duplicate copy of the statement in his office. Since 1835 all costs collected in penitentiary cases which have been paid by the state or which are to be so paid, have been certified into the treasury as belonging to the state. (33 O. L. 44; 67 O. L. 103.)

Since 1831, the auditor has kept an account current with the county treasurer showing the payments of money into the treasury listing the time, by whom paid, and on what fund. Upon receiving the treasurer's daily statement he was, and is, directed to enter on his account current as a charge to the treasurer the amount shown. (29 O. L. 280-291; 67 O. L. 103.)

In 1902 the legislature was made provision for a system of uniform accounting and auditing for all public offices, under the director of a bureau of inspection in the office of the auditor of state. The act provided, also, for the annual examination of the finances of all public offices. (85 O. L. 511-515.) Since 1904 liquor, cigarette, and inheritance taxes have constituted separate funds. All other taxes are credited to the general fund. (97 O. L. 457.) Semiannually, the auditor makes a settlement with the treasurer ascertaining the amount of taxes the treasurer is to "stand charged." Semiannual settlements began in 1859; previous to that time, settlements had been made annually. (G. C. sec. 2596; 56 O. L. 132; 78 O. L. 226.)

Since 1904 the auditor has been required to report to the commissioners on the state of county finances. On the first business day of each month the auditor prepares, in duplicate, a statement of the finances of the county for the preceding month. After comparing it with a treasurer's balances, the statement is submitted to the commissioners, who, in turn, post one copy of it in the auditor's office where it remains for at least thirty days for the inspection and examination of the public. (67 O. L. 103; 97 O. L. 457.)

During the development of the office other duties have been conferred upon the auditor with great diversity. For example, since 1833 he has been authorized to discharge from imprisonment, any person can find in jail for the nonpayment of any fine or amercement due to the county, when, in his opinion, the fine appears to be on collectible. (G. C. sec. 2576; 31 O. L. 18; 67 O. L. 103.) The present duty of reporting to the auditor of state statistics of deaf, dumb, blind, insane, and idiotic persons in his county with the names and post office addresses of their parents or guardians, head it's beginning in 1861. (58 O. L. 40.) Eight years later saw the beginning of the practice of reporting to the same officer statistics of livestock in his county, as returned to his office by assessors, and an abstract of the funded and unfunded indebtedness of his county, and for each township, city, village, and school district. (G. C. sec. 2604.) A year later, in 1862, the auditor was given his present duty of issuing peddlers' licenses to persons who filed a statement of his stock in trade in conformity with the law requiring the listing of such stock for taxation, and since 1917 he has issued dog licenses. (59 O. L. 67; 79 O. L. 96; 107 O. L. 535.)

Until 1908 the auditor served as clerk to the county commissioners, and he was required to keep an accurate record of their proceedings and preserve all documents, books, records, maps, and papers which might be required to be filed in his office. (G. C. sec. 2566; 67 O. L. 103. See also page 4.) After 1908 such duties were delegated to the purchasing clerk. (See page 176.) Since 1850 he has been the official custodian of the reports submitted to the commissioners by the prosecuting attorney, the clerk of courts, the sheriff, and the treasurer. These reports have been recorded by the auditor in books especially for that purpose. (G. C. sec. 2504; R. S. 886; 48 O. L. 66.)

Then, too, since Six, the auditor has served as the sealer of weights and measures, and is responsible for the preservation of the copies of the original standards delivered to his office. He enforces all state laws regulating weights and measures in his county. (G. C. sec. 2615; 44 O. L. 55; 58 O. L. 78; 101 O. L. 234.) The auditor is a member of the county board of revision (see page 171) and serves as a trustee of the sinking fund. (see page 181).

In recent years there has been much criticism of the auditor's office. The chief complaint is, of course, that there is a duplication of work in the auditor's and in the treasurer's offices. The daily registers are, in all respects, similar.

Real Estate Division

The real estate division of the county auditor's office, which include the assessment, plaiting, public utilities, settlement, and transfer departments were not created by statute, but was established by the county auditor by virtue of the powers vested in him under the Ohio General Code to facilitate the work of his office. The function of this division is to list and superintendent the transferring of all lands subject to taxation in the county as provided for under sections 2558-2631 of the general code. The board of revision (see page 171) was arbitrarily made a department of this division.

General Records

354. ABSTRACT OF TAX DUPLICATE
1899. 34 volumes. (1-34).
Lists land valuation, personal property valuation, general tax, and delinquent tax. Chronologically arranged. No index. Handwritten. Volumes average 250 pages. 24

x 20 x 2, County Courthouse, 1899-1930, 31 volumes, Auditor's storeroom, basement; 1931—. 3 volumes, Room 112.

355. APPLICATION FOR TAX EXEMPTIONS
1916—. 12 file boxes (1-801).
Applications for real estate tax exemptions showing approval or rejection; also miscellaneous papers pertaining thereto. Numerically arranged by application numbers. No index. Handwritten on printed forms. 10 x 4.5 x 2 County Courthouse, Room 109.

356. EXEMPT REAL ESTATE
1912—. 3 volumes.
Abstracts of auditors list of real estate exempted from taxation in Hamilton County showing name of owner, description of property, valuation of land, and buildings and grounds upon which exemptions are allowed. Alphabetically arranged by names of owners. No index. Handwritten and typed on printed forms. Volumes average 200 pages. 16 x 12 x 2. County Courthouse, Room 109.

357. EXEMPT REAL ESTATE TAX DUPLICATES
1924—. 4 volumes.
Auditor's list of exempted real property, both publicly and privately owned in Hamilton County; property of the United States, state of Ohio, county, townships, municipalities, schools and colleges, houses of worship, cemeteries and monuments, institutions of learning, charitable institutions, and American Legion and Disabled World War Veterans. Alphabetically arranged by titles of properties. No index. Handwritten and typed. Volumes average 500 pages. 15 x 8 x 3. Room 112.

358. TAX EXEMPTIONS
1929—. 1 volume.
Record of publicly owned property on which no tax payment is required. Alphabetically arranged by titles of properties. No index. Handwritten on printed forms. 100 pages. 18 x 18 x 1. County Courthouse, Room 109.

359. REAL ESTATE CARDS
1925—. 600 volumes. System of recording initiated 1925.
Records ownership, valuation, size, location, tax rate and amount of tax on residences, apartments, farms, and Industrial properties in the various townships, villages and cities in Hamilton County. Numerically arranged by plat numbers. No index. Typed on printed forms. Volumes average 3,000 pages. 12 x 10 x 8. County Courthouse, 1925-1930, 300 volumes, Auditor's storeroom, basement; 1931—, 300 volumes, Room 109.

360. DELINQUENT RECORD, FIDUCIARY, PERSONAL, AND REAL ESTATE
1932—. 30 volumes. (1-300).
Records names of owners of estates, foreign and domestic; also reason estate is in trust. Numerically arranged by estate numbers. No index. Handwritten on typed and printed forms. Volumes average 500 pages. 14 x 8.5 x 2. County Courthouse, 1932-1933, 28 volumes, Auditor's storeroom, basement; 1934—, 2 volumes, Room 114.

361. PLANS AND ESTIMATES ON STREET IMPROVEMENTS
1878—. 30 volumes.
Shows plat of property to benefit by improvement, copy of published ordinance, and copy of estimated cost. Chronologically arranged. Index by subject in front of each volume. Handwritten on printed forms. Volumes average 200 pages. 18 x 12 x 2.5. County Courthouse, 1878-1899, 12 volumes, Auditor's storeroom, basement; 1900—, 18 volumes, Room 114.

362. BUILDING CARDS
1920—. 62 file boxes. Prior records destroyed.
Lists description of property, name of owner, and location; also book and plat numbers. Alphabetically arranged by wards and townships. No index. Handwritten. 24 x 13 x 9.5. County Courthouse, 1920-1932, 48 file boxes, Auditor's storeroom, basement; 1933—, 14 file boxes, Room 109.

363. SUBSEQUENT ADDITIONS IN HAMILTON COUNTY
1925—. 8 volumes 51 file boxes (1-5700). Prior records destroyed.
Additions of buildings to real estate since regular real estate appraisement; also additional taxes to be paid. Chronologically arranged. No index. Handwritten and

typed on printed forms. Volumes average 1,000 pages.10 x 8 x 5. File boxes, 12 x 10 x 4.5. County Courthouse, 1925-1929, 43 file boxes, Auditor's storeroom, basement; 1930-1932,8 file boxes; 1930—, 8 volumes, Room 109.

364. DESTROYED BUILDINGS AFFIDAVITS
1932—. 27 file boxes (1-10000).
Records name of owner, case number, description, value, and deductions of taxes to be paid. Numerically arranged by case numbers. No index. Handwritten on printed forms. 12 x 10 x 4.5. County Courthouse, Room 109.

365. LO9NGVIEW HOSPITAL BUILDING COMMISSION RECORD
1915-1924. 1 volume.
Record of bills and accounts for the construction of a new addition to the hospital listing nature of work, name of firm supervising work, time and cost accounts. Alphabetically arranged by names of contractors. No index. Handwritten. 74 pages. 16 x 13 x 1. County Courthouse, Auditor's storeroom, basement.

366. BIDS FOR TUBERCULOSIS HOSPITAL
1928—. 4 bundles. Record initiated 1928.
Tabulations of bids on buildings at tuberculosis hospital. Alphabetically arranged by names of bitters. No index. Handwritten and typed. 12 x 8 x 3. County Courthouse, Room 109.

367. MINUTES, HAMILTON COUNTY TUBERCULOSIS HOSPITAL BUILDING COMMISSION
1928—. 1 volume.
Records minutes and proceedings of Hamilton County tuberculosis hospital commission. Record is kept in the auditor's office as he is an ex officio member of the commission. Chronologically arranged. No index. Typed. 600 pages. 18.5 x 12.5 x 3. County Courthouse, Room 109.

368. GENERAL CORRESPONDENCE, HAMILTON COUNTY TUBERCULOSIS HOSPITAL COMMISSION
1928—. 3 file boxes.
All correspondence of and with the commission pertaining to tuberculosis hospital. Record is kept in the auditor's office as he is an ex-officio member of the

commission. Alphabetically arranged by names of correspondents. No index. Handwritten and typed. 24 x 15 x 10. County Courthouse, Room 109.

369. CONFIDENTIAL WORK SHEETS
1925—. 16 file boxes.

Work sheets pertaining to real estate appraisals. Records are not accessible to general public. Alphabetically arranged by names of property owners. No index. Typed on printed forms. 26 x 12 x 10. County Courthouse, Room 109.

370. ATLAS, CITY OF CINCINNATI
1883-1884. 1 volume.

Shows city of Cincinnati by divisions. Index by divisions in front of volume. Published by E. Robinson, Philadelphia, Pennsylvania. Hand drawn. 28 pages. 28 x 20 x 2. County Courthouse, Room 109.

371. ATLAS, HAMILTON COUNTY
1869. 1 volume.

Shows cities, townships, and villages of Hamilton County. Index by townships and villages in front of volume. Published by E. Titus, Philadelphia, Pennsylvania. Hand drawn in colors. 117 pages. 30 x 18 x 1. County Courthouse, Room 109.

372. VALUATION MAP, CINCINNATI
1934—. 1 volume.

Shows valuation of land in various sections of Cincinnati. Published by Sanborn Map Company, New York. Printed in black and white. Scale, 1 inch equals 100 feet. 100 pages. 30 x 20 x 1.5. County Courthouse, Room 109.

Platting Department

373. INDEX MAPS TO PLAT BOOKS
1931—. 1 file of 14 shutters. Record initiated 1931.

Index maps of all cities, villages, and townships in Hamilton County. Records plat book and page numbers, size and location of property, and school district; also names and owners of farms. Alphabetically arranged by names of cities, villages, and townships. Hand drawn in colors. File, 28 pages. 60 x 54. County Courthouse, Room 109, west wall.

374.INDEX MAP TO PLAT BOOKS, CITY OF CINCINNATI
1933—. 1 map.
Political index map to plat books, City of Cincinnati. Author and publisher not indicated. Printed in color and framed. Scale, 1 inch equals 1,000 feet. 72 x 54. County Courthouse, Room 109.

375. PLAT BOOKS, VILLAGES
1880—. 24 volumes.
Plats of Hamilton County, villages of Addyston, Arlington Heights, Cheviot, Cleves, Deer Park, Elmwood Place, Glendale, Harrison, Lockland, Loveland, Madison, Milford, Montgomery, Mt. Healthy, Newton, North Bend, North College Hill, Reading, Sharonville, Silverton, St. Bernard, Terrace Park, and Wyoming. For index see entry 373. Hand drawn. Volumes average 6 pages. 32 x 24 x .25. County Courthouse, Room 109.

376. PLAT BOOKS, CITY, COUNTY, TOWNSHIPS
1880—. 39 bundles. (13 bundles labeled City and County; 26 bundles labeled Cincinnati).
Shows size of property, lot numbers, location, name of property owner, and to whom transferred. These are damaged pages which have been replaced by new pages that are now in use in Room 109. For index see entries 373 and 374. Hand drawn. 20 x 16 x 2. County Courthouse, Auditor's storeroom, basement.

377. PLAT BOOKS, CITY OF CINCINNATI
1880—. 110 volumes. (21-130). Prior records, volumes 1-20, missing.
Shows name and size of subdivisions and location; also streets and lot numbers. For index see entry 374. Hand drawn. Volumes average 60 pages. 24 x 20 x 2. County Courthouse, Room 109.

378. PLATS, TOWNSHIPS IN HAMILTON COUNTY
n. d. 23 file boxes.
Duplicate plats of these separately bound in volume form. Author or publisher not indicated. Hand drawn in colors. Scale, 1 inch equals 300 feet. 34 x 30 x 1. County Courthouse, Room 109.

379. INDEX MAP TO PLAT BOOKS, TOWNSHIPS OF HAMILTON COUNTY
1932. 1 map.

Political index map to plat books of townships and villages in Hamilton County. Prepared by J. A. Stewart. Published by Strobridge Lithographing Company, Cincinnati, Ohio. Printed in color and framed. Scale 1 inch equals 2,000 feet. 72 x 48. County Courthouse, Room 109.

380. PLAT BOOKS
n. d. 26 volumes.

Shows villages and cities in Hamilton County, excepting Cincinnati. Author or publisher not indicated. Hand drawn in colors. No index. Scale, 2.5 inches equals 100 feet. Volumes average 40 pages. 24 x 18 x 1.5. County Courthouse, Room 109.

381. PLATS
1931—. 10 file boxes.

Plants of villages townships, and new subdivisions; also field maps. Alphabetically arranged by names of villages, townships, and subdivisions. No index. Hand drawn in black and white. Scales vary. 26 x 24 x 2. County Courthouse, Room 109.

382. PLATS
1931—. 9 file boxes.

Plats of buildings and lands by township and villages in Hamilton County. Alphabetically arranged by names of villages and townships. No index. Hand drawn. Scales vary. Size of maps vary. County Courthouse, Room 109, west wall.

383. INDEX MAP TO PLAT BOOKS OF NORWOOD
1931. 1 map.

Index to plat books of the City of Norwood showing streets, lots, and size; also plat book and page numbers. Hand drawn. Black and white with numbers in colors. Scale, 1 inch equals 200 feet. 72 x 60.County Courthouse, Room 115, west wall.

For subsequent index to plat books of Norwood see entry 424.

384. INDEX PLAT BOOK

1932—. 1 volume. System of recording initiated 1932.
Revolving counter index to Cincinnati and Norwood plats. Numerically arranged
by house and plat numbers; typed. 20 x 9 x 5. County Courthouse, Room 109.

385. PLATS, COPIES, FIELD NOTES

1884—, 4 file boxes.
Plats of subdivisions, copies of plats, and engineers' field notes. Alphabetically
arranged by names of subdivisions. No index. Handwritten and hand drawn. 26 x
16 x 12. County Courthouse, Room 109.

386. FIELD PLATS, UNION TERMINAL AND VILLAGES.

1925—. 9 file boxes.
Records plans and diagrams of the union terminal and Hamilton County villages.
Chronologically arranged. No index. Hand drawn. 24 x 24 x 6. County Courthouse,
Room 112.

387. RAILROAD MAPS AND PLANS

1931—. 11 file boxes. Prior records missing.
Maps and plans of railroad property improvements and repairs. Alphabetically
arranged by names of railroads. No index. Hand drawn and blueprint. Scales vary.
26 x 16 x 4.5. County Courthouse, Room 109.

Transfer Department

388. REAL ESTATE TRANSFER RECORDS

1892—. 568 volumes. Prior records missing.
Record of real estate transfers showing names of grantors and grantees, description,
valuation, consideration, and date of transfer; also number and time of recording.
Chronologically arranged. No index. Handwritten and typed. 534 volumes average
350 pages. 17 x 14 x 2; 32 volumes average 1000 pages. (loose-leaf in post binders)
11 x 7 x 5. County Courthouse, 1892-1929, 532 volumes, Auditor's storeroom,
basement; 1930—. 34 volumes, Room 109.

389. PERMANENT DUPLICATE CARDS, VOIDED
1932—. 7 file boxes. System of recording initiated 1932.
Record of real estate transfers listing property owner, description, valuation of property, and assessments. Alphabetically arranged by names of property owners. No index. Handwritten on printed forms. 26 x 14 x 10. County Courthouse, Room 109.

390. AFFIDAVIT OF TRANSFERS
1906—. 18 file boxes.
Affidavits of transfers of real estate where deeds are lost before recording. Chronologically arranged. No index. Handwritten and typed. 18 x 10 x 5. County Courthouse, Room 109.

391. TRANSFER BOOKS
1930—. 194 volumes. (1930-1931, 1-45; 1932—, 1-43; 1933—, 1-19; 1934—, 1-23; 1935—, 1-27; 1936—, 1-37).
Records transfers of city and county real estate in Hamilton County. Alphabetically arranged by names of property owners. No index. Typed on printed forms. Volumes average 150 pages. 12 x 9 x 2 County Courthouse, Room 109.

392. REAL ESTATE TRANSFER SHEETS
1932—. 24 volumes. Prior records destroyed.
Departmental copies of real estate transfers. Chronologically arranged. No index. Handwritten. Volumes average 1000 pages. 11 x 7 x 5. County Courthouse, Room 109.

393. MISCELLANEOUS REAL ESTATE RECORD HAMILTON COUNTY
1906—. 816 file boxes.
Miscellaneous real estate plats listing board book, plat, parcel, building specifications, and total. Chronologically arranged; also numerically arranged by ward numbers. No index. Handwritten. 30 x 11 x 5. County Courthouse, 1906-1928, 610 file boxes, Auditor's storeroom, basement; 1929—, 206 file boxes, Room 109.

394. TOWNSHIP PLAT BOOKS
1880—. 46 volumes. (Volumes numbered by townships in order listed below respectively, 1-8, 1-5, 1-3, 1-3, 1-4, 1-2, 1-2, 1-6, 1-6, 1-3, 1-4).
Plat books for Anderson, Colerain, Crosby, Delhi, Green, Harrison, Miami, Springfield, Sycamore, Symmes, and White Water townships showing sizes of properties, names of subdivisions and property owners, and to whom titles were transferred. Alphabetically arranged by names of townships. For index see entry 373. Hand drawn. Volumes average 6 pages. 32 x 26 x .25. County Courthouse, Room 109.

395. PLAT BOOKS, CITY OF CINCINNATI
1880—. 247 volumes. (1-247).
Plat books showing sizes of properties, lot numbers, location, names of subdivisions and property owners, and to whom titles were transferred. Chronologically arranged. For index see entry 373. Hand drawn. Volumes average 6 pages. 32 x 26 x .25. County Courthouse, Room 109.

396. PLAT BOOKS, CITY OF NORWOOD
1880—. 6 volumes.
Plat books of city of Norwood showing names of streets, size of lots, lot numbers, names of property owners, to whom titles were transferred, boundaries of subdivisions in color and names of original owners of subdivisions. Chronologically arranged. For index see entries 373 and 383. Hand drawn and printed. Volumes average 20 pages. 34 x 24 x 1. County Courthouse, Room 109.

Assessment Department

397. TAX DUPLICATES
1884—, 1226 volumes. Prior records missing.
Auditor's real estate tax duplicates of Cincinnati and Norwood; also villages and townships of Hamilton County, recording name of property owner, size and location of property, December and June taxes, and extra levies. Alphabetically arranged by names of property owners. No index. Typed. Volumes average 600 pages. 24 x 20 x 5. County Courthouse, 1884-1928, 122 volumes, Auditor's storeroom, basement; 1929—, 1,104 volumes, Room 109.

398. TAX DUPLICATES
1897—. 11 volumes.

Records names and addresses of corporations, value of property, December and June taxes, extra levies, and total tax. Alphabetically arranged by names of Corporations. No index. Typed. Volumes average [—] pages. 18 x 16 x 3. County Courthouse, 1897-1930, 4 volumes, Auditor's storeroom, basement; 1931—, 7 volumes, Room 112.

399. EXEMPT TAX DUPLICATE
1917—. 6 volumes. System of recording initiated 1917.

Records name of property owner, description of property, evaluation of building and land, and reason for tax exemption. Alphabetically arranged by names of property owners. No index. Handwritten and typed on printed forms. Volumes average 200 pages. 22 x 18 x 2. County Courthouse, Room 109.

400. PERMANENT DUPLICATE CARDS
1932—. 99 file boxes (1-99 and A-Z; 57 file boxes labeled Cincinnati, 42 file boxes labeled by names of townships and villages). System of recording initiated 1932.

Shows name of owner, description, valuation, and assessments on property. Alphabetically arranged by names of owners. No index. Handwritten on printed forms. 26 x 14 x 10. County Courthouse, Room 109.

401. ADDITIONS AND DEDUCTIONS TO TAX DUPLICATE
1874—. 85 volumes.

Records additions and deductions to tax duplicate giving number of record, name of owner, identification of real estate, amount of tax on duplicate, and amount of additions or deductions. Numerically arranged by case numbers. No index. Handwritten on printed forms. Volumes average 125 pages. 16 x 6 x 1. County Courthouse, Auditor's storeroom, basement.

402. MISCELLANEOUS ASSESSMENTS
1908-1933. 1 volume.

Record of miscellaneous Assessments in Hamilton County, including streets and sewers, listing lot numbers, address, date due, and date of assessment

Alphabetically arranged by names of property owners. No index. Handwritten. 350 pages. 18 x 16 x 4. County Courthouse, Auditor's storeroom, basement.

For subsequent records of see entry 403.

403. INDEX TO ASSESSMENT BY STREETS
1933——. 3500 file boxes.

Index record of assessments on property in Cincinnati and townships give the name of owner, address, description of property, and amount of taxes and assessments. Alphabetically arranged by names of streets. No index. Typed. 24 x 20 x 12. County Courthouse, Room 109.

404. CENTRAL PARKWAY ASSESSMENTS
1927——. 1 volume. System of recording initiated 1927.

Assessments for improvements of Central Parkway, Cincinnati, as posted against real estate tax list showing name of owner, description of property, and date of payment. Alphabetically arranged by name some property owners. No index. Typed. 500 pages. 24 x 24 x 4. County Courthouse, Room 109.

405. CENTRAL PARKWAY ASSESSMENT PLATS
1927——. 1 volume.

Records size of lot and lot numbers of all property assessed as benefited by the Central Parkway, Cincinnati. Chronologically arranged. Alphabetical index by names of property owners. Hand drawn. 250 pages. 24 x 16 x 2. County Courthouse, Room 109.

406. MIAMI CONSERVANCY ASSESSMENT BOOKS, HAMILTON COUNTY
1934-1935. 2 volumes.

Assessment for the bond issue and maintenance fund Miami Conservancy District. Numerically arranged by case numbers; also alphabetically arranged under initial letters of names of property owners. Typed on printed forms. Volumes average 50 pages. 24 x 18 x .5. County Courthouse, Room 109.

407. VILLAGE CERTIFICATIONS
1929—. 5 volumes. Prior records missing.
Village assessments for improvements as certified to the county auditor to be paid with real estate taxes. Alphabetically arranged by names of property owners. No index. Handwritten. Volumes average 100 pages. 22 x 10 x 1. County Courthouse, Room 109.

408. COUNTY WATER BOOKS
1925—. 7 volumes. (1-7). System of recording initiated 1925.
Record of assessments for installation of water mains in Hamilton County. Chronologically arranged. Alphabetical index by names of property owners in front of each volume. Handwritten on printed forms. Volumes average 300 pages. 24 x 24 x 3. County Courthouse, Room 109.

409. ORDERS TO RECEIVE
1898—. 45 volumes. (1-45).
Warrant stubs of street assessments, sewers, and direct inheritance fees. Numerically arranged by warrant numbers. No index. Handwritten on printed forms. Volumes average 200 pages. 12 x 6 x 1.5. County Courthouse, 1898-1930, Auditor's storeroom, basement; 1931—, 8 volumes, Room 112.

410. STREET ASSESSMENTS
1894—. 5 file boxes. Prior records missing.
Certified reports of Village clerks for street assessments listing names of property owner, and amount of assessments. Arranged by names of villages of Cincinnati and environs: Carthage, Westwood, St. Bernard, Home City, Delhi, Bond Hill, Riverside, Harrison, College Hill, Arlington Heights, Hartwell, and Glendale. No index. Handwritten on printed forms. 15 x 6 x 5. County Courthouse, Auditor's storeroom, basement.

411. STREET ASSESSMENTS, CINCINNATI ONLY
1902—. 12 volumes, 20 file boxes (9 volumes A-G, 2 volumes H, 1 volume, H-K).
Shows amount of street assessments as a portion to property owners according to benefit received; also date due and date paid. File boxes are a Kardex system. Alphabetically arranged by names of property owners. No index. Handwritten and

typed on printed forms. Volumes average 950 pages. 20 x 18 x 4. File boxes, 24 x 9 x 1. County Courthouse, 1902-1933, 12 volumes, Auditor's storeroom, basement; 1934—, 20 file boxes, Room 109.

412. OIL ASSESSMENTS, CINCINNATI
1921-1929. 2 volumes. System of recording initiated 1921. Subsequent records kept by city treasurer.
Records of paid assessments for oiling streets in Cincinnati giving names of persons assessed, subdivisions, and dates paid. Alphabetically arranged by names of taxpayers. No index. Handwritten. Volumes average 250 pages. 20 x 16 x 2. County Courthouse, Auditor's storeroom, basement.

413. SEWER ASSESSMENTS
1907—. 9 volumes (A-Z and 1-4). System of recording initiated 1907.
Records of assessments for installation of sewers in Hamilton County. Chronologically arranged. Alphabetical index by names of property owners in front of each volume. Handwritten on printed forms. Volumes average 600 pages. 24 X 24 X 3. County Courthouse, 1907-1923, 5 volumes, Auditor's storeroom, basement; 1924, 4 volumes, Room 109.

414. SEWER ASSESSMENTS
1910—. 3 volumes. System of recording initiated 1910.
Special assessments of the city of Cincinnati as posted to real estate tax list. Chronologically arranged. Handwritten and typed on printed forms. Volumes average 200 pages. 20 x 16 x 2. County Courthouse, 1910-1930, 2 volumes, Auditor's storeroom, basement; 1931—, 1 volume, Room 109.

415. INDEX TO SEWER ASSESSMENTS
1910—. 1 volume.
Index to sewer assessment record as certified to county auditor. Alphabetically arranged by names of property owners. No index. Handwritten. 200 pages. 16 x 12 x 1.5. County Courthouse, Room 109.

416. DELINQUENT SIDEWALK ASSESSMENTS
1931—. 1 volume. Prior records missing.
Record of sidewalk assessments as posted on real estate tax list of Hamilton County. Chronologically arranged. Handwritten and typed. 200 pages. 20 x 16 x 2. County Courthouse, Room 109.

417. INDEX TO DELINQUENT SIDEWALK ASSESSMENTS
1931. 1 volume.
Index to sidewalk assessment record as posted to real estate tax list. Alphabetically arranged by names of property owners. Handwritten. 200 pages. 16 x 12 x 1.5. County Courthouse, Room 109.

418. SIDEWALKS AND SEWERS
1904-1932. 3 volumes. System of recording initiated 1904.
Miscellaneous assessments against property owners for sidewalks and sewers in Hamilton County listing name of owner and amount of assessment. Alphabetically arranged by names of property owners. No index. Handwritten and typed. Volumes average 300 pages. 20 x 20 x 3. County Courthouse, 1904-1927, 2 volumes, Auditor's storeroom, basement; 1929-1932, 1 volume, Room 109.
For subsequent records see entry 421.

419. INTER-COUNTY HIGHWAY ASSESSMENTS
1908—. 16 volumes. (1908-1928, 10 volumes, A-Z; 1929—, 6 volumes, no labeling).
Records of assessments for improvements and repairs of highways and streets in Hamilton County listing plants of improvements, newspaper clippings of advertisements, amount of assessments, and date of payment. Chronologically arranged. Alphabetical index by names of landowners in front of each volume. Handwritten. Volumes average 300 pages. 20 x 15 x 3. County Courthouse, 1908-1933, 14 volumes, Auditor's storeroom, basement; 1934—, 2 volumes, Room 109.

420. BOULEVARD LIGHTS ASSESSMENTS
1925, 2 volumes. Record initiated 1925.
Record of assessments against property owners for boulevard lights showing names of property owners, amounts, and date of payment. Alphabetically arranged by

names of property owners. No index. Typed. 200 pages. 24 x 24 x 2. County Courthouse, Room 109.

521. ENJOINED ASSESSMENTS
1932—. 1 volume. Record initiated 1932.
Enjoined assessments for boulevard lights, street, sewer, water, sidewalk, boulevard, and miscellaneous assessments. Alphabetically arranged under initial letters of names of property owners. Alphabetical thumb tab index attached to margins. Handwritten. 1,000 pages. 14 x 9 x 5. County Courthouse, Room 109.

422. ASSESSORS' RECORD, PERSONAL TAX
1913-1932. 4 volumes. Prior records missing. Discontinued.
Lists assessors' record of personal property. Alphabetically arranged by names of wards and townships. Alphabetical index by names of property owners. Handwritten. Volumes average 100 pages. 14 x 9 x 2. County Courthouse, Auditor's storeroom, basement.

423. SPECIAL ASSESSMENTS, COUNTY, DELINQUENT PENALTIES
1929—. 1 volume.
Shows delinquent tax penalties on special assignments, name of owner, lot number, and amount of penalties. Alphabetically arranged by names of property owners. No index. Handwritten. 125 pages. 24 x 16 x 1. County Courthouse, Room 114.

424. CORRESPONDENCE AND AGREEMENTS
1928. 4 file boxes. Prior records missing.
General correspondence and agreements on real estate tax assessment. Alphabetically arranged by names of correspondents. No index. Handwritten and typed. 26 x 16 x 12. County Courthouse, Room 109.

425. SUBDIVISION INDEX
1892—. 5 volumes.
Index to subdivisions showing names of subdivision and owner; also plat book and page numbers. Counter revolving index, alphabetically arranged by names of subdivisions. Handwritten and typed. Volumes average 500 pages. 16 x 12 x 4. County Courthouse, Room 109.

426. ASSESSMENT PLAT BOOKS
1906—. 5 volumes.

Plat books covering city of Cincinnati assessments on sewers, boulevard lights, streets, and sidewalks. Alphabetically arranged by names of property owners. No index. Handwritten. Volumes average 300 pages. 20 x 12 x 3. County Courthouse, Room 109.

427. CUT-UP RECORDS, CITY AND COUNTY
1932—. 3 volumes (1 volume labeled City; 2 volumes County). System of recording initiated 1932.

Division of original lots into one or more parcels giving dimensions and legal descriptions. Alphabetically arranged by names of property owners. No index. Handwritten. Volumes average 400 pages. 14 x 9 x 3. County Courthouse, Room 109.

Public Utilities Department

428. PUBLIC UTILITIES REAL ESTATE APPRAISEMENTS
1903—. 3 volumes, 3 file boxes. 1910-1930, missing. (volumes labeled chronologically; 1 file box labeled Active; 2 file boxes labeled Voided.)

Appraisements of real estate public utilities and other corporations for purpose of taxation. Alphabetically arranged by names of companies. No index. Handwritten and typed on printed forms. Volumes average 200 pages. 18 x 14 x 2. File boxes, 24 x 14 x 10. County Courthouse, 1903-1909, 3 volumes, Auditor's storeroom, basement; 1931—, 3 file boxes, Room 109.

429. PUBLIC UTILITIES REAL ESTATE CARDS
1932—. 24 volumes, 2 file boxes.

Shows public utility ownership, land and building values, size of property, and amount of tax. Cards voided in cases where property is sold, divided, or consolidated. Chronologically arranged. Some tab index by names of companies attached to margins. Handwritten and typed on printed forms. Volumes average 150 pages. 18 x 10 x 1.5. File boxes, 24 x 12 x 10. County Courthouse, Room 109.

430. PLANS AND PLATS, NEW SUBDIVISION

1933—. 3 file boxes.

Shows new and proposed improvements to public utilities property. These are duplicate plans and plats of those kept in the real estate division. Alphabetically arranged by names of utilities. For index see entry 425. Hand drawn and blueprint. 25 x 14 x 10. County Courthouse, Room 109.

For prior records see entries 426 and 427.

Settlement Department

431. FINANCIAL SETTLEMENTS, BOARD OF EDUCATION

1922—. 5 file boxes. System of recording initiated 1922.

Board of education records of settlements for real estate. Chronologically arranged. No index. Handwritten and typed on printed forms. 14 x 10.5 x 4. County Courthouse, Auditor's storeroom, basement.

432. TAX BILLS ISSUED

1933—. 108 file boxes (1-108).

Shows duplicates of tax bills issued giving date, name and address, and amount due. Chronologically arranged. No index. 12 x 12 x 5. County Courthouse, Auditor's storeroom, basement.

433. TREASURER'S RETURNS ON DELINQUENT REAL ESTATE TAXES

1899—. 59 volumes (1-59). System of recording initiated 1899.

Record listing name of property owner, amount of taxes paid, location of real estate, valuation, and size a lot. Chronologically arranged. No index. Handwritten. Volumes average 500 pages. 19.5 x 5.75 x 2.75. County Courthouse, Room 109.

434. RECORD OF DELINQUENT TAX SETTLEMENTS

1917—. 488 volumes. (labeled chronologically). System of recording initiated 1917.

Record listing name property owner, month, and year of settlement. Chronologically arranged. No index. Handwritten. Volumes average 500 pages. 21 x 15 x 2. County Courthouse, 1917-1931, 366 volumes, Auditor's storeroom, basement; 1932—, 122 volumes, Room 109.

154 AUDITOR

435. FORFEITURE TAX DUPLICATES
1884——. 84 volumes

Record listing properties sold for nonpayment of taxes, name of property owner, amount of delinquent taxes, penalties, and tax title purchaser. Alphabetically arranged by names of property owners. No index. Handwritten and typed. Volumes average 125 pages. 22 x 17 x 1. County Courthouse, 1884-1928, 83 volumes, Auditor's storeroom, basement; 1929——, 1 volume, Room 109.

436. PENALTY REFUNDS OR REMITS
1931-1935.87 file boxes, 16 volumes. Prior records missing. Refund for 1936 yet to be made.

Refunds of penalty, interest, or other charge for payment of real estate taxes or assessments when do. Alphabetically arranged by names of property owners. No index. Handwritten on printed forms. File boxes 14 x 10.5 x 4. Volumes average 375 pages. 11 x 6 x 3. County Courthouse, 1931, 1935, 65 boxes and 7 volumes, Room 112; 1932, 27 file boxes, Room 109; 1933-1934, 9 volumes, Auditor's storeroom, basement.

437. REFUND STUBS
1910——. 21 volumes (1-10000).

Refunds on overcharges on real estate taxes listing name of taxpayer, description of property, and voucher number. Numerically arranged by voucher numbers. No index. Handwritten on printed forms. Volumes average 100 pages. 8 3 x 1. County Courthouse, Room 109.

438. TREASURER'S DUPLICATE OF TAXES PAID, RECEIPTS
1916——. 8 volumes.

Records date, number, name of property owner, classification, valuation, and rate of payment. Numerically arranged by serial numbers. No index. Handwritten on printed forms. Volumes average 500 pages. 9 x 4 x 2. County Courthouse, 1916-1929, 6 volumes, Auditor's storeroom, basement; 1930——, 2 volumes, Room 112.

439. TREASURER'S LEDGER
1918——. 8 volumes. Prior records missing.

Auditor's record of county treasurer's accounts listing credits, debits, and balances of county funds with various depositories; also funds of various county departments. Chronologically arranged. Alphabetical index by names of departments in front of each volume. Handwritten on printed forms. Volumes average 600 pages. 12 x 6 x 2. County Courthouse, 1918-1929, 4 volumes, Room 109; 1930—, 4 volumes, Room 114.

440. SUMMONSES AND INJUNCTIONS
1935—. 3 file boxes (1-5000). Prior records destroyed.
Duplicates of summonses and injunctions in actions of common pleas court in foreclosure cases. Alphabetically arranged by names of property owners. No index. Handwritten on printed forms. 10 x 12 x 4.5. County Courthouse, Room 109.

441, SHEEP AND ANIMAL CLAIMS
1906—. 5 volumes. Prior records destroyed.
Claims and judgments for injured or killed animals showing name and address of owner; also amount and disposition of claim. Chronologically arranged. No index. Handwritten on printed forms. Volumes average 300 pages. 16 x 11 x 2. County Courthouse, 1906-1924, 3 volumes, Auditor's storeroom, basement; 1925—, 2 volumes, Room 112.

Tangible and Intangible Tax Division

This division of the auditor's office, which includes the license and inheritance tax departments, was not created by statute but established by the county auditor by virtue of powers vested in him under the Ohio General Code, to facilitate the work of his office. The functions of this division are to administer and enforce the provisions of sections 2583-2608 of the General Code.

442. CITY AND COUNTY PERSONAL TAX
1918—. 200 volumes. (1918-1927, 45 volumes labeled County; 1918-1927, 81 volumes labeled City; 1928—, 74 volumes labeled City and County).
Lists city of Cincinnati and county real and personal property, consecutive number of ward or subdivision, name of property owner, address, description of property, date of tax payment, and amount. Numerically arranged by ward numbers; also alphabetically arranged by names of townships. No index. Typed on printed forms. Volumes average 350 pages. 20 x 16 x 3. County Courthouse, 1918-1930, 145 volumes, Auditor's storeroom, basement; 1931—, 60 volumes, Room 109.

443.UNPAID DUPLICATES, GENERAL TAX
1934——. 7 volumes. (1-58999).
Shows description, location of property, and amount of tax. Alphabetically arranged
by names of property owners. No index. Handwritten and typed on printed forms.
Volumes average 500 pages. 14 x 8.5 x 2. County Courthouse, Auditor's storeroom,
basement.

444, TAX RETURNS, FINANCIAL INSTITUTIONS AND PUBLIC
UTILITIES
1932. 4 volumes (A-Z). System of recording used for 1 year only.
Shows name of owner, districts, domestic or foreign value, computation, and
summary. Alphabetically arranged by names of property owners. No index.
Handwritten on printed forms. Volumes average 500 pages. 14 x 8.5 x 2. County
Courthouse, Auditor's storeroom, basement.

445. DELINQUENT TAXES, PERSONAL, CORPORATION,
UNINCORPORATED
1932. 19 volumes (A-Z). System of recording used for 1 year only.
Shows name of owner, domestic or foreign, property value, computation, and
summary. Alphabetically arranged by names of corporations or individuals. No
index. Handwritten and typed on printed forms. Volumes average 500 pages. 14 x
8.5 x 2. County Courthouse, Auditor's storeroom, basement.

446. INTANGIBLE TAXES, PERSONAL, CORPORATE, AND
UNINCORPORATED
1932——. 891 volumes. (1932-1934, 570 volumes labeled Personal, 1932-
1934, 138 volumes labeled Corporations, 1932-1934, 183 volumes labeled
Unincorporated, 1932——, loose sheets, as yet unbound, covering separate
taxes as listed in title).
Gives returns, name of owner, district, domestic or foreign values, computations,
and summary. Alphabetically arranged by names of Corporations or individuals. No
index. Handwritten. Volumes average 500 pages. 14 x 8.5 x 2. County Courthouse,
Auditor's storeroom, basement.

447. PERSONAL TAX DUPLICATES

1932. 16 volumes. (A-Z). System of recording used for one year only. Shows amount and valuation of personal property, name of owner, rate of taxation, and amount. Alphabetically arranged by names of owners. No index. Typed. Volumes average 1,000 pages. 5 x 4 x 4. County Courthouse, Auditor's storeroom, basement.

448. PERSONAL PROPERTY TAX RETURNS

1920-1932, 275 volumes. (A-Z). Discontinued. Shows personal property tax returns of townships, balance sheets, unincorporated companies and firms, and companies and Partnerships engaged in business. Alphabetically arranged by names of owners. No index. Handwritten. Volume Savage 200 pages. 14 x 8 x 1. County Courthouse, Auditor's storeroom, basement.

449. PERSONAL PROPERTY TAX RETURNS, NORWOOD, OHIO

1929-1930, 10 volumes. (228-235, 309-310). Discontinued. Tax returns on personal property of unincorporated companies, firms, and Partnerships in Norwood, Ohio. Alphabetically arranged by names of owners. No index. Handwritten on printed forms. Volumes average 200 pages. 14 x 8 x 1. County Courthouse, Auditor's storeroom, basement.

450. PERSONAL TAX RETURNS, INCORPORATED COMPANIES

1920-1930. 85 volumes. Discontinued. Shows personal tax returns of individuals in incorporated companies in townships and cities of Cincinnati and Norwood, Ohio alphabetically arranged by names of owners. No index. Handwritten. Volumes average 200 pages. 14 x 8 x 1. County Courthouse, Auditor's storeroom, basement.

451. DELINQUENT TAX LIST

1904-1930. 40 volumes. (1-40). Discontinued. Shows record of delinquent personal taxes of Hamilton County giving date, name and address, bill number, and amount delinquent. Alphabetically arranged by names of wards and townships. No index. Handwritten. Volumes average 200 pages. 25 x 10 x 1. County Courthouse, Auditor's storeroom, basement.

452. DELINQUENT PERSONAL TAX DUPLICATE
1926-1930. 4 volumes. Prior records missing. Discontinued.
Delinquent tax duplicates of personal property. Alphabetically arranged by names of individuals. No index. Handwritten on printed forms. Volumes average 150 pages 18 x 18 x 1.5. County Courthouse, Room 109.

453. PERSONAL TAX REMITS
1895-1929. 34 volumes. Discontinued.
Shows personal tax penalties charged in error. Alphabetically arranged by names of owners. No index. Handwritten. Volumes average 100 pages. 12.5 x 6 x 1. County Courthouse, Auditor's storeroom, basement.

454. PERSONAL PROPERTY TAX CORRECTIONS
1907–1932. 3 volumes. Discontinued on amendment of personal property tax statute.
Shows personal property tax corrections by deputy auditor. Alphabetically arranged by names of owners. No index. Handwritten on printed forms. Volumes average 100 pages. 11.5 x 9 x 1, County Courthouse, Auditor's storeroom, basement.

455. INCOME TAX, SPECIAL ASSESSMENTS
1919-1925. 65 volumes. Discontinued.
Shows income tax records, special assessments, street assessments, and penalties. Numerically arrange by ward numbers. No index. Handwritten. Volumes average 50 pages. 19 x 12 x .5. County Courthouse, Auditor's storeroom, basement.

456. CIGARETTE TRAFFIC DUPLICATES
1901—. 30 volumes, 2 file boxes (1901-1931, 30 volumes labeled chronologically). 1915, missing.
Shows assessments which are to be made, name of Village, town, name of owner of business, date of assessment, amount of assessment, when do, penalty for nonpayment, and remarks. Numerically arranged by city ward numbers. No index. Handwritten. Volumes average 150 pages. 17 x 12 x 1.5. File boxes, 19 x 8 x 4. County Courthouse, 1901-1931, 30 volumes, Auditor's storeroom, basement; 1932—, 2 file boxes, Room 112.

457. AFFIDAVITS FOR CIGARETTE TAX REFUNDS
1927-1931. Discontinued
Certificates of tax refunds showing name, address, and amount. Chronologically arranged. No index. 14 x 10.5 x 5. County Courthouse, Auditor's storeroom, basement.

458. TAX DUPLICATES, DOW-AIKEN
1898-1917. 24 volumes. Discontinued.
Assessment duplicates of traffic in intoxicating liquors listing name of assessor, name of village, town, and township, names of owner of business, date of assessment, amount due, penalty for nonpayment, and remarks. Arranged by names of townships and wards. No index. Handwritten. Volumes average 150 pages. 18 x 14 x 2. County Courthouse, Auditor's storeroom, basement.

459. REFUNDED TAX, LIQUOR TRAFFIC
1907-1915. 8 volumes (N-Q). Discontinued.
Shows name of person receiving refund, date, and amount. Alphabetically arranged by name some taxpayers. No index. Handwritten on printed forms. Volumes average 200 pages. 15 x 6 x 1.5. County Courthouse, Auditor's storeroom, basement.

460. AUDITOR'S SPECIAL REPORT BLOTTER
1931. 1 volume. Discontinued.
Shows receipts from taxation for general county purposes. Chronologically arranged. No index. Handwritten. 35 pages. 19 x 15 x 1.5. County Courthouse, Auditor's storeroom, basement.

461. CORRESPONDENCE, INSURANCE AND PUBLIC UTILITY COMPANY ASSESSMENTS
1917—. 3 volumes (A-Z) Prior records missing.
Correspondence relating to assessments against insurance and public utility companies and records of intangible tax returns on stocks and bonds. Alphabetically arranged by names of correspondents. No index. Handwritten and typed on printed forms. Volumes average 80 pages. 23 x 16 x 1. County Courthouse, 1917-1932, 2 volumes, Auditor's storeroom, basement; 1933—, 1 volume, Room 112.

Inheritance Tax Department

462. INHERITANCE TAX SETTLEMENTS
1919—. 261 file boxes. (1-27063).
Record of tax on estates of deceased persons showing name of decedent, description of a state, valuation, and amount of assessment. Chronologically arranged. Typed. 12 x 10 x 4.5. 1919-1930, 207 file boxes, Auditor's storeroom, basement; 1931—, 54 file boxes, Room 109.

463. INDEX TO INHERITANCE TAX SETTLEMENTS
1919—. 14 file boxes (A-Z and 16601-27083).
Card index to inheritance tax settlements. Alphabetically arranged by names of taxpayers. Typed. 16 x 5 x 3. County Courthouse, Room 109.

464. INHERITANCE TAX CHARGES
1919—. 43 file boxes (1-11700, A-Z).
Inheritance tax charges showing amount of tax as determined by the probate court. Alphabetically arranged by names of estates. No index. Handwritten and typed. 10 x 4.5 x 2. County Courthouse, 1919-1930, 35 boxes, Auditor's storeroom, basement; 1931—, 13 file boxes, Room 109.

465. INHERITANCE TAX CHARGES PAID
1919—. 15 volumes. (1-15).
Record of paid inheritance tax charges. Numerically arranged by case numbers. 1919-1929, Alphabetical index by names of estates; 1919-1929, no index. For separate index, 1930—, see entry 466. Typed on printed forms. Volumes average 800 pages. 12 x 9 x 4. County Courthouse, 1919-1929, 10 volumes, Auditor's storeroom, basement; 1930—, 5 volumes, Room 109.

466. INDEX TO (Inheritance Tax) CHARGES PAID
1930—. 1 volume.
Index to paid inheritance tax charges. Alphabetically arranged by names of estates. Handwritten on printed forms. 300 pages. 12 x 9 x 3. County Courthouse, Room 109.

467. COPIES OF INVENTORIES
1919—. 161 file boxes (1-131, 614).
Copies of inventories in settlements of estates through probate court. Numerically arranged by case numbers. 1919-1927, alphabetical index by names of estates. For separate index, 1928—, see entry 468. Typed. 12 x 9 x 4.5. 1919-1927, 100 file boxes, Auditor's storeroom, basement; 1928—, 61 file boxes, Room 109.

468. INVENTORIES, INDEX
1928—. 15 file boxes (A-Z).
Card index to estate settlements administered through probate court. Alphabetically arranged. Handwritten. 12 x 5 x 3. County Courthouse, Room 109.

469. CINCINNATI ESTATES, SUBSEQUENT ADDITIONS
1915—. 46 volumes. (A-Z).
Tax returns on personal property in settlement of estates. Chronologically arranged. No index. Handwritten on printed forms. Volumes average 500 pages. 14 x 10 x 3. County Courthouse, 1915-1922, 30 volumes, Auditor's storeroom, basement; 1923—, 16 volumes, Room 109.

License Department

470. LICENSES TO DEALERS IN INTANGIBLES
1932-1933. 2 volumes. (A-Z). Discontinued. System of recording initiated 1932.
Records name of owner, district, domestic or foreign, computation, and summary. Alphabetically arranged by names of dealers. No index. Handwritten. Volumes average 500 pages. 14 x 8.5 x 2. County Courthouse, Auditor's storeroom, basement.

471. APPLICATIONS FOR CIGARETTE LICENSES
1931—. 25 file boxes.
Applications for licenses to sell cigarettes and cigarette papers showing name and address of applicant and date of application. Alphabetically arranged by names of applicants. No index. Typed on printed forms. 15 x 11 x 5. County Courthouse, 1931-1932, 14 file boxes, Auditor's storeroom basement; 1933—. 11 file boxes, Room 112.

472. REFUND RECEIPTS, CIGARETTE TAX
1927—. 9 volumes.
Records refunds on cigarette tax for overcharges and returns on unearned tax due
to discontinuance of business before expiration of license. Chronologically
arranged. No index. Handwritten. Volumes average 200 pages. 18 x 15 x 1.5.
County Courthouse, Auditor's storeroom, basement.

473. DOG LICENSES AND KENNEL REGISTER
1918-1931. 145 volumes. System of recording initiated 1918.
Records application number, name and address of applicant, number of dogs kept
or harbored, and date of registration. Alphabetically arranged by names of
applicants. No index. Handwritten. Volumes average 500 pages. 17 x 14 x 5.
County Courthouse, Auditor's storeroom, basement
For subsequent records see entry 474.

474. DOG LICENSE RECEIPTS
1931—. 460 volumes. (A-Z).
Certificates of registration of dogs showing name and address of owner, number of
license, and amount paid. Numerically arranged by license numbers. No index.
Handwritten on printed forms. Volumes average 100 pages. 10.5 x 4.5 x 1. County
Courthouse, Room 114.
For prior records see entry 473.

475. FREE LICENSES, PRODUCE PEDDLERS
1916-1929. 6 volumes. (1-6). Discontinued. System of recording initiated
1916.
Records date; also name and address of person entitled to free license to peddle
produce. Alphabetically arranged by name of peddlers. No index. Handwritten on
printed forms. Volumes average 200 pages. * x 6 x 1.5. County Courthouse, 1916-
1920, 4 volumes, Auditor's storeroom, basement; 1921-1929, 2 volumes, Room
101.

Accounting Division

This division of the auditor's office was not created by statute, but was established by the county auditor to facilitate the work of his office, by virtue of powers vested in him under sections 2567-2572 of the Ohio General Code. The function of this division is to keep an accurate account currently with the county treasurer showing all money paid into and out of the treasury, and to keep an accurate record of all taxes collected.

General Accounts

476. TOWNSHIP AND CORPORATION FUNDS
1884—. 7 volumes.
Apportionment of corporation and township funds collected from tax imposed. Alphabetically arranged by names of funds. Alphabetical index by names of townships or corporations in front of each volume. Handwritten on printed forms. Volumes average 160 pages. 15 x 11 x 2.5. County Courthouse, 1884-1926, 5 volumes, Auditor's storeroom, basement; 1927—, 2 volumes, Room 114.

477. RECEIPTS
1928—. 18 file boxes.
Record of taxes received. Numerically arranged by the receipt numbers. No index. Handwritten on printed forms. 19 x 14 x 4. County Courthouse, Room 114.

478. AUDITOR'S LEDGERS
1918—. 6 volumes.
Record of various accounts county treasurer has deposited or drawn from county department funds or banks. Chronologically arranged. Alphabetical index by names of banks in front of each volume. Handwritten on printed forms. Volumes average 600 pages. 18 x 12 x 3. County Courthouse, 1918-1929, 4 volumes, Room 109; 1930—, 2 volumes, Room 114.

479. CONDENSED DISBURSEMENTS LEDGER
1884-1904. 18 volumes. Discontinued.
Record showing public funds paid out by vouchers. Numerically arranged by voucher numbers. No index. Handwritten. Volumes average 135 pages. 24 x 17 x 2. County Courthouse, Auditor's storeroom, basement.

480. EXPENSE AND DRAYAGE LEDGER
1910—. 6 volumes (1-6).
Itemized expense accounts listing amount paid, to whom, and for what purpose. Chronologically arranged. Alphabetical index by names of pays in front of each volume. Handwritten. Volumes average 350 pages. 20 x 12 1930, 3 volumes, Auditor's storeroom, basement; 1931—, 3 volumes, Room 114.

481. DOCKETS, BILLS FILED
1904—. 29 volumes. (1-29).
Infirmary, commissary, and commissioners bills showing names of commissioners, bill number, specific purpose, amount, date of filing, date of approval, and entry. Numerically arranged by bill numbers. No index. Handwritten. Volumes average 300 pages. 19 x 18 x 3. County Courthouse, 1904-1923, 19 volumes, Auditor's storeroom, basement; 1924—, 10 volumes, Room 112.

482. MISCELLANEOUS COUNTY DISBURSEMENTS
1919—. 62 file boxes. System of recording initiated 1919.
Treasurer's daily statements, payrolls, and school settlements. Chronologically arranged. No index. Handwritten and typed. 14 x 10 x 5. County Courthouse, 1919-1932, 50 file boxes; Auditor's storeroom, basement; 1933—, 12 file boxes, Room 109.

Payrolls, Vouchers, and Warrants

483. APPROPRIATION LEDGER
1901—. 38 volumes.
Record of county auditor's judiciary fund listing salaries of court officials. Chronologically arranged. Handwritten. Volumes average 400 pages. 17 x 13 x 2.5. County Courthouse, 1901-1926, 24 volumes, Auditor's storeroom, basement; 1927—, 14 volumes, Room 114.

484. INDEX TO APPROPRIATION LEDGER
1901—. 38 volumes.
Index to judicial salaries as recorded in appropriate ledger. Alphabetically arranged by names of funds. Handwritten. Volumes average 100 pages. 17 x 13 x 1. County Courthouse, 1901-1926, 24 volumes, Auditor's storeroom, basement; 1927—, 14 volumes, Room 114.

485. ELECTION BOARD PAYROLLS
1926—. 6 bundles. Prior records destroyed.
Payrolls for judges, clerks, and election officers. Chronologically arranged. No index. Handwritten. 32 x 22 x 12. County Courthouse, 1926-1935, 5 bundles, Auditor's storeroom, basement; 1936—, 1 bundle, Room 112.

486. RECEIPTED PAYROLLS
1912—. 18 volumes, 37 file boxes. Prior records missing.
Check stubs showing amount of board of assessor's fees, names of payee and deputies, date, and amount. Volumes, numerically arranged by pay roll numbers. File boxes, numerically arranged by check numbers. No index. Handwritten on printed forms. Volumes average 400 pages. 15 x 6 x 1.5. File boxes, 15 x 10 x 5. County Courthouse, 1912-1932, 18 volumes, 16 file boxes, Auditor's storeroom; basement; 1933—, 21 file boxes, Room 114.

487. COURT WARRANTS
1906—. 26 volumes. Prior records missing.
Auditor's record of warrants issued by common pleas, juvenile, police, superior, probate, circuit, insolvency, and magistrate courts. Numerically arranged by warrant numbers. No index. Handwritten. Volumes average 450 pages. 15 x 12 x 3.5. County Courthouse, 1906-1932, 22 volumes, Auditor's storeroom, basement; 1933—, 4 volumes, Room 114.

488. AUDITOR'S JOURNAL OF WARRANTS
1906—. 23 volumes. Prior records missing.
Record listing name of person to whom warrant was issued, amount, purpose, and from which fund. Chronologically arranged. No index. Handwritten on printed forms. Volumes average 250 pages. 23.5 x 17 x 2. County Courthouse, 1906-1917, 6 volumes, Auditor's storeroom, basement; 1918—, 17 volumes, Room 109.

489. MISCELLANEOUS WARRANTS AND VOUCHERS
1906—. 184 volumes, 6 bundles, 169 file boxes. Prior records missing.
Tuberculosis hospital, engineering, county home, schools, and miscellaneous warrants; also miscellaneous vouchers of Department of Public Welfare. Volumes chronologically arranged. File boxes and bundles, numerically arranged by voucher numbers. Volumes, alphabetical index by names of pays. File boxes and bundles, no index. Handwritten and typed and printed forms. Volumes average 200 pages. 15 x 6 x 1.5. Bundles, 12 x 10 x 8. File boxes average, 19 x 10 x 6. County Courthouse, 1906-1935, 184 volumes, 150 file boxes, 6 bundles, Auditor's storeroom, basement; 1936—, 19 file boxes, Room 114.

490. MISCELLANEOUS VOUCHERS, COUNTY CORPORATIONS
1911—. 103 file boxes (numbering varies).
Vouchers, welfare payrolls, and invoices. Chronologically arranged. No index. Typed on printed forms. File boxes average 19 x 17 x 8. County Courthouse, 1911-1932, 33 file boxes, Auditor's storeroom, basement; 1933—, 79 file boxes, Room 112.

491. COUNTY WARRANTS
1930-1932, 11 file boxes (1-10000). Discontinued. System of recording initiated 1930.
Warrants on county treasurer for salaries and fees paid. Numerically arranged by warrant numbers. No index. Typed on printed forms. 10.5 x 8 x 14. County Courthouse, Auditor's storeroom, basement.

492. COURT AND WITNESS WARRANTS
1930—. 4 file boxes. Prior records missing.
Record of court and grand jury witness fees listing warrant number, date issued, names of witnesses, and amount. Numerically arranged by warrant numbers. No index. Handwritten and typed on printed forms. 15 x 10 x 5. County Courthouse, Auditor's storeroom, basement.

493. CANCELLED WARRANTS

1931—. 15 file boxes (1-16221).
Warrants for salaries, also witness and miscellaneous fees, listing name of person, date issued, and date paid. Numerically arranged by warrant numbers. No index. Handwritten on printed forms. 15 x 1 x 5. County Courthouse, 1931-1932, 6 file boxes, Auditor's storeroom, basement; 1933—, 9 file boxes, Room 112.

494. MISCELLANEOUS RECEIPT RECORDS

1929-1931, 1 volume. Discontinued. System of recording initiated 1929. Copies of receipts for payment of miscellaneous bills. Chronologically arranged. Alphabetical index by names of payers in front of each volume. 200 pages. 15 x 11 x 3. County Courthouse, Auditor's storeroom, basement.

Miscellaneous

495. REPORTS, INSTITUTION FOR THE FEEBLE-MINDED

1913-1915. 1 file box. Discontinued. System of recording initiated 1913. Reports on the support of inmates of institution for feeble-minded and correspondence pertaining thereto. Chronologically arranged. No index. Handwritten and typed. 10 x 5 x 4. County Courthouse, Room 108.

496. CANCELLED BOND COUPONS

1904—. 62 volumes. (A-Z). Prior records missing.
Cancelled coupons on bridge, courthouse, hospital, road, sewer, turnpike, and soldiers' memorial bonds. Numerically arranged by bond numbers. No index. Handwritten on printed forms. Volumes average 400 pages. 18 x 14 x 4. County Courthouse, Auditor's storeroom, basement.

497. SECURITIES DEPOSITED WITH COUNTY COMMISSIONERS

1933—. 1 volume, 1 file rack of 20 steel shutters.
Record listing name of bank issuing security for safe keeping of county funds deposited by county commissioners; also listing name of security, total value of security, and date of maturity. Chronologically arranged. No index. Handwritten and typed on printed forms. Volume, 100 pages. 15 x 10 x 1. Steel shutters, 8 x 18. County Courthouse, Room 114.

498. CORRESPONDENCE

1933—. 8 file boxes.

Miscellaneous correspondence pertaining to department of county welfare. Alphabetically arranged by names of correspondents. No index. Handwritten. 24 x 12 x 12. County Courthouse, 1933-1934, 6 file boxes, Auditor's storeroom, basement; 1935—, 2 file boxes, Room 109.

General Office Division

499. VOUCHER RECORDS

1908—. 11 volumes. Prior records missing.

Voucher record and journal of courthouse building commission giving date, name of payee, township, and amount. Chronologically arranged. No index. Handwritten on printed forms. Volumes average 200 pages. 16.5 x 13 x 1.25. County Courthouse, 1908-1922, 6 volumes, Auditor's storeroom, basement; 1923—, 5 volumes, Room 109.

500. CORRESPONDENCE

1931—. 1 file box. Prior records missing.

General office correspondence. Alphabetically arranged by names of correspondents. No index. Handwritten and typed. 26 x 14 x 10. County Courthouse, Room 109.

Weights and Measures Division

This division of the county auditor's office was created by statute under an act of the Ohio General Assembly, passed April 11, 1861, entitled "An act to provide for uniform standard of weights and measures," designating the county auditor as county sealer of weights and measurer. The functions of this office are set forth in section 2615 of the Ohio General Code (10 O. L. 234).

All records of this division are in the County Courthouse basement, drafting room.

501. ANNUAL REPORT OF SEALER

1912—. 1 volume. Prior records missing.

Copies of annual reports of sealer to Ohio state department of weights and measures listing activities during the year, number of inspections made, seizures, and replacements. Chronologically arranged. No index. Typed. 100 pages. 12 x 6 x .5.

502. DAILY RECORDS OF INSPECTIONS

1912—. 5 volumes. (1-5).

Daily record of inspections made by sealer of scales and measuring devices, showing names of owner, location, date of inspection, serial number, and types. Chronologically arranged. No index. Handwritten. Volumes average 15 x 12 x 1.

503. INSPECTION RECORD OF GASOLINE PUMPS

1912—. 1 volume.

Record of regular inspections of gasoline pumps in Hamilton County showing name of owner, location and type of pump, date, and serial number. Chronologically arranged. No index. Handwritten on printed forms. 300 pages. 8 x 6 x 4.

Although the legislature, in 1911, made provision for the establishment of a budget commission in each county composed of the county auditor, the mayor of the largest municipality, and the prosecuting attorney (162 O. L. 266), it was not until after the World War, when county expenditures steadily increased, that the importance of improved methods of finance were forcibly brought to its attention. This new need was met, in 1927, by the establishment of a budget commission in each county. This commission, consisting of the county auditor, county treasurer, and county prosecuting attorney, receives and examines the annual budget of the county, municipal, township, and school authorities, with an estimate of the amount to be raised for state purposes in each subdivision. (112 O. L. 399.) If the total amount exceeds the sum authorized to be raised, the commission adjusts the amount to be raised and may change and revise the estimates. The commission may reduce all items in the budget, but it is prohibited from increasing the total of any budget or any item.

The adjusted budget is certified to the taxing authority in each subdivision. If the work of the commission is satisfactory, each taxing authority by ordinance or resolution authorizes the necessary tax levies and certifies them to the county auditor. (G. C. sec. 5625-25.) On the other hand, the taxing authority in any subdivision may appeal, through its fiscal officer, from the decision of the budget commission to the state tax commission of Ohio, which is empowered to adjust the estimates of revenues and balances in fixing this tax rates. (G. C. sec. 5625-28.)

The county auditor, as secretary to the commission, is required to keep a full and accurate record of the proceedings of the commission.

504. COUNTY BUDGET COMMISSION MINUTES
1911—. 14 volumes. Prior records missing.
Record of meetings of county budget commission of which the auditor has by law been appointed the secretary. Chronologically arranged. No index. Typed. Volumes average 50 pages. 20 x 17 x .5. County Courthouse, 1911-1923, 13 volumes, Auditor's storeroom, basement; 1924—. 1 volume, Room 112.

The county board of revision, the object of which was to correct some of the defects and inequalities of assessments, was established by the legislature in 1825. The first board of revision, or equalization as it was sometimes called, was composed of the county commissioners, county auditor, and the assessor. The board was authorized to meet at the seat of justice on the first Monday in June annually "to hear and determine the complaint of any owner of property listed and valued by the assessor. . . and correct any list or valuation made by the assessor, either by adding to or deducting from valuation." (23 O. L. 66.) The act of 1831, repealing the act of 1825, left the duties and personnel of the board unchanged. (29 O. L. 278.)

In 1859 the legislature made provision for two county boards of equalization. One board, composed of the county auditor and the county commissioners, was directed to meet annually for the purpose of equalizing real and personal property, and moneys and credit in the county. The other board, composed of the county auditor, county surveyor, and county commissioners, was authorized to meet sexennially for the same purpose. At the same time, two special boards of equalization for the city of Cincinnati were created. One, composed to the county auditor and six citizens of Cincinnati appointed by the city council, was authorized to meet annually to equalize the real and personal property, and the moneys and credit of that city; the other, consisting of the same personnel, and having the same duties, was directed to meet sexennially. (56 O. L. 57, 60.)

The act of 1863, amending the act of 1859, left the personnel and duties of the annual county board unchanged. The second county board, although it continued without alteration in composition or duties, was directed to meet decennially, rather than sexennially. Furthermore, the provisions creating the special boards of equalization, which, under the act of 1859, had applied to Cincinnati only, were extended to all cities of the first and second class. In addition, there were created two boards of equalization, each consisting of the county auditor and six citizens selected by the city council, one to meet annually, the other, decennially (60 O. L. 57, 69.) The legislative act of 1868, amending the act of 1863, left practically unchanged the membership and duties of the annual and special boards in the county and in the cities of the first and second class.

The annual and special boards of equalization in both county and city were abolished, when, in 1913, the state tax commission of Ohio was given the task of supervising the assessment of real and personal property in the state. Under this arrangement each county constituted a district. It each district containing less than

60,000 inhabitants one state tax commissioner was to be appointed by the governor. In all other districts there were appointed, in the same manner, two state deputy tax commissioners. In each district a district board of complaints, appointed by the state tax commission with the consent of the governor, took over the duties and powers formerly vested in the boards of equalization. The county auditor made secretary to the board of complaints, was required to be present at each meeting in person or by deputy, and to keep in a book for that purpose, and accurate record of the proceedings. (103 O. L. 791.) Moreover, the board was directed to take full minutes of all evidence given before it and allowed to have such evidence taken in shorthand and extended into typewritten form. The auditor was required to preserve in his office separate records of all minutes and documentary evidence offered in each complaint. (*Ibid.*,)

After being in operation for two years, this arrangement was abolished by the legislature in 1915, when the county auditor, under the supervision of the tax commission of Ohio, became the chief assessing officer in the county. The county treasurer, county prosecutor, probate judge, and the president of the county commissioners were to constitute a board for the purpose of appointing three members to constitute a board of revision. The county auditor was made secretary to the board and directed to keep a record of the proceedings and to preserve in his office a separate record of all minutes and documentary evidence offered in each complaint. (105 O. L. 257-258.)

Under the present system, inaugurated in 1917, the county treasurer, county auditor, and the president of the county commissioners constitute a board of revision. This board organizes annually, on the second Monday in June, by electing a chairman for the ensuing year. The county auditor serves as secretary to the board. (G. C. sec. 5587, 5592.) The county board of revision may, with the consent and approval of the tax commission of Ohio, employee experts, clerks, and other employees. (G. C. sec. 5587.)

The duties of the board, similar in detail to those prescribed in 1825, include the hearing of all complaints related to valuation or assessments of real property as it appears upon the tax duplicate of the "then current year." The board is authorized to investigate all complaints and may increase or decrease any valuation or correct any assessment complained of, or order a reassessment by the original assessing official. (G. C. sec. 5597.) However, no valuation is increased without notice being given to the person in whose name the property affected is listed. (G. C. sec. 5599.) The board of revision is always governed by the laws pertaining to the valuation of real property and makes no change of any valuation "except in accordance with such laws." (G. C. sec. 5596.)

On the second Monday in June, annually, the county auditor lays before the board of revision the returns of assessments of any real property for the current year, and the board proceeds to review the assessment. The board of revision certifies its action to the county auditor, who corrects the tax list and duplicate according to the additions and deductions ordered by the board. The auditor is prohibited by statute from making up his tax list in duplicate until the board has completed its work and he's remitted to him with revisions all the returns laid before it. (G. C. sec. 5605.) But in the event the tax duplicate has been delivered to the county treasurer, the auditor is required to certify such corrections to him and enter them in his tax duplicate. (G. C. sec. 5605.)

In its investigations the board may examine persons, under oath, as to their or others' real property. In the event witnesses fail to appear or refuse to testify, the board through its chairman is authorized to make a complaint in writing to the probate judge, who is directed by statute to institute proceedings against them. (G. C. sec. 5596.) Decisions may be appealed to the tax commission of Ohio within thirty days after they are served. (G. C. sec. 5610.)

The chairman of the board is required to keep "an accurate record of the proceedings of the board in a book to be kept for that purpose." (G. C. sec. 5592.) The county auditor, as in 1913, is required to preserve in his office separate records of all minutes and documentary evidence offered in each complaint. (G. C. sec. 5603.) The records of the board are open to the inspection of the public. (G. C. sec. 5591.)

505. MINUTES.
1884——. 29 volumes. (1-29).
Shows all business transacted at meetings of Hamilton County Board of revision; gives decisions on real estate tax complaints and all other business transacted. Chronologically arranged. No index. Handwritten and typed. Volumes average 50 pages. 18 x 14 x 1.5. County Courthouse, 1884-1930, 22 volumes, Auditor's storeroom; 1931——, 7 volumes, Auditor's office.

506. RECORD OF CITY DECENNIAL

1901-1902. 1 volume. Discontinued.

Record of proceedings and orders of the city of Cincinnati decennial Board of Equalization listing details of real estate appraisals made at ten-year periods (as customary at that time) showing names of owners, addresses, assessments, and taxes. Chronologically arranged. Alphabetical index by names of property owners in back of each volume. Handwritten and typed. 260 pages. 24 x 19 x 2. County Courthouse, Auditor's storeroom, basement.

507. COMPLAINTS

1931—. 91 volumes, 12 bundles. System of recording initiated 1931.

Lists complaints and requests for reductions in real estate taxes on special assessments. Chronologically arranged. Handwritten on printed forms. Volumes average 200 pages. 14 x 9 x 2. Bundles, 14 x 9 x 5. County Courthouse, Room 109.

508. INDEX TO COMPLAINTS, BOARD OF REVISION

1931—. 15 file boxes. Prior records missing.

Card index to complaints showing date of filing, complaint number, and board of revisions action on applications for tax reduction. A new system of indexing was initiated in 1934 giving a double index, 1934—. Alphabetically arranged by names of complainants. Handwritten on printed forms. File boxes average 14 x 9 x 5.5. County Courthouse, Room 109.

509. BOARD OF REVISION NOTICES

1931—. 14 file boxes.

Copies of notices to taxpayers showing action of board of revision on applications for reductions in taxes. Alphabetically arranged by names of taxpayers. No index. Typed on printed forms. 10 x 8 x 6. County Courthouse, Room 109.

510. TAX REFUNDS

1919-1934. 8 file boxes. Prior records missing.

Record of tax refunds by board of revision listing date of refund, amount, case number, and to whom refund was made. Numerically arranged by case numbers. No index. Typed on printed forms. 16 x 11 x 5. County Courthouse, 1919-1932, 7 file boxes, Commissioners' storeroom, basement; 1933-1934, 1 file box, Room 204.

For subsequent records see entry 437.

511. GENERAL CORRESPONDENCE

1928—. 8 file boxes. Record initiated 1928.

Correspondence of board of revision and real estate division of auditor's office. Alphabetically arranged by name of correspondents. No index. Handwritten and typed. 24 x 15 x 10. County Courthouse, Room 109.

512. ATLAS OF CINCINNATI REAL ESTATE

1922. 2 volumes.

Actual surveys and official records of city of Cincinnati and Norwood. Index by names and numbers of streets in front of each volume. Author unknown. Published by Sanborn Map Company, New York. Hand drawn in colors. Scale, 1 inch equals 100 feet. 75 pages. 24 x 18 x 2. County Courthouse, Room 109.

513. INSURANCE MAPS OF CINCINNATI

1904. 3 volumes. (1-3).

Maps of Cincinnati by sections and streets showing types of buildings, size, location, and improvements. Numerical index by section numbers. Author unknown. Published by Sanborn Map Company, New York. Hand drawn in colors. Scale, 1 inch equals 50 feet. Volumes average 100 pages. 24 x 32 x 1.5. County Courthouse, Room 109.

The Hamilton County purchasing department, a branch office of the board of county commissioners, established in 1908 under provisions of those sections of the General Code which defined the powers and duties of the board of county commissioners serves all departments of county government. (99 O. L. 337; G. C. sec. 2395-2557-4.)

The purchasing department, functioning as a division of county government, is headed by a purchasing clerk appointed by the commissioners, who serves also as a clerk of the commissioners. (See page 4.) The department contracts for as many as 3,000 various items each year, constituting forty-seven general divisions of commodities.

Since January, 1933, the Hamilton County purchasing department coordinates with the city of Cincinnati, board of education, University of Cincinnati, and public library in contracting for materials and supplies which are used and purchased by all, thereby reducing both testing expense and purchase costs. Also, because of the uniformity of specifications under this collective system, both time and expenses are saved in the operations of bidding and purchase.

The department employees and assistant to the purchasing clerk and several other clerks, all appointed by the county commissioners. (G. C. secs. 2409-2410.)

Records prior to 1932 destroyed, see page 29.

514. ADDRESSOGRAPH VENDING RECORDS
1932—. 30 file boxes.
Records giving name and address plates of vendors requested to submit bids. Chronologically arranged; also arranged by bids on various commodities. No index. Typed. 25 x 4 x 2. County Courthouse, Room 120.

515. SPECIFICATIONS
n. d. 2 file boxes.
Record of standard specifications comprising more than 500 items. Alphabetically arranged by names of items. No index. Typed on printed forms. 25 x 13 x 11. County Courthouse, Room 120.

516. CLOSED BIDS AND INQUIRIES
1932—. 6 file boxes.
Active and suspended bids for miscellaneous merchandise. Alphabetically arranged by names of bitters. No index. Typed. 25 x 13 x 11. County Courthouse, 1932-1934, 5 file boxes, Purchasing department storeroom, basement; 1935—, 1 file box, Room 120.

517. CONTRACTS
1932—. 3 file boxes.
Contracts for purchases of commodities. Alphabetically arranged by name so commodities. No index. Typed on printed forms. 25 x 13 x 11. County Courthouse, Room 120.

518. INSURANCE POLICIES
1933-1939. 1 file box.
Insurance policies covering general hazards are issued for a three-year period and cover all county offices and their respective contents. Arranged by departments into groups, 1933-1936 and 1936-1939. No index. Typed on printed forms. 25 x 13 x 11. County Courthouse, Room 120.

519. INTERDEPARTMENTAL CHARGES
1935—. 1 file box.
Record of interdepartmental charges for supplies. Chronologically arranged; also alphabetically arranged by names of departments. No index. Typed on printed forms. 25 x 13 x 11. County Courthouse, Room 120.

520. ORDERS
1932—. 41 file boxes.
Orders for merchandise to be delivered to various county departments. Alphabetically arranged by names of vendors. No index. Typed. 25 x 13 x 11. County Courthouse, 1932-1934, 21 file boxes, Purchasing department, basement; 1935—, 20 file boxes, Room 120.

521. REQUISITIONS
1932—. 11 file boxes.
Requisitions for supplies which were received from various county departments.

Alphabetically arranged by names of departments. No index. Typed on printed forms. 25 x 13 x 11. County Courthouse, 1932-1935, 6 file boxes, Purchasing department, storeroom, basement; 1936——, 5 file boxes, Room 120.

522. SUSPENSE FILES AND ACTIVE REQUISITONS
1936——. 1 file box.

Suspense orders and active requisitions. Suspense orders, chronologically arranged; also arranged by bids on various commodities. Active requisitions, alphabetically arranged by departments. No index. Typed on printed forms. 25 x 13 x 11. County Courthouse, Room 120.

523. OFFICIAL CORRESPONDENCE
1934——. 1 file box.

Letters received and copies of outgoing mail. Alphabetically arranged by names of correspondents. No index. Typed. 25 x 13 x 11. County Courthouse, Room 120.

The Hamilton County board of control was established under provisions of an act of the legislature, passed March 13, 1872. This act provided that in each county in the state containing a city of the first class, having a population exceeding 180,000, "there shall be, in addition to the board of county commissioners, a board of control, to consist of five members, who shall be elected. . .by the qualified electors of any county. . .and they shall hold their office for three years, . . . and [they] shall meet with the board of county commissioners, . . . at their regular meeting on the first (1) Monday of March, June, September, and December, and at such other times as may be necessary, and as may be provided for by said board of control." (69 O. L. 40.) The members of the board of control received no compensation for their services.

By a majority vote the board of control elected one of their members as president of the board. In the same manner the board elected a clerk, whose duty it was to keep a correct journal of all proceedings of the board, and perform such other duties as might be prescribed. (*Ibid.*, 41.)

The board of control had "final action and jurisdiction on all matters involving the expenditure of money or the awarding of contracts, or the assessing or levying of taxes" by the county commissioners. No contract, release, appropriation, or allowance made, or liability incurred, or taxes levied or assessed by the county commissioners was considered valid and binding unless favored by the boat of a majority of the board. (*Ibid.* 41.) The act provided that the county commissioners, at each meeting of the board of control, should present to the board a true and accurate statement of all matters that came before them which involved the expenditure of money, or the awarding of contracts, or the assessing or levying of taxes; and they were required to present to the board at their meetings, all bids on contracts, and all plans and specifications received by them. (*Ibid.*, 42.)

Between 1881 and 1908 certain amendments were made to sections of the original act. On January 31, 1881, an act passed by the legislature extended the term of board members from three to five years. (78 O. L. 21.)

In 1886 the legislature amended the act of 1881 and added a section to provide for the election of district assessors of real property in counties having a city of the first class. (83 O. L. 87.)

In 1889 an amendment transferred certain of the powers and duties of the board to the county commissioners (86 O. L. 296); and on May 9, 1908, the legislature passed a measure which abolished the board of control and authorized the county auditor to pass upon and approve all actions of the county commissioners relating to the expenditure of money. (99 O. L. 520.)

524. MINUTES OF BOARD OF CONTROL
1891-1907. 8 volumes. Prior records missing.
Minutes and resolutions of board of control. Chronologically arranged. No index.
Handwritten. Volumes average 575 pages. 19 x 14.5 x 3. County Courthouse,
Superintendent of buildings, storage, basement.

For subsequent records see entry 1.

525. RECORDS OF BOARD OF CONTROL
1881-1891. 5 volumes. Subsequent records missing.
Records of business entries showing names of persons concerned, voucher numbers,
description of accounts, amounts, and action taken by the board. Chronologically
arranged. No index. Handwritten. Volumes average 300 pages. 17 x 15 x 1.5.
County Courthouse, Superintendent of buildings, storage, basement.

The board of sinking fund trustees, composed of the prosecuting attorney, auditor, and treasurer, was organized in 1919 in each county owing a bonded debt. The county prosecuting attorney serves as president of the board and the auditor as secretary. It is the duty of the trustees to provide for the payment of all bonds issued by the county and the interest maturing thereon.

Oh bonds issued by the county must be recorded in the office of the trustees of the sinking fund, bear a stamp containing the words "Recorded in the office of the sinking fund trustees," and signed by the secretary before they become valid in the hands of any purchaser. Since 1922, in the event the secretary is unable to act, by reason of absence or disability, such recording and authenticating is performed by the county treasurer. (G. C. sec. 2976-25.)

On or before the first Monday in May of each year, the trustees certify to the county commissioners the rate of tax necessary to provide a sinking fund both for the payment at maturity of bonds heretofore issued by the county and for the payment of interest on the bonded indebtedness. The amount certified by the trustees is set forth without diminution in the annual budget of the commissioners. (G. C. sec. 2976-26.) Then, after each semiannual settlement of taxes and assessments, the county auditor reports to the trustees the amount of money in the treasury of the county charge to the credit of the sinking fund. Money drawn from the county treasury for investment or disbursement is by the issuance of a voucher signed by all the members of the board and directed to the county auditor. The trustees are directed, by statute, to invest all moneys subject to their control in United States bonds, Ohio bonds, or bonds of municipal corporation, school district, township, or county in the state.

The board members are required to keep "a full and complete record of their transactions, complete record of the funded debt of the county specifying the dates, purposes, amounts, numbers, maturities, and rates and maturities of interest and installments thereof, and where payable, and an account exhibiting the amount held in the sinking fund for the payment thereof." (G. C. sec. 2976-24.)

The meetings of the trustees are open to the public. All questions relating to the purchase or sale of securities or the payment of bonds or interest are decided by a yea and nay vote, which is recorded in their journal.

All records of this office are located in County Courthouse, Auditor's office, Room 109.

526. MINUTES.
1884—. 5 volumes
Transactions of the county commissioners relative to the sinking fund and transactions of the trustees since the establishment of the board of sinking fund trustees in 1919. Chronologically arranged. No index. Handwritten. Volumes average 300 pages. 16 x 12 x 3.

527. GENERAL LEDGER
1884-1927. 43 volumes.
Record of all moneys received and paid out on bond issues listing date of receipt and from what source received; also date paid out and for what purpose. Numerically arranged by warrant numbers. No index. Handwritten. Volumes average 200 pages. 14 x 12 x 2.

For subsequent records see entry 528.

528. LEDGER
1927—. 1 volume.
Records nature of bonds bought and sold, date of issue, date of maturity, amount of bonds, by what authority issued, by whom issued, when paid, interest collected, and amount paid. Numerically arranged by warrant numbers. No index. Handwritten. 500 pages. 14 x 12 x 5.

For prior records see entry 527.

The county board of education, a modern administrative and supervisory agency developed during the last two decades, supplanted the smaller educational units, which, established during the early period of Ohio history, became inefficient and unable to meet the modern requirements as demanded by rural communities.

During the earlier period of Ohio history educational administration, because of the newness of the state, the sparseness of the population, and the undeveloped means of transportation was, by necessity, local in character. For fourteen years after the accession of Ohio to statehood though the constitution stated that means of education should be encouraged by the general assembly no legislation was an active for public schools. (*Ohio Const. 1802*, Art. VIII, sec. 3, 25, 27.) It was not until 1817 that the legislature authorized six or more people in the townships to form associations to build school houses and to be incorporated for educational purposes. (15 O. L. 407.) This was a beginning, but as yet the values of an educational system were not rapidly perceived by those engaged in subduing a stubborn wilderness.

The first permanent law for the organization of schools in Ohio was passed in 1821. Under the provisions of this act, the electors of the township were authorized to vote on the proposition of dividing the townships into school districts. If the proposal carried, there were to be elected three school commissioners, who, in turn, were authorized to select a clerk and a collector who should act as a treasurer. They were instructed also, to levy taxes for the support of schools and to hire teachers. (19 O. L. 54.)

As education began to advance in the early years of the nineteenth century some kind of state control was needed. Accordingly, in 1837, the office of state superintendent of schools was established. A year later an act was passed making the county auditor also the county superintendent of schools; and in each township the clerk became superintendent of the smaller unit. The county superintendent was made responsible to the state superintendent in all educational affairs. In the same year each incorporated city, town, or borough not regulated by the charter was made a separate school district. The voters in each division were authorized to elect three directors. (31 O. L. 21.) The effectiveness of this organization, however, was destroyed in 1840, when the legislature abolished the office of state superintendent and the secretary of state took over his functions of tabulating and transmitting school statistics. (38 O. L. 130.) Seven years later, twenty-five counties were allowed to have county superintendents, and in 1848 the provisions of the previous act wee extended to all counties in the state. (46 O. L. 86.)

Although marked changes were made in the curriculum of the schools, the history of education in Ohio from 1850 to the earlier part of the twentieth century was largely one of the gradual transference of powers from districts to townships, and from townships to county in the interest of a better system of education. It was not, however, until within the last three decades that the county became the unit for educational administration. (70 O. L. 195, 204; 97 O. L. 354.)

Although the county superintendent was known as early as 1838, the first permanent law for the establishment of a county board of education was enacted in 1914. Under this act the school districts were classified, and provision was made for a county school district, exclusively of the territory embraced in any city or village desiring exemption. The county district was to be under the supervision of five board members elected by the presidents of the village and rural school boards. The members were to hold office for one, two, three, four, and five years respectively, and each year one member wish to be selected.

The county board of education was authorized to change school district lines; for transportation for children living more than two miles from a schoolhouse; appoint a county superintendent; and certify annually to the county auditor the number of teachers and superintendents employed, their salaries, and the amount apportioned for each school district. The county superintendent, acting as secretary of the board, was required to keep in a book provided for that purpose a full record of the proceedings of the board properly indexed. Each motion, together with the name of the person making it and the vote thereon, was to be entered on the record. (104 O. L. 133; 108 O. L. pt. i, 704.)

The county was divided into administrative divisions containing one or more villages or rural school districts. Each district was to be under the supervision of a district superintendent, who was required to visit the schools in his charge, direct and assist teachers in the performance of their duties, and classify and control promotions of pupils. Moreover, he was required to report annually to the county superintendent on matters under his charge, and assemble teachers for the purpose of conferring on curricular matters, discipline, and school management. (104 O. L. 133-145.)

Significant changes were made by the act of 1920, under which the county board members became elective. They were authorized to a point one or more assistant county superintendents for a term of three years. The board was authorized to publish, with the advice and consent of the county superintendent, a minimum course of study to serve as a guide to local board members. The same act abolished the office of district superintendent. (G. C. secs. 4728-1 4729; 108 O. L, pt. I, 706.)

The county organization has placed the rural schools on a plane of equality with the city schools. The consolidation of the smaller units has eliminated the small, ill-equipped schools, and provides under one roof facilities and instruction suited to the needs of the rural children under the supervision of educational specialists.

529. REPORT OF COMMISSION OF EDUCATION
1914—. 1 volume.
General survey made by commissioners of education in 1914. Chronologically arranged. No index. Printed. 300 pages. 8 x 5 x 2. County Courthouse, Room 545

530. REPORT OF OHIO STATE SCHOOL SURVEY COMMISSION TO GOVERNOR
1924. 1 volume.
Cooperative field study of 659 rural village schools; also extensive study of 900 school rooms and 395 school systems. Numerically arranged by school district numbers. No index. Printed. 352 pages. 9 x 5 x 2. County Courthouse, Room 545.

531. MINUTES OF ASBURY SCHOOL NO. 15, ASBURY, OHIO
1903-1924. 1 volume. Discontinued as a county record in 1924. Subsequent records kept by local school board.
Record of all transactions of school board. Chronologically arranged. No index. Handwritten. 100 pages. 9 x 5 x 2. County Courthouse, Room 545.

532. MINUTES OF JOHN S. CONNOR SCHOOL, NORTH BEND, OHIO
1917-1923. 1 volume. Discontinued as a county record in 1923. Subsequent records kept by local school board.
Record of all transactions of school board. Chronologically arranged. No index. Handwritten. 100 pages. 9 x 89 x .5. County Courthouse, Room 532.

533. MINUTES OF SCHOOL BOARD, NEWTON, OHIO
1911-1912. 1 volume. Discontinued as a county record in 1912. Subsequent records kept by local school board.
Record of all transactions of school board. Chronologically arranged. No index. Handwritten. 100 pages. 12.5 x 12.5 x 1. County Courthouse, Room 545.

534. MINUTES OF SCHOOL BOARD, PLAINSVILLE NO. 16, ANDERSON TOWNSHIP

1895-1921. 1 volume. Discontinued as a county record in 1921. Subsequent records kept by local school board.

Record of all transactions of school board. Chronologically arranged. No index. Handwritten. 100 pages. 12.5 x 8.5 x .5. County Courthouse, Room 545.

535. CERTIFICATES OF BUS DRIVERS AND PHYSICIANS

1925—. 2 volumes.

Record of certificates issued to school bus drivers and physicians giving names, addresses, ages, and date issued. Alphabetically arranged by names of bus drivers and physicians. No index. Handwritten on printed forms. Volumes average 200 pages. 10 x 4 x 1. County Courthouse, Room 532.

536. TEACHERS' CERTIFICATES EXPIRED

1915-1935. Subsequent records kept by Ohio State Department of Education.

Teachers' certificates listing name and address, age, and date issued. Chronologically arranged; Also alphabetically arranged by names of teachers. No index. Handwritten on printed forms. 24 x 18 x 8. County Courthouse, Room 542.

537. INTELLIGENCE TEST, CARD SYSTEM

1935—. 21 file boxes.

Group test cards listing names and addresses, dates, and average grades. Alphabetically arranged by names of pupils. No index. Typed. 16 x 4 x 3. County Courthouse, Room 532.

538. MISCELLANEOUS CORRESPONDENCE
1915—. 23 file boxes.

Correspondence pertaining to board of education. Alphabetically arranged by names of correspondents. No index. Handwritten and typed. 14 x 28 x 14. County Courthouse, Room 532.

539. TOWNSHIP AND SCHOOL DISTRICT MAPS
1934. 8 maps.

Maps showing names of owners and acreage of each plot of ground of township, and school districts; also street index in upper left and lower right corners. Prepared by county engineer's office; published by C. O. Titus, Philadelphia, Pennsylvania. Hand drawn and colored. No scale. 60 x 48. County Courthouse, Room 532, mounted on map rack.

Hillcrest School for problem girls and the Glenview School for problem boys were established in 1915. The two institutions replaced the Cincinnati House of Refuge, a corrective and reform school for both girl and boy delinquents, which was established by the city of Cincinnati under the provisions of the city ordinance passed March 12, 1845 entitled "An act to authorize the city of Cincinnati to erect a house of correction."

Under provisions of this ordinance, any male under sixteen or female under fourteen years of age, who, under the then existing laws, was liable to confinement in the county jail, or in the state penitentiary, might, at the discretion of the court or magistrate pronouncing sentence, be placed in the house of correction. When so placed until of legal age such persons were to be subject to the exclusive control of the directors of the house of correction, and were either to be apprenticed, or, with the written consent of the court or magistrate giving sentence, to be discharged.

The act, furthermore, authorized the directors of the house of correction to receive all males under sixteen and females under fourteen when parents or guardians, or the township trustees, represented them to be proper subjects for the institution.

Under the measure, the city council of Cincinnati was empowered to levy a tax or taxes for the building or support of the house of correction, and also to receive subscriptions, either annual or otherwise, to be used for the same purpose. The city of Cincinnati alone was made liable for any debts incurred by the institution, and provision was made that no tax should ever be loving on the institution for any state or county purpose.

Expenses of those minors committed by a court or magistrate of the county were paid by the county; those of minors committed by township trustees were paid by the township; and those of minors committed by parents or guardians were paid by the parents or guardians, excepting in cases where the directors of the home might determine otherwise.

The institution was under the control of a board of directors, consisting of nine members, three of whom were appointed by the city council, three by the Hamilton County court of common pleas, and three from among those contributing toward the support of the institution. The directors thus appointed serve terms of three years, and had full power to make contracts, and to establish and enforce regulations for the government in control of the institution and its inmates. (*Ordinances of Cincinnati*, 1845, sec. 3-11; G.C. sec. 4097-4124.)

Upon the closing of the Cincinnati House of Refuge, and following an act of the legislature in 1913 creating a board of state charities and amending certain sections of the General Code to provide for the cooperation of city and county with the juvenile court in the board of state charities in the maintenance and operation of schools for problem children, the Hillcrest and Glenview schools were established in 1915. The schools at this time, known as the Girls' Opportunity Farm and the Boys' Opportunity Farm, were under the control of the county commissioners and the city of Cincinnati. (103 O. L. 871.)

On March 7, 1917, the legislature passed an act, amending and repealing sections of certain other acts passed in 1878, 1879, and 1883, and providing for the control and management of such correctional schools by the board of education, with the city and county sharing the cost of maintenance. (75 O. L. 513; 76 O. L. 75; 80 O. L. 217; 107 O. L. 61.)

The act of 1917 provided in part that "the inmates of a county, semi-public or district children's home shall have the advantage of the privileges of the public schools, and... whenever a school is maintained at such a home, such school shall be under the control and supervision of the city, township, village or special board of education, having jurisdiction over the school district within which such home is located." (107 O. L. 61.)

Until the two schools were tentatively closed on January 1, 1937, because of the defeat, November 3, 1936, of a special tax levy for their support, the two institutions were operated under the provisions set forth in the acts of 1913 and 1917. They were closed by the board of education by virtue of the power vested in that board under the act of the legislature which provides that "the Board of Education is authorized to keep in operation such schools until the full share of all the school funds for the township or district belonging to said children, on the basis of enumeration, shall have been expended." (75 O. L. 513.)

As provided by statute, each of the schools, prior to closing, was in charge of a principal and a teaching staff appointed by the board of education, a parole officer representing and appointed by the juvenile court, and certain other attendance necessary for the operation of the schools. Commitments to the two schools were through the juvenile court as provided under Sections 1652, 1652-1, and 1653 of the General Code, and discharge of those under legal age was by parole to parents or guardians.

The Hillcrest School comprises 130 acres, seventy-five of which are under cultivation, while the Glenview School has 379 acres, with 225 acres under cultivation.

Although the schools were closed in January 1937, they're reopening by the city and county is contemplated, when means are devised for their support. The time of such reopening has not yet been determined.

Hillcrest School

Case Records

540. COMMITMENTS, INSTITUTIONS
1915—. 1 file box.
Copies of original commitments from court of common pleas division of domestic relations listing commitment number, name and age of inmate, date of order issuance by court, offense charged, signature of deputy, and signature of school superintendent acknowledging receipt of girl. Alphabetically arranged by names of children. No index. Typed on printed forms. 26 x 14 x 11.5. Hillcrest School, Administration Building, Parole and record office.

541. CASE HISTORY
1915—. 3 file boxes.
Complete case history of each girl committed to institution giving commitment data, complete report of the findings of central clinic in respect to the girl's physical and mental condition, hereditary background, recommendations of clinic, observation by superintendent and attendance of the child's conduct in school, record of child's conduct and progress after being released on parole from institution, and correspondence relating to child. Alphabetically arranged by names of inmates; each case in separate folder. No index. Typed on printed forms. 26 x 14 x 11.5. Hillcrest School, Administration Building, Parole and record office.

542. DENTAL RECORD CARDS
1928—. 1 file box.
Card record of dental treatment given inmates by the public dental service society of the Cincinnati board of education listing name and address, page, nationality, room number, and grade of girl treated; date, time, and number of teeth treated;

remarks and chart showing teeth treated. Alphabetically arranged by names of inmates. No index. Handwritten and typed on printed forms. 9 x 8.5 x 4.25. Hillcrest School, Administration Building, Parole and record office.

Reports

543. MONTHLY POPULATION REPORTS
1935—. 2 folders.
Report giving name and date, new commitments, names of children escaping from school, of those returned to school, and of those transferred; also placements and returns from placements. Chronologically arranged. No index. Typed. 12 x 9 x .25. Hillcrest School, Administration Building, Parole and record office.

544. MONTHLY REPORTS TO DIVISION OF CHARITIES, STATE DEPARTMENT OF PUBLIC WELFARE
1935—. 1 folder.
Copies of monthly reports of superintendent of school to department of public welfare, Columbus, Ohio, giving complete record of additions and reductions in school roll; also reports on children place in foster homes, and a statistical and financial summary for month. Chronologically arranged. No index. Handwritten on printed forms of 8 pages each. 12 x 9 x .25. Hillcrest School, Administration Building, Parole and record office.

545. PRINCIPAL'S MONTHLY ATTENDANCE REPORTS
1934—. 1 folder.
Complete report of monthly attendance of all grades, enrollments in city public schools, fire drills, and description of any changes in class organization. Chronologically arranged. No index. Typed on printed forms. 12 x 9 x .25. Hillcrest School, Administration Building, Parole and record office.

546. TEACHERS' MONTHLY ATTENDANCE REPORTS
1934—. 1 folder.
Complete report of monthly attendance of pupils in all grades, enrollments in city public schools, and daily average attendance. Chronologically arranged. No index. Typed on printed forms. 12 x 9 x .25. Hillcrest School, Administration Building, Parole and record office.

547. PHYSICIANS' REPORTS, GIRLS TRANSFERRED TO HOSPITAL
    1933—. 1 folder.
Daily reports of physician covering, in detail, patient's condition after periodic examinations; listing name of girl, date of examination, impression of physician, and prescription. Chronologically arranged. No index. Typed. 12 x 9 x .25. Hillcrest School, Cottage A, Doctor's office.

548. MONTHLY MEDICAL AND HEALTH SERVICE REPORTS
    1932—. 1 folder.
Monthly reports of medical and health service rendered by institution hospital listing number of girls received at institution and examined, number requiring hospitalization, number referred to hospital clinics, number dismissed from hospital, number of periodic examinations, number treated for various ailments, number of girls showing gain and loss of weight, and number of calls made by visiting physician in dentist. Chronologically arranged. No index. Typed. 12 x 9 x .25. Hillcrest School, Cottage A, Doctor's office.

549. NURSE'S WEEKLY REPORTS OF PHYSICIAN'S VISITS
    1931—. 1 folder.
Resident nurse's weekly reports of examinations and treatments by visiting doctor listing names of girls treated, nature of their ailment, and type of treatment prescribed. Chronologically arranged. No index. Typed. 12 x 9 x .25. Hillcrest School, Cottage A, Doctor's office.

550. SCHOOL PHYSICIAN'S SEMIANNUAL REPORTS
    1928—. 1 folder.
Health reports by institution physician covering six-month periods, listing number and types of examinations during period, number of girls requiring hospital care, number of girls visiting special clinics, laboratory work done, dental treatments, preventative measures taken during period to check contagious diseases, remarks concerning plans for future, and comment upon care of equipment and records of hospital. Chronologically arranged. No index. Typed. 12 x 9 x .25. Hillcrest School, Cottage A, Doctor's office.

551. ANNUAL SCHOOL HEALTH REPORTS
1929—. 1 folder.
Annual health report of attending physician covering work performed during year, with remarks concerning plans and improvements for ensuing year. Reports list number and types of examinations for year, number of girls requiring hospital care, number of girls visiting special clinics, laboratory work performed, dental treatments, and preventative measures taken to check contagious diseases. Chronologically arranged. No index. Typed. 12 x 9 x .25. Hillcrest School, Administration Building, Parole and record office.

552. PAROLE OFFICER'S MONTHLY REPORTS OF GIRLS PAROLED
1927—. 1 folder.
Reports of parole officer covering conduct and progress of girls released from institution on parole listing name and address of girl employed, name of employer, and observations and recommendations of parole officer. Chronologically arranged. No index. Typed. 12 x 9 x .25. Hillcrest School, Administration Building, Parole and record office.

553. PAROLE OFFICER'S SEMIANNUAL REPORTS OF GIRLS RECEIVED
1927—. 1 folder.
Reports cover the general conduct of girls in the institution for six month period after commitment listing, in detail, all infractions of rules, characteristic traits and moods manifested, personal habits observed, girl's reaction to discipline, and recommendation of officer in each case. Chronologically arranged. No index. Typed. 12 x 9 x .25. Hillcrest School, Administration Building, Parole and record office.

Miscellaneous

554. ANNUAL HOSPITAL AND DRUG ROOM INVENTORY
1930—. 1 folder.
Annual inventory of stock and equipment on hand in hospital and drug room. Chronologically arranged. No index. Typed. 12 x 9 x .25. Hillcrest School, Cottage A, Doctor's office.

555. PURCHASE ORDERS, REQUISITIONS, RECEIPTED BILLS, CORRESPONDENCE
1934—. 3 file boxes.

Miscellaneous record of orders for material and supplies, Bill's covering same, and general correspondence pertaining their two. Alphabetically arranged by names of merchants or firms. No index. Handwritten and typed. 26 x 14 x 11.5. Hillcrest School, Administration Building, Secretary's office.

556. GENERAL CORRESPONDENCE
1934—. 1 file box.

General correspondence pertaining to institution and inmates. Alphabetically arranged by names of individuals. No index. Typed and handwritten. 26 x 14 x 11.5. Hillcrest School, Administration Building, Parole and record office.

Glenview School

All records are in Glenview School office, Glendale, Ohio.

557. PHYSICAL EXAMINATIONS
1930—. 1 file box.

Record giving name and address of each boy in school, result of his physical examination, name a position, and date on which examination was made. Alphabetically arranged by names of pupils. No index. Handwritten on printed forms. 16 x 14 x 26.

558. MEDICAL RECORD OF EMPLOYEES
1933—. 1 file box.

Record of medical examinations of all employees giving name, date, position held, and name of physician. Alphabetically arranged by names of employees. No index. Handwritten on printed forms. 16 x 14 x 26.

559. MEDICAL RECORDS, BOYS RELEASED
1930—. 2 file boxes.

Record showing names, addresses, and physical condition of boys released, name of physician, dates of examinations, and date of each boy's release. No index. Handwritten on printed forms. 16 x 14 x 26.

560. DEPARTMENT OF PUBLIC WELFARE RECORDS

1930—. 1 file box.

Annual report of the Department of Public Welfare of each boy is school showing name, address, names of parents or guardian, live in conditions, and progress made since attending school. Alphabetically arranged by names of pupils. No index. Handwritten on printed forms. 16 x 14 x 26.

561. RECORD OF VISITS, GRADES, AND CLOTHES

1933—. 1 file box.

Record showing number of visits by boys, grade made in school, and clothes received from home. Alphabetically arranged by names of boys. No index. Handwritten on printed forms. 14 x 8 x 6.

562. GRADE RECORDS

1930—. 6 file boxes. (A-Z).

Record giving name of boy, age, address, names of parents or guardian, school tests, examinations, grades, and short review of boy's conduct. Alphabetically arranged by names of boys. No index. Handwritten on printed forms. 16 x 14 x 26.

563. EDUCATIONAL TESTS

1930—. 1 file box.

Record giving name and address, names of parents or guardian, time of entry in school, and mental test. Alphabetically arranged by names of boys. No index. Handwritten on printed forms. 16 x 14 x 26

564. CONFIRMATIONS

1930—. 4 file boxes.

Record of all bills approved by board of directors showing name of person, amount, date paid, and for what purpose. Alphabetically arranged by names of payees. No index. Handwritten on printed forms. 16 x 14 x 26.

565. PAYROLLS

1930—. 1 file box.

Record of payrolls, petty cash, and delivery receipts showing name of payee, service rendered, cash on hand, from what source received, and delivery receipts for all farm products. Alphabetically arranged by names of payees. No index. Handwritten on printed forms. 16 x 14 x 26.

566. CORRESPONDENCE

1933—. 1 file box.

Correspondence of an executive nature and copies of replies. Alphabetically arranged by names of correspondents. No index. Handwritten and typed. 16 x 14 x 26.

567. CORRESPONDENCE

1930—. 1 file box.

Correspondence in reference to boys and their grades. Alphabetically arranged by names of correspondents. No index. Handwritten and typed. 16 x 14 x 26.

One of the recent developments in county health administration has been the establishment of the general health district, or county health department. By an act of the legislature, in 1919, the townships and municipalities in each county, exclusive of any city having a population of 25,000 or more, were to constitute a general health district. Cities having a population of 25,000 or more were to constitute a municipal health district. On the other hand, municipalities of not less than 10,000 or more than 25,000 which maintain a board of health meeting the qualifications and set by the legislative act were authorized, after examination by the state health department, to continue operation as a separate health district. (108 O. L. pt. i, 238.) An amendment passed in December 1919, made each city a health district. The townships and villages in each county were combined into a general health district. Provision also was made whereby a city and general health district might combine for administrative purposes. (108 O. L. pt. ii, 1086.)

Under the latter act, the provisions of which are still in force, the mayor of each municipality not constituting a city health district, and the chairman of the trustees of each township were authorized to meet at the seat of justice and organize by selecting a chairman and a secretary. The organization, known as the district advisory council, selects and appoints a district board of health composed of five members one of whom must be a physician. The members serve without compensation. (108 O. L. pt. ii, 1085.)

Within thirty days after the appointment the members of the district or "county board of health" organized by selecting one of their members as president and another member as president pro tempore. The board is authorized to appoint a licensed physician as district health commissioner. This officer, serving as secretary to the board, is designated as deputy state registrar of vital statistics, and is required to report monthly to the state registrar of vital statistics. (G. C. sec. 1261-32; 108 O. L. pt. i, 242.)

The duties of the county board of health include, among other things, the appointment, upon the recommendation of the health commissioner, a "whole-time" public health nurse, a clerk, and such additional public health nurses, physicians, and other persons as may be necessary for the proper conduct of its work. Moreover, the board makes a study of the prevalence of disease, especially communicable diseases, within the county, and provides for the treatment of venereal diseases and inspection of public charitable, benevolent, correctional, and penal institutions. In addition to this, the board may provide inspection of dairies, stores, restaurants, hotels, and other places where food is manufactured, handled, stored, sold, or offered for sale. (108 O. L. pt. ii, 1088-1089.) The board is authorized to make any and all regulations it deems necessary for the prevention or restriction of disease and the prevention, abolition, or suppression of a nuisance. (*Ibid.*, 1089.) The county prosecuting attorney represents the board in legal matters. (See page 102.)

The board may provide for carrying on such laboratory work as may be necessary for the conduct of its work by establishing a laboratory or contracting with existing laboratories. All state institutions, supplied in whole or in part by public funds, must furnish such laboratory service to a county board of health under the terms agreed upon. (108 O. L. pt. ii, 1089.)

The work of the health department is financed by public taxation. The board annually estimates, in itemized form, the amount needed for the next fiscal year. Such estimates, certified by the county auditor, are submitted to the county budget commissioners, who may reduce any items in such an estimate, but cannot increase any item or the aggregate of all items. The aggregate amount, is fixed by the budget commissioners, is apportioned by the county health district on the basis of taxable valuations in such townships and municipalities. (*Ibid.*, 1091.)

568. VITAL STATISTICS, BIRTHS, HAMILTON COUNTY
1920—. 18 volumes. (1-18).

Certificates of birth in Hamilton County listing name of child, sex, color, date of birth, birthplace, and names of parents. Chronologically arranged. Typed on printed forms. Volumes average 800 pages. 8.5 x 7.5 x 2.5. County Courthouse, Room 404.

569. INDEX TO VITAL STATISTICS, BIRTHS, HAMILTON COUNTY
1920—. 1 file box.

Card index to vital statistics of birth. Alphabetically arranged by names of infants. Typed.5 x 6 x 20. County Courthouse, Room 404.

570. VITAL STATISTICS, DEATHS, HAMILTON COUNTY
1920—. 10 volumes. (1-10).

Certificates of deaths in Hamilton County listing name of decedent, sex, color, marital status, and cause of death. Chronologically arranged. Typed on printed forms. Volumes average 800 pages. County Courthouse, Room 404.

571. INDEX TO VITAL STATISTICS, DEATHS, HAMILTON COUNTY
1920—. 1 file box.
Card index to vital statistics of deaths. Alphabetically arranged by names of decedents. Typed. 5 x 6 x 24. County Courthouse, Room 404.

572. HEALTH BULLETIN
1920—. 60 pamphlets (labeled chronologically).
Milk reports, vital statistics, contagious disease reports, help hints for distribution to teachers, social workers, and departmental officers. Alphabetically arranged by subjects. No index. Mimeographed and clipped. Pamphlets average 4 pages. 8.5 x 11 x .0625. County Courthouse, Room 404.

573. SCHOOL RECORDS
1920—. File boxes (labeled chronologically).
Records of health conditions of all children in elementary grades in Hamilton County. Alphabetically arranged by names of schools; also numerically arranged by numbers of school grades. No index. Typed on printed cards. 5 x 8 x 17. County Courthouse, Room 404.

574. MEDICAL REPORTS
1920—. 6 file boxes.
Individual records of public school children covering infant welfare, dental records, crippled cases, tuberculosis, and other communicable diseases. This record is discontinued after child's fourteenth birthday. Chronologically arranged. No index. Handwritten and typed on credit forms. 5 x 8 x 17. County Courthouse, Room 404.

575. LABORATORY REPORTS
1930—. 2 file boxes. Record initiated 1930.
Clinic reports showing nutritional value of foods. Chronologically arranged. No index. Typed on printed forms. 12 x 12 x 20. County Courthouse, Room 404.

576. MISCELLANEOUS RECORDS
1920—. 14 bundles (labeled by subjects).
General correspondence; also dental, public school, and sanitary records. Chronologically arranged. No index. Handwritten and typed on printed forms. 6 x 4 x 10. County Courthouse, Room 404.

The Hamilton County tuberculosis hospital was established in 1927 under the provisions of the legislative act of 1919 (supplemented the legislation of 1908), which authorized the county commissioners in any county wherein there was situated a municipal tuberculosis hospital, to provide for the purchase or lease of the necessary buildings thereon for the operation and maintenance of a county hospital for the treatment of tubercular patients. (108 O. L. pt. i, 253; see also 99 O. L. 62.) The hospital was to be separate and apart from the county home, which, in previous years, had housed not only the county's indigent but its tubercular patients as well. (99 O. L. 62.)

The management and control of this hospital is vested in a board of trustees, appointed by the county commissioners for a period of three years. This board has the usual powers and duties by law upon the board of trustees of the district hospitals, for the care of persons suffering from tuberculosis. All laws applicable to the leasing, maintenance, and operation of the district hospitals apply to the tuberculosis hospitals.

The board of hospital trustees is directed to hold meetings at least once a month, adopt necessary rules and regulations for its business, and keep a complete record of its proceedings. Moreover, the board is empowered to employ a superintendent, upon whose nomination it shall confirm the appointment of such positions, nurses, and other employees as may be necessary for the proper care, control, and management of the hospital and its inmates.

The trustees are required annually, on the first Monday of March, to file with the commissioners a statement of their receipts and expenditures for the preceding year and to submit to the same body and estimate of the financial requirements of the hospital for the ensuing year. (108 O. L. pt. i, 258.)

577. CENSUS BOOK

1910—. 2 volumes.

List of yearly admissions, discharges, death, classification of patients as to sex, race, and age, x-ray, medical, surgical, dental, eye, ear, nose, and throat examination reports; also laboratory autopsies. Alphabetically arranged by names of patients. No index. Handwritten and typed on printed forms. Volumes average 100 pages. 13.5 x 9.5 x 1. Tuberculosis Hospital, Superintendent's office.

578. MEDICAL AND STATISTICAL RECORD

1924—. 1 volume.

List of yearly admissions, discharges, and deaths showing classification according to diagnosis of adults and children, race, sex, and age. Alphabetically arranged by names of patients. No index. Handwritten. 200 pages. 13.5 x 10 x 1.5. Tuberculosis Hospital, Superintendent's office.

The Hamilton County home at Hartwell was established in 1852, under provisions of an act of the council of Cincinnati passed March 23, 1850, and was known as the city infirmary. (*Ordinances of Cincinnati*, 1850, 95.) On January 1, 1924, the county home was combined with the county infirmary, which had been established at Carthage, Ohio, in 1873. This merger was affected under provisions of an act of the legislature, passed as early as March 1911, which authorized the county commissioners to acquire land for an infirmary. (102 O. L. 54.)

Upon amalgamation of the two institutions, the name "Hamilton County Infirmary," was substituted for "City Infirmary," and the Hamilton County commissioners were, from that date, empowered to govern the operation of the combined institutions. Since that time, the classifying term, "infirmary,' which in earlier years had been used to describe an institution caring for the aged only, was changed to the "Hamilton County Home," meaning merely a haven of rest for the aged, and having no connection with the hospitalization system which had been set up by city, county, and state to care for those people who have insufficient funds to employ a physician.

The chronic disease hospital was established as part of the county home in 1929, under provisions of an act of the legislature passed April 21, 1927. (112 O. L. 381.)

Under direct supervision of the county commissioners, the institution is in charge of a superintendent. The medical personnel of the hospital section comprises three physicians, three interns, a chief nurse, and a core of eleven registered nurses, a dietitian, a laboratory technician, and a pharmacist.

Case Records

579. CASE RECORDS
1852-1933. 16 volumes.

Records giving names and former addresses of all inmates, names of their children or relatives, and dates of admittance, death, or discharge. Alphabetically arranged by names of inmates. No index. Handwritten. Volumes average 250 pages. 16 x 12 x 3. County Home, storeroom, 1st floor.

For subsequent records see 580 and 581.

580. SOCIAL SERVICE HISTORY
1928—. 4 file boxes.

Complete case history of each inmate showing name, age, former address, names of relatives, education, and former occupation; also admittance date and physical condition. Alphabetically arranged by names of inmates. No index. Typed. 20 x 16 x 12. County Home, office.

581. DEATHS AND DISCHARGES
1928—. 4 file boxes.

Record of discharges or deaths of inmates showing name, date of discharge or death, and cause of death. Alphabetically arranged by names of inmates. No index. Handwritten and typed on printed forms. 30 x 16 x 12. County Home, office.

582. KARDEX SYSTEM
1928—. 33 file box sections. (14 sections labeled History, 11 sections labeled Deaths, 8 sections labeled Discharges).

Complete card record of each inmate. Alphabetically arranged by names of inmates. No index. Typed on printed forms. 30 x 8 x 1. County Home, office.

583. MEDICAL CHARTS
1929—. 6 file boxes.

Medical charts of patients showing name, age, residence, names of relatives, date, and treatment. Alphabetically arranged by names of patients. No index. Handwritten on printed forms. 30 x 16 x 12. Chronic Disease Hospital office.

Business Administration of Office

584. BUDGET
1933—. 1 file box.

Yearly budgets of monthly receipts, expenses, and disbursements. Chronologically arranged. No index. Typed. 20 x 10 x 10. County Home, office.

585. MAINTENANCE ORDERS
1933—. 24 volumes.
Orders for maintenance and repairs on county home and hospital showing name of contractor and amount of supplies furnished. Numerically arranged by order numbers. No index. Handwritten. Volumes average 150 pages. 8 x 6 x 2. County Home, office.

586. REQUISITIONS
1933—. 1 file box.
Original requisitions for supplies showing detailed list of articles ordered, name of vendor, and cost price. Numerically arranged by order numbers. No index. Typed. 30 x 16 x 12. County Home, office.

587. FILLED ORDERS
1933—. 2 file boxes.
Filled supply orders showing name of vendor, amount, and date of payment. Alphabetically arranged by names of vendors. No index. Typed. 30 x 16 x 12. County Home, office.

588. PETTY CASH
1933—.1 volume.
Record of all cash payments showing amount on hand, from what source received, to whom paid, purpose, date, and balance on hand. Chronologically arranged. No index. Handwritten. 300 pages. 14 x 9 x 2. County Home, office.

589. VOUCHER REGISTER
1933—. 1 file box.
Vouchers for all money disbursed showing for what purpose, number, date, amount, and to whom paid. Numerically arranged by voucher numbers. No index. Handwritten on printed forms. 30 x 16 x 12. County Home, office.

590. VOUCHER REGISTER
1933—. 2 volumes.
List of purchases for county home and hospital showing order number, date, amount of supplies ordered, and amount paid. Numerically arranged by voucher numbers. No index. 23 x 18 x 2. County Home, office.

591. CANCELLED CHECKS
1933. 1 file box.
Cancelled checks showing date, amount, name of payee, and for what issued. Alphabetically arranged by names of payees. No index. Handwritten and typed on printed forms. Alphabetically arranged by names of payees. No index. Handwritten and typed on printed forms. 16 x 12 x 6. County Home, office.

592. PAYROLLS
1933—. 1 file box.
Payrolls of allowances paid to inmates of county home giving name, date, and amount. Chronologically arranged. No index. Handwritten. County Home, office.

593. CURRENT PAYROLLS
1933—. 2 file boxes.
Payroll of all employees and cash allowances to inmates showing name, date, amount, and purpose. Chronologically arranged. No index. Handwritten. 16 x 26 x 30. County Home, office.

Miscellaneous

594. STOREROOM INVENTORY
1933—. 2 volumes.
Inventory of storeroom supplies in storage such as groceries, incidentals, and household supplies. Chronologically arranged. No index. Handwritten. Volumes average 250 pages. 26 x 14 x 4. County Home, office.

595. LINEN ROOM SUPPLIES
1933—. 2 volumes.
List of supplies kept in linen room for county home and hospital. Chronologically arranged. No index. Handwritten. Volumes average 200 pages. 17 x 14 x 2. County Home, office.

596. MISCELLANEOUS RECORDS
1852-1933. 27 bundles.

Records containing bills paid, payrolls, receipts, and disbursements. Chronologically arranged. No index. Handwritten and typed. 12 x 10 x 6. County Home, storeroom, 1st floor.

597. CORRESPONDENCE AND REPORTS
1933—. 6 file boxes

Correspondence relative to inmates, reports on consultations, medical service, and social service investigations. Alphabetically arranged by names of inmates. No index. Handwritten and typed. 30 x 16 x 12. County Home, office.

County relief for the indigent, one of the most pressing problems of the twentieth century was met in frontier Ohio. As early as 1805 there was passed an act, modeled from the territorial law which was, in all respects, similar to the poor laws of seventeenth century England. (3 O.L. 272.) Under the early enactments of the township trustees were authorized to appoint overseers of the poor. Then, in 1816, the county commissioners were authorized to construct "poor houses" for the care of the county's indigent. As the system developed and succeeding decades the county was made responsible for those who had become permanently disabled, and for paupers who could not be satisfactorily cared for except at the county infirmary, now called the county home. The township trustees and officials of municipal corporations were made responsible for providing temporary relief to needy persons who were residents of the state, or the county, township, or city. In the event any person became chargeable to the township in which he had not gained a legal settlement, it was the duty of the overseers, later the township trustees, to remove him to the township where he was legally settled. With slight alterations, the principles of this system, continued until the twentieth century. (For an excellent study, but biting criticism of the administration of relief in Ohio prior to 1934 see Aileen Elizabeth Kennedy, *The Ohio Poor Law and Its Administration*. University of Chicago Press, *Social Service Monographs*, no. 22.)

The Hamilton County department of public welfare was established in 1928 under provisions of an act of the legislature, passed April to 8, 1913, entitled "An act to supplement section 2419 of the General Code by an additional section authorizing county commissioners to contract with cities for the maintenance of the county poor." Under provisions of the act and Article 15 of the Cincinnati Administrative Code, which authorizes the appointment of a director of welfare for the city of Cincinnati, the county commissioners established the county department of welfare to coordinate and correlate the work of caring for the indigent and unemployed of the county. (103 O. L. 577.)

When in the third decade of the twentieth century, the state was enveloped in an unprecedented depression the antiquated system, without a centralized organization, proved entirely inadequate. As a result of the abnormal employment and the crop failures owing to the drought of 1930, many local subdivisions of the county charged by law to administer support and medical relief to the indigent were unable to discharge their obligations. Accordingly, in 1931, the legislature passed an emergency act authorizing the county, township, and Municipal taxing authorities to borrow money and issue bonds for poor relief, providing the state tax commission found that no other funds were available. (114 O. L. 11-12.)

During the early months of 1932 the governor, aware of the widespread suffering in the state, called the legislature into special session. (See message of governor to Eighty-ninth General Assembly in 114 O. L. pt. ii, 6-8.) At this session the legislature authorized him to appoint a state relief commission composed of five members, to study the relief situation. This commission was permitted to cooperate with the national, state, or local relief commissions, which, in many counties, had been established and were already functioning. Since the county and township treasuries were depleted, because of the excessive drain caused by the mounting relief load and the steady decline of tax collections, the legislature authorized an excise tax on utilities, for the years 1932-1937, to be used for relief purposes. This state tax was to be allocated to the counties on the basis of population, the tax duplicate, and the value of utilities property in the county as of 1930. (114 O. L. pt. ii, 19-20.) The funds allocated to each county under this act were to be credited to the "county poor relief excise fund."

Moreover, the county commissioners were authorized to borrow money for emergency relief and evidence such indebtedness by the issuance of negotiable bonds and notes. Upon submission of such a resolution to the state tax commission, the commission was directed to an estimate the amount which would probably be allocated to the county from the public utility excise taxes, and was directed to calculate the total amount of bonds, the principal and interest on which might be paid out of such estimated allocation. The date of maximum maturity of such bonds was to be on or before March 15, 1938. If, in the year 1932, additional funds were needed for four relief, the county commissioners were authorized, after the state tax commission found that no other funds were available, to issue additional funds in the amount not exceeding one-tench of one percent of the general tax list and duplicate of the county. The maturity date of such additional bonds was to be on or before September 15, 1940.

Proceeds of the sale of such bonds were to be placed in a special fund, denominated the "emergency relief fund." No expenditures were to be made from this fund except in accordance with the method and under uniform regulations prescribed by the state relief commission, and in no case after December 31, 1933. The county commissioners were authorized to distribute, prior to the first of March 1933, portions of the fund to the political subdivisions of the county, according to their needs for poor relief determined by the county and set forth in such an approved budget. The money distributed to the subdivisions was to be expended in them for poor relief, including the renting of lands and the purchase of seeds for gardening by the unemployed. (*Ibid.*, 22.) For the county, poor relief included mother's pensions, soldiers' relief, temporary assistance to nonresident, maintenance of a county and a children's home, and work and direct relief. In the townships and municipalities poor relief was interpreted to be the support of the poor and burial of the indigent. (*Ibid.*, 17.) Each subdivision administering funds under the act was expected to require labor in exchange for relief given to any family where there resided and able-bodied wage earner. (*Ibid.*, 17.)

In February 1933, the tenure of the state relief commission was extended to March 1, 1935. (115 O. L. 22.) In the same year, the legislature levied an additional stamp tax on the sale of bottled and bulk beer, malt, cosmetics, and toilet preparations to furnish additional funds for emergency relief. (115 O. L. 642-646, 649; 115 O. L. pt. ii, -33, 83, 247, 5, 177, 200, 256.) The state treasurer was authorized to appoint the county treasurer as his deputy for the purpose of selling tax stamps to be affixed to such articles. (115 O. L. 642-646.)

When, in 1935, the state relief commission ceased to exist by reason of the term of the act creating it, the legislature passed a measure designed to coordinate and correlate all emergency poor relief work, activities and administration with the federal emergency relief administration which was authorized to administer and direct the distribution and expenditure of federal funds for relief in the state. Accordingly, all powers previously vested in the state relief commission were transferred to the county commissioners. Whenever in their discretion such action was necessary in order to continue the coordination and correlation of state, local, and federal funds they were authorized to appoint, with the approval of the director of finance of the state of Ohio, of such emergency poor relief. If such an officer were appointed, the representative succeeded to all powers and functions, which, under the act, were delegated to the county commissioners. This representative, however, was subject to such terms and conditions in respect to auditing, examinations, and reports as were directed by the county commissioners and such a federal agency. The county commissioners were directed to conduct relief activities outside limits of municipal corporations through the township trustees, insofar as practicable, and were to be guided by the recommendations of the township trustees with respect to relief need in such a political subdivision. Again, as in 1932, the commissioners were authorized, if the state tax commission found that no other means existed to provide funds, to borrow money, and issue bonds in the year 1935-1936. The maximum maturity date of such bonds was to be on or before March 1, 1944. (116 O. L. 572.) Other bonds, in addition to those secured by the county's share of the excise tax, might be issued not to exceed one-fifth of one percent of the general tax list of the county. (*Ibid.*, 575.) If the county was unable to issue bonds by raisin of the limitations imposed by the constitution (Art. XII, sec. 2), the taxing authority of each subdivision was authorized to submit the question of issuing bonds to the electorate either at a general or special election. (116 O. L. 578.)

The year 1936 saw the re-creation of the state relief commission. Consisting of four persons appointed by the governor, this body was authorized to serve until January 31, 1937. Again, the commission was directed to study problems of relief, to receive advice from federal, state, and local governmental departments, to cooperate with agencies of the national and local governments and private agencies engaged in the administration or financial support of direct or indirect relief, to administer moneys appropriated to the commission for poor relief, to examine the conduct of local governmental agencies in administering relief, and to order the distribution and payment of moneys from the state treasury.

The county commissioners were authorized to administer all advances by the state to the relief commission and were directed to operate through duly authorized agencies of townships, municipalities, and school districts. Of the funds allocated to the county by the state relief commission for direct relief, the commissioners were authorized, when they deemed it expedient for a reduction of cost, to reallocate the funds on a percentage basis, of the relief requirements of a political subdivisions. Within the appropriations made by the commissioners and subject to the rules and regulations of the state relief commission, the commissioners were instructed to appoint assistants and other employees as were necessary.

The county commissioners, like the state relief commission, were directed to cooperate with all agencies of the federal, state, and county governments, and with private agencies which were engaged in administering relief or financial support to the needy. It was made the duty of all county, township, and municipal governments administering relief or assistance to dependence to report to the county commissioners, at its request, the names and addresses of all persons to whom they were providing aid and the amount and character thereof. (116 O. L. pt. ii, 133-148.)

The principle of issuing bonds and securing them by the county's share of the utility taxes was continued. Moreover, there was appropriated to the state relief commission from the general revenue fund the sum of $3,000,000 which was designated as the "state relief rotary fund." The various counties of the state which had not issued bonds and were not authorized to do so without the consent of the people, were empowered to obtain an advance from the state relief rotary fund in an amount equal to that of bonds which were permitted to be issued. If the county failed to repay the total of all advances and interest at two percent before June 1936, the state relief commission was directed to refuse to make further allocations or distributions to the county. (*Ibid.*, 133-148.)

In the early months of 1937 the legislature authorized the state relief commission to serve until April 1937. Under this act the county commissioners are authorized to give temporary support and medical relief to nonresident and to all persons possessing a legal residence in the county and in need of relief. Funds may be expended for both direct and work relief. However, all persons on relief able and competent to perform labor who refuse to accept private employment under prevailing conditions and prevailing wages, may be dropped from the relief rolls. This does not apply, however, to areas where strikes are prevalent. On the other hand, any person receiving relief in the county is permitted to engage in any business without losing his relief status. During the period of such employment, he is required to forfeit the prorated amount of relief received by him, and is eligible to his former relief status upon the conclusion of such employment.

The county commissioners are required to file with the state relief commission a budget and a detailed statement and plan showing how the funds to be received are to be expended, the purpose for which they are to be used, the nature and kind of work to be carried on, and the number of persons to be aided by such relief. Besides this, the county commissioners must file a complete analysis of their proposed expenditures, together with an estimate of all available resources, including the unencumbered proceeds of any bonds here to four issued and the amount of bonds which the county commissioners have a right to issue without a vote of the people on the approval of the state tax commission of Ohio as authorized in 1935.

Of the funds allocated to the county by the state relief commission for direct relief, the commissioners may, when they believe that the cost of administration may be reduced, reallocate the funds on a percentage basis, of relief requirements of the various subdivisions. (Page's *Ohio Cumulative Code Service*, Cincinnati, 1937, no. 20, 65-67.)

The emergency relief measures, passed during the period 1932-1937, gave the counties for the first time in the history of Ohio a centralized relief administration.

Intake and Registration Department

All records of this department are located on the first floor, 1316 Pendleton Street, Cincinnati, Ohio.

Case Records

598. FAMILY RELIEF INDEX
1933—. 112 file boxes (A-Z).
Master card index of all county relief cases in all district offices, whether current or closed, giving case number, opening and closing dates, name of each member of family, name of district, and date of transfer. Alphabetically arranged by names of clients. For cross index see entry 599.Typed on printed cards. 24 x 6 x 4.

599. DIRECT RELIEF INDEX
1933—. 100 file boxes
Master index of all county active relief cases in all district offices giving case number, names of husband and wife, date case was opened, and case number. Numerically arranged by case numbers. For cross index see entry 598. Typed on printed forms. 24 x 10 x 1.

600. RELIEF APPLICATION FILE
1933—. 20 file boxes (A-Z).
Relief application slips giving name of each member of family, address, and names of agencies from whom relief had been previously obtained. Alphabetically arranged by names of clients. No index. Handwritten on printed forms. 24 x 7 x 5.5.

601. CLOSED FILE
1933—. 94 file boxes.
Papers and reports giving complete case histories of all closed relief cases handled by all district offices. Numerically arranged by case numbers. No index. Handwritten and typed on printed forms. 25 x 13 x 11.

602. INTAKE ACTIVE CASES
1933—. 2 file boxes.
Active relief cases of intake department containing all papers and reports giving

complete case histories since cases were opened. Alphabetically arranged by names of clients. No index. Handwritten and typed on printed forms. 25 x 13 x 11.

603. CASE FINANCIAL AND STATISTICAL RECORD
1933—. 1 bundle.

Condensed case histories of active cases carried by intake department with notations of dates and amounts of relief vouchers given in each case. Alphabetically arranged by names of clients. No index. Typed on printed forms. 15 x 12 x 1.

604. ACTIVE CCC CASES
November 1934—. 2 file boxes (A-Z).

Card file of persons enlisted in CCC camps giving name, address, parents' names, case number, date enrolled, number of company, location of camp, and name of person to whom money was sent. Alphabetically arranged by names of enlisted. No index. Typed on printed cards. 18 x 6 x 4.

605. CLOSED CCC CASES
November 1934—. 6 file boxes (A-Z).

Card file of persons enrolled in CCC camps and discharged giving name, address, parents' names, case number, date enrolled, dated and reason for discharge, number of company, location of camp, and name of person to whom money was sent. Alphabetically arranged by names of enlisted. No index. Typed on printed cards. 18 x 6 x 4.

606. FILE OF COUNTY CHARGES IN STATE INSTITUTIONS
1933—. 2 file boxes.

Card file of persons committed to state institutions, such as death, blind, and feeble-minded, giving name, address, date of commitment, probate court docket identification, and name of person responsible for commitment. Alphabetically arranged by names of persons committed. No index. Handwritten and typed on printed forms. 16 x 6 x 4.

607. REFERRALS TO DISTRICTS
1935—. 1 file box.

Memoranda of correspondence referred to relief districts concerning out-of-town information requested about persons who have a relief record here. Alphabetically arranged by names of clients. No index. Typed. 15 x 8 x 6.

608. OUT-OF-TOWN INVESTIGATION FILE
1935—. 3 file boxes.

Records and papers giving complete case histories of active cases under investigation about whom information has been requested by relief agencies outside county. Alphabetically arranged by names of clients. Handwritten and typed. 25 x 13 x 11.

609. FILE INDEX
1933—. 4 file boxes (A-Z).

Card index of active and closed cases about which information has been requested by relief agencies outside county giving name, address, and brief history of case. Alphabetically arranged by names of clients. Handwritten and typed on printed forms. 25 x 6 x 5.5.

610. INELIGIBLE FILE
1935. 3 file boxes.

Registration cards of persons on relief who were ineligible for WPA and PWA employment giving name, address, case number, brief family history, occupational classifications, and occupational histories of employable members of each family. Numerically arranged by case numbers. No index. Handwritten and typed on printed forms.

Complaints and Adjustments

611. COMPLAINT AND ADJUSTMENT INDEX
1935—. 12 file boxes (A-Z).

Card index record giving name, address, case number, date and nature of complaint; and where and to whom referred for adjustment. Alphabetically arranged by names of clients. Typed on ruled cards. 15 x 6 x 4.

612. DAY SHEETS
June 1936—. 1 file box.
Record giving names, addresses, dates, caseworkers names, and dates and nature of complaints. Chronologically arranged. No index. Handwritten on mimeograph forms. 25 x 13 x 11.

613. CORRESPONDENCE
1935—. 8 file boxes.
Correspondence pertaining to adjustment and complaint cases. Alphabetically arranged by names of claimants. No index. Typed. 25 x 13 x 11.

Miscellaneous

614. REFUND LEDGER
February 1935-April 30, 1936. 1 volume.
Entries of money refunded to Department of Public Welfare by relief clients. Alphabetically arranged by names of clients. No index. Typed. 25 pages. (loose-leaf). 12 x 9.5 x .25.

615. DAILY RECORD OF CAR TICKETS ISSUED
December 1935—. 1 bundle.
Record of car tickets issued by Department of Public Welfare giving dates, names of persons, number of tickets, and purpose for which issued. Numerically arranged by serial numbers. No index. Typed on mimeograph form. 14 x 8.5 x 3.

616. CAR TICKETS, DISTRIBUTION RECORD
December 1935—. 2 volumes.
Monthly record of car tickets distributed by relief districts showing number of car tickets issued by each case worker. Chronologically arranged. No index. Handwritten on printed forms. 25 pages. (loose-leaf). 16 x 11 x .25.

617. GENERAL CORRESPONDENCE
1934—. 12 file boxes.
General correspondence of county welfare director. Alphabetically arranged by subjects. No index. Typed. 25 x 13 x 11.

618. CORRESPONDENCE FILE
1935. 8 file boxes.
Interoffice communications; also correspondence with clients and with districts. Alphabetically arranged by subjects. No index. Handwritten and typed. 25 x 13 x 11.

Financing and Auditing Department

All records of this department are located on the third floor, 1316 Pendleton Street, Cincinnati, Ohio.

Budget and Vouchers

619. BUDGET REGISTER
December 1935—. 2 volumes.
Monthly budget for each district and record of relief orders given date, account, total amount of orders, and detailed purposes for which amount of each order was to be spent. Chronologically arranged. No index. Handwritten on printed forms. Volumes average 40 pages. (loose-leaf). 18 x 11 x 1.5.

620. FUND CONTROL LEDGER
September 1936—. 1 volume. Prior records missing.
Various funds available for expenditure by department of public welfare against which requisition orders may have been charged, giving dates and total amounts of funds, order numbers, names of persons credited, and specific amount of each order and comfort against funds. Chronologically arranged. No index. Handwritten on printed forms. 40 pages. (loose-leaf). 15 x 11 x .75.

621. DISTRICT DISTRIBUTION REPORT
January 1-April 1, 1936. 1 volume.
Reports listing names of districts, number and names of caseworkers in each district, number and names of clients assigned each case worker, and detailed amounts and purposes for which case worker may spend a lot of budget for each two-week payroll period. Chronologically arranged. No index. Handwritten on printed forms. 150 pages. 18 x 9 x 1.

622. RELIEF SUPPLY ORDER VOUCHERS AND BUDGET RECORD
May 1, 1936-December 31, 1936. 1 volume.
Record of vouchers sent to each district and of vouchers cancelled giving amounts, detail entries of amounts, and monthly budget for each relief district. Chronologically arranged. No index. Handwritten on printed forms. 200 pages. 11.5 x 17.5 x 1.5.

623. AUTHORIZATION FOR VOUCHERS
December 1, 1935—. 15 file boxes.
Authorization to cashier from caseworkers to issue vouchers to relieve clients giving amounts and purposes for which vouchers were to be made. Numerically arranged by districts. No index typed on printed forms. 25 x 13 x 11.

624. RELIEF SUPPLY ORDERS
December 1, 1935-January 8, 1936. 17 file boxes.
Relief order vouchers given to relief clients for food, clothing, and other supplies. Numerically arranged by voucher numbers. No index. Typed on printed forms. 25 x 13 x 11.

625. YELLOW VOUCHERS
January 8, 1936—. 107 file boxes.
Yellow copy of relief order vouchers given to relieve clients for food, clothing, and other necessities. Numerically arranged by voucher numbers. No index. Typed on printed forms. 25 x 13 x 11.

626. EMERGENCY VOUCHERS
December 1, 1935—. 2 file boxes.
Emergency vouchers issued to clients by department of public welfare for emergency purposes. Chronologically arranged; also numerically arranged by voucher numbers. No index. Typed on printed forms. 25 x 13 x 11.

Cash Books

627. CASH JOURNAL
December 1935—. 6 volumes.
Cash expenditures of department of public welfare. Records are entered according

to funds available for expenditures. Chronologically arranged. No index. Handwritten on printed forms. Volumes average 40 pages. (loose-leaf). 15 x 11 x .75.

628. SCHEDULES OF DISBURSEMENTS
May 1, 1936—. 1 bundle.
Detail record of entries, total amounts of which are entered in entry 627. These schedules must be approved by the state examiner. Chronologically arranged. No index. Handwritten and typed on printed forms. 11 x 12 x 8.5.

Vendors' Records

629. VENDORS' FILE, WARRANTS
March 1934-April 1935, December 1, 1935—. 71 file boxes (A-Z).
Vendors' warrants of sales to relieve clients on authority of public welfare department relief vouchers. Alphabetically arranged by names of vendors. No index. Typed on printed forms. 25 x 13 x 11.

630. INVOICES PAID THROUGH DECISION "A"
1934-1935. 5 file boxes (A-Z).
Invoices of purchases made by county department of public welfare and warrants of sales to relieve clients on authority of county welfare relief orders paid to vendors through decision "A." Alphabetically arranged by names of vendors. No index. Typed on printed forms. 25 x 13 x 11.

631. VENDORS' LEDGERS
December 1935-May 1936. 7 volumes.
Entries debited and credited to each vendor on purchases by the department and on purchases by relief clients on authority of relief order vouchers. Alphabetically arranged by names of vendors. No index. Handwritten and typed on printed forms. Volumes average 300 pages. (loose-leaf). 12.5 x 10 x 6.

Purchasing Department

All records of this department are located on the third floor, 1316 Pendleton Street, Cincinnati, Ohio.

632. PURCHASE ORDER INDEX

January 1, 1935—. 1 file box.

Card index of purchases made by department of public welfare. Numerically arranged by order numbers. For cross index see entry 633. Typed on ruled cards. 18 x 5.5 x 4.5.

633. PURCHASE ORDER INDEX

January 1, 1935—. 1 file box (A-Z).

Card index of purchases made by department of public welfare. Alphabetically arranged by names of vendors. For cross index see entry 632. Typed on ruled cards. 18 x 5.5 x 4.5.

634. REQUISITIONS, ACTIVE

1935—. 1 file box.

Requisitions for supplies and materials with notations of fund number against which they are encumbered. Numerically arranged by requisition numbers. No index. Handwritten and typed on printed forms. 25 x 13 x 11.

635. REQUISITIONS FILLED

1935—. 3 file boxes.

Filled requisitions for supplies and materials purchased by department. Numerically arranged by requisition numbers. No index. Handwritten and typed on printed forms. 25 x 13 x 11.

636. VENDORS' REQUISITIONS

1935—. 1 file box (A-Z)

Purchase orders for supplies and materials giving complete details. Alphabetically arranged by names of vendors. No index. Handwritten and typed on printed forms. 25 x 13 x 11.

637. REQUISITION REGISTER
1935—. 1 volume.
Current record of requisitions giving date, requisition number, purchase order number, purpose of requisition, encumbrance fund, and district credited. Chronologically arranged. No index. Handwritten on printed forms. 40 pages. (loose-leaf). 18 x 12 x 2.

638. REQUISITION BOOK
December 1, 1935—. 2 volumes.
Records of requisitions of Department of Public Welfare entered according to relieve districts, giving date, requisition number, total amount of requisition, and purpose for which money is to be spent. Chronologically arranged. No index. Handwritten on printed forms. Volumes average 40 pages. (loose-leaf). 15 x 11 x .5.

Statistical Department

All records of this department are located on the third floor, 1316 Pendleton Street, Cincinnati, Ohio.

639. STATISTICAL REPORTS AND SURVEYS
1933—. 37 file boxes.
Daily, weekly, monthly, and yearly summaries, reports and surveys (general and special) of all social and financial activities of the county public welfare department. Alphabetically arranged by subjects. No index. Typed. 25 x 13 x 11.

640. CORRESPONDENCE
1933—. 2 file boxes.
Requests for statistical information, general and special reports, and surveys. Alphabetically arranged by subjects. No index. Typed. 25 x 13 x 11.

Investigation Department

All records of this department are located on the third floor, 1316 Pendleton Street, Cincinnati, Ohio.

641. INDEX
1934—. 4 file boxes (A-Z).
Card index of cases of fraud under investigation (entries 642 and 643) giving name, address, and case number. Alphabetically arranged by names of clients. Typed. 18 x 6 x 5.

642. ACTIVE FILE
1934—. 1 file box.
Records, papers, and documents of active cases of fraud under investigation. Numerically arranged by case numbers. For index see entry 641. Handwritten and typed on printed forms. 25 x 13 x 11.

643. CLOSED FILE
1934—. 1 file box.
Records, papers, and documents of closed cases investigated for fraud. Numerically arranged by case numbers. For index see entry 641. Handwritten and typed. 25 x 13 x 11.

Central District Division

All records of this department are located on the third floor, 1316 Pendleton Street, Cincinnati, Ohio.

644. FINANCIAL AND STATISTICAL CASE RECORD
1934—. 3 file boxes, 29 volumes (Volumes A-Z).
Condensed case history and record of financial assistance given in each case. Alphabetically arranged by names of clients. No index. 1934-1936, typed on printed forms; 1937—, typed. File boxes, 25 x 12 x 10. Volumes average 150 pages. 15 x 12 x 1.

645. ACTIVE CASE FILE
June 1933—. 29 file boxes (A-Z).
Complete case history of all active cases carried by the district. Alphabetically arranged by names of clients. Typed on printed forms. 12 x 13 x 11.

646. CASE WORKER INDEX OF ACTIVE CASES
June 1933—. 3 file boxes.
Card system giving name, address, case number, name of caseworker, date of opening, number persons in family, and name of district. Alphabetically arranged by names of clients in each case workers' stack boxes. Handwritten and typed. 18 x 6 x 4.5.

647. INACTIVE CASES, INDEX
June 1933—.2 file boxes.
Card system giving name, address, case number, name of caseworker, date of opening, number of persons in family, and name of district, with notations on the back of each card of amounts of relief given and other sources of income of family. Alphabetically arranged by names of clients. Typed. 18 x 6 x 4.5.

648. MASTER INDEX, ACTIVE CASES
June 1933—. 3 file boxes (A-Z).
Card index of all active cases carried by district giving name, address, case number, date case was opened, and number of persons in family. Alphabetically arranged by names of clients. Typed. 18 x 6 x 4.5.

649. MASTER INDEX, INACTIVE AND TRANSFERRED CASES
June 1933—. 10 file boxes (A-Z).
Card index of closed and transferred cases in district giving name, address, case number, date case was opened, date closed or transferred, and number of persons in family. Alphabetically arranged by names of clients. Typed. 18 x 6 x 4.5.

650. MONTHLY STATISTICAL REPORT
June 1933—. 1 file box.
Monthly summary reports of casework activities carried on by district. Chronologically arranged. No index. Handwritten on mimeograph forms. 23 x 13 x 11.

651. CORRESPONDENCE FILE
1934—. 3 file boxes.
Correspondence of district relating to case work. Alphabetically arranged by subjects. No index. Typed. 25 x 13 x 11.

Northside District Division

All records of this department are located on the third floor, 1316 Pendleton Street, Cincinnati, Ohio.

652. FINANCIAL AND STATISTICAL CASE RECORD
1934—. 3 file boxes, 31 volumes (volumes A-Z).
Condensed case history and record of financial assistance given in each case. Alphabetically arranged by names of clients. No index. 1934-1935, typed on printed forms; 1937—, typed. File boxes, 25 x 12 x 10. Volumes average 150 pages (loose-leaf). 15 x 12 x 1.

653. ACTIVE CASE FILE
1933—. 27 file boxes (A-Z).
Complete case history of all active cases carried by district. Alphabetically arranged by names of clients. Typed. 25 x 13 x 11.

654. CASE WORK INDEX OF ACTIVE CASES
June 1933—. 4 file boxes.
Card system giving name, address, case number, name of caseworker, date of opening of case, number of persons in family, and name of district. Alphabetically arranged by names of clients in each case workers stack boxes. Handwritten and typed. 18 x 6 x 4.5.

655. INACTIVE CASE INDEX
June 1933—. 4 file boxes.
Card system giving name, address, case number, name of caseworker, date of opening of case, number of persons in family, and name of district, with notations on back of each card of amounts of relief given and other sources of income of family. Alphabetically arranged by names of clients. Typed. 18 x 6 x 4.5.

656. MASTER INDEX, ACTIVE CASES
June 1933—. 4 file boxes (A-Z).
Card index of all active cases carried by district giving name, address, case number, date case was opened, and number of persons in family. Alphabetically arranged by names of clients. Typed. 15 x 4.5 x 4.5.

657. MASTER INDEX, INACTIVE AND TRANSFERRED CASES
June 1933—. 8 file boxes.
Card index of closed and transferred cases in district giving name, address, case number, date case was opened, days close or transferred, and number of persons in family. Alphabetically arranged by names of clients. Typed. 18 x 6 x 4.5.

658. MONTHLY STATISTICAL REPORT
1934—. 4 file boxes.
Correspondence of district relating to case work. Alphabetically arranged by subjects. No index. Typed. 25 x 13 x 11.

Terminal District Division

All records of this division are located in this office, Dalton and Kenner Streets, Cincinnati, Ohio.

660. FINANCIAL AND STATISTICAL CASE RECORD
1934—. 3 file boxes, 29 volumes (volumes A-Z).

661. ACTIVE CASE FILE
1933—. 28 file boxes (A-Z).
Complete case histories of all active cases carried by district. Alphabetically arranged by names of clients. Handwritten and typed. 25 x 13 x 11.

662. CASE WORKER INDEX OF ACTIVE CASES
June 1933—. 4 file boxes.
Card system giving name, address, case number, name of caseworker, date of opening, number of persons in family, and name of district. Alphabetically arranged by names of clients in each case workers stack boxes. Handwritten and typed. 6 x 4.5 x 18.

663. INACTIVE CASE INDEX

June 1933——. 4 file boxes.

Card system giving name, address, case number, name of caseworker, date of opening, number of persons in family, and name of district; notations on back of each card of amounts of relief given and sources of income of family. Alphabetically arranged by names of clients. Typed. 6 x 4.5 x 18.

664. MASTER INDEX, ACTIVE CASES

June 1933——. 4 file boxes (A-Z).

Card index of all active cases carried by district giving name, address, case number, date case was opened, and number of persons in family. Alphabetically arranged by names of clients. Typed. 6 x 4.5 x 18.

665. MASTER INDEX, INACTIVE AND TRANSFERRED CASES

June 1933——. 5 file boxes (A-Z)

Card index of closed and transferred cases in district giving name, address, case number, date case opened, date closed or transferred, and number of persons in family. Alphabetically arranged by names of clients. Typed. 6 x 4.5 x 18.

666. MONTHLY STATISTICAL REPORT

June 1933——. 1 file box.

Monthly summary reports of casework activities carried on by district chronologically arranged. No index. Handwritten on mimeograph forms. 25 x 13 x 11.

337. CORRESPONDENCE FILE

1934——. 6 file boxes.

Correspondence of district relating to casework. Alphabetically arranged by subjects. No index. Typed. 25 x 13 x 11.

Local Homeless and Transient Division

All records of this division are located on the second floor, 411 Lincoln Park Drive, Cincinnati, Ohio.

668. ACTIVE FILE INDEX
1933—. 1 file box (A-Z).
Card index of current cases giving name, address, date, case number, age, race, marital status, and name of caseworker. Alphabetically arranged by case names. For cross index see entry 669. Typed on ruled cards. 25 x 6 x 5.

669. ACTIVE FILE INDEX
1933—. 1 file box.
Card index on current cases giving name, address, date, case number, age, race, marital status, and name of caseworker. Numerically arranged by case numbers. For cross index see entry 668. Typed on ruled cards. 25 x 6 x 5.

670. INACTIVE CASE INDEX
1933—. 11 file boxes (A-Z).
Card index of closed cases giving name, address, date, case number, age, race, marital status, date case closed, and name of case worker. Alphabetically arranged by names of clients. Typed on ruled cards. 25 x 6 x 5.

671. TRANSFER SLIPS
n. d. 3 file boxes.
Slips giving details of movements of original case records within office. Chronologically arranged. No index. Handwritten. 25 x 6 x 5.

672. ACTIVE CASE FILE
1933—. 6 file boxes (A-Z).
Records and papers giving complete case history of each active case. Alphabetically arranged by case numbers. No index. 25 x 13 x 11.

673. MASTER INDEX, NONRESIDENT CASES
1933—. 48 file boxes (A-Z).
Card index of all cases giving name, address, date opened, date closed, age, race, marital status, and name of case worker. Alphabetically arranged by names of clients. Typed on ruled cards. 25 x 6 x5.

674. ACTIVE NRS FILE
1933—. 1 file box (A-Z).
Current card file of active nonresident single and family cases, and state single cases giving essential history of each case. Alphabetically arranged by case names. No index. Handwritten on mimeographed cards. 25 x 8.5 x 6.

675. REJECTED NRS FILE
1933—. 1 file box (A-Z).
Current card file of rejected nonresident single and family cases, also state single cases giving essential history of each case and reason for rejection of service. Alphabetically arranged by case numbers. No index. Handwritten on mimeographed cards. 25 x 8.5 x 6.

676. CLOSED NRS FILE
1933—. 12 file boxes.
Card file of closed cases including nonresident single and family cases; also state single cases giving essential history of each case. Nope numerically arranged by case numbers. No index. Handwritten on mimeographed cards. 25 x 8.5 x 6.

677. EXTENDED NRS AND SS ACTIVE FILE
1933—. 1 file box (A-Z).
Records and papers giving complete case history of active cases accepted for extended service. Alphabetically arranged by case names. No index. Typed. 25 x 13 x 11.

678. SS CLOSED CASES
September 21, 1935—. 2 file boxes.
Records and papers giving complete case history of all state single cases accepted for extended service now closed. Numerically arranged by case numbers. No index. Handwritten on printed forms. 25 x 13 x 11.

679. NRS CLOSED CASES
September 21, 1933—. 9 file boxes.
Records and papers getting complete case history of closed nonresident single and family cases accepted for extended service. Numerically arranged by case numbers. No index. Handwritten on printed forms. 25 x 13 x 11.

680. TS CLOSED FILE
December 1, 1933-September 21, 1935. 70 file boxes.
Records and papers give in complete case history of closed transient service cases. Numerically arranged by case numbers. Handwritten on printed forms. 25 x 13 x 11.

681.REGISTRATION CARD INDEX
December 1, 1933-September 21, 1935. 7 file boxes (A-Z).
Double file boxes containing registration cards of closed transient service cases giving essential history of transience. It serves as an index to the TS closed file, entry 680. Alphabetically arranged by case names. Handwritten on printed forms. 25 x 20 x 6.

682. TS REGISTRATION FACE CARDS
December 1, 1933-September 21, 1935. 14 file boxes (A-Z).
Registration face cards of transient service cases giving brief histories of transience. Alphabetically arranged by case numbers. No index. Handwritten and typed on printed forms. 25 x 13 x 11.

The soldiers' relief commission was established by an act of the legislature passed May 19, 1886, entitled "An act to provide for the relief of indigent Union soldiers, sailors and marines, and the indigent wives, widows and minor children of indigent or deceased Union soldiers, sailors and marines." Under provisions of this act the commissioners of each county were authorized to levy a specified tax for the purpose of creating a fund for the relief of those beneficiaries mentioned above. This act further provided that the judge of the court of common pleas appoint three county residents, at least two of whom are honorably discharged Union soldiers, to serve for a term of three years as members of the commission, which, when organized by the selection of a chairman and a secretary, was to be known as the soldiers' relief commission. (83 O. L. 232.)

This act was amended in part on March 4, 1887, providing that councilman of city wards, as well as the board of trustees of the township, certify to the soldiers' relief commission names of those requiring and entitled to aid under the act. (84 O. L. 100.)

By act of the legislature, passed April 28, 1890, the soldiers' relief commission was required to appoint annually a committee of three in each township and a committee of three in each ward in any city in the county, whose duty it was to receive all applications for aid and to certify them to the soldiers' relief commission. (87 O. L. 352.)

By legislative enactment April 14, 1900, provision was made for the employment of an assistant to the secretary of the commission in counties maintaining a soldiers' home or those having a city of the first class. (94 O. L. 159.)

On March 6, 1917, sections 2930 and 2933-4 of the General Code where amended to provide for the appointment to each county commission of one member who is the wife or widow of an honorably discharged soldier, sailor, or marine of the Civil War or of the Spanish-American War, the other two members to be honorably discharged soldiers, sailors, or marines of the United States. The act further provided for the appointment to each township and ward committee of a wife or widow or a soldier, sailor, or marine of the United States. (107 O. L. 27.) Two years later, in 1919, relief was extended to indigent veterans of the World War or to indigent parents, wives, widows, or minor children of such veterans. (108 O. L. pt. i, 633.)

On April 6, 1929, sections 2930 and 2934 of the General Code were amended by an act of the legislature providing for the appointment by the court of common pleas in each county of a soldiers' relief commission, to consist of three members, one to be the wife, widow, son or daughter of an honorably discharged soldier, sailor, or marine of the Civil War, of the Spanish-American War, or of the World War, the other two members to be honorably discharged soldiers, sailors, or marines of the United States– one of whom, wherever possible, to be a member of the Spanish-American War Veterans, the other a member of the American Legion. (113 O. L. 466.)

All records are located in the County Courthouse, Room 415.

683. MINUTE BOOKS
1886—. 10 volumes.
Record of weekly transactions by the relief commissioners showing new applications granted and amount disbursed on relief of all types. Chronologically arranged. No index. Handwritten. Volumes average 300 pages. 16 x 14 x 2.

684. ACTIVE APPLICATIONS
1930—. 8 file boxes.
Records name and address of relief recipient, period granted aid, amount, and dates of payments. Alphabetically arranged by names of recipients. No index. Typed on printed forms. 26 x 14 x 12.

685. NEW APPLICATIONS
1932—. 5 volumes (labeled chronologically).
Record of new applications for relief showing name, address, name of each member of applicant's family, and name a caseworker in charge of application. Chronologically arranged. Alphabetical index by names of applicants in front of each volume. Handwritten. Volumes average 300 pages. 12 x 10 x 3.

686. RENEWAL APPLICATIONS
1934—. 1 volume.
Records names and addresses of all applicants for renewal of aid, date, and case number. Chronologically arranged. Alphabetical index by names of applicants in front of each volume. Handwritten. 200 pages. 14 x 12 x 3.

687. RECOMMENDATIONS
1936—. 4 file boxes.

Recommendations on relief cases by Red Cross and Hamilton County department of public welfare. Alphabetically arranged by names of persons recommended. No index. Typed on printed forms. 26 x 16 x 14.

688. ACTIVE CASES
1930—. 4 file boxes.

Card record of all cases showing name of applicant, names and ages of members of family, time application filed, caseworker's recommendation, and amount of aid allowed. Alphabetically arranged by names of recipients. No index. Typed on printed forms. 14 x 6 x 6.

689. INACTIVE CASES
1930—. 5 file boxes.

Records of cases where payments have been discontinued showing name, address, reason for discontinuance, date and amount. Alphabetically arranged by names of recipients. No index. Typed on printed forms. 13 x 10 x 5.

690. DECEASED MEMBERS
1930—. 1 file box.

Record of deceased members showing name, address, amount of relief, and date of demise. Alphabetically arranged by names of descendants. No index. Typed. 13 x 10 x 5.

691. FINANCIAL LEDGER
1930—. 6 volumes.

Daily, weekly, and yearly receipts and disbursements. Records name of recipient, amount, date, and case number. Chronologically arranged. Alphabetical index by names of recipients in front of each volume. Handwritten. Volumes average 300 pages. 14 x 14 x 3.

692. MILK RECORD
1934—. 2 volumes.
Record of milk given to dependent children showing name, address, amount, and name of company supplying milk. Numerically arranged by order numbers. No index. Handwritten. Volumes average 250 pages. 14 x 14 x 2.

693. VOUCHER STUBS
1930—. 18 volumes.
Stubs showing time voucher issued, to whom issued, and amount. Numerically arranged by voucher numbers. No index. Handwritten on printed forms. Volumes average 200 pages. 14 x 12 x 3.

In 1884 the legislature made provision for a soldiers' burial commission in each county in the state. The burial commission, consisting of three persons in each township appointed by the county commissioners, was directed to attend to and defray the expense incurred in the interment of any honorably discharged Union soldier, sailor, or a marine who died in poverty. The commission, serving at the pleasure of the appointing power, was required to report to the county commissioners the name, rank, and command of the decedent which report was transcribed by the county commissioners in a book kept for that purpose. (81 O. L. 146-147.) The original act, amended in 1891, extended the provisions of the act so as to include the interment of the wives or widows of the Union soldiers. (88 O. L. 330-331.) In 1893 the act was again amended so as to include the interment of mothers of Union soldiers, sailors and marines, and army nurses. (90 O. L. 177.) In 1908 the personnel of the commission was reduced to two.

Under the present law which became effective in 1921, the county commissioners are directed to appoint two suitable persons in each township and ward in the county who are directed, with the approval of the family or friends of the deceased, to contract with an undertaker, and direct the burial in a respectable manner, of the body of any honorably discharged soldier, sailor, or marine having at any time served in the army of the United States, or the mother, wife or widow of any soldier, sailor, or marine or any war nurse who did service at any time in the army of the United States who died in poverty. (G. C. sec. 2950; 108 O. L. pt. i, 211-212; 109 O. L. 212.)

The burial commission is instructed to enforce all laws relative to the burial of indigent veterans, investigate the financial status of the decedent's family, and report its findings to the county commissioners, together with the name, rank, and command to which the deceased belonged, date of death, place of burial, occupation while living, and an itemized statement of the cost of burial (99 O. L. 100.)

Upon receiving the report of the burial commission, the county commissioners transcribe the information in a book kept for that purpose, and certify the expense to the county auditor who draws his warrant for payment to the person or persons specified by the county commissioners. (*Ibid.*, 101.)

The amount contributed by the county for the burial of an indigent veteran set by the legislature $35 in 1884 was increased to $75 in 1908, and to $100 in 1921. (81 O. L. 146-147; 99 O. L. 99; 109 O. L. 212; G. C. sec. 2951.) Since 1908, each member of the burial commission has been allowed one dollar for each service performed. (99 O. L. 99; G. C. sec. 2951.)

694. BURIAL RECORDS INDIGENT SOLDIERS AND SAILORS
1907—. 7 volumes. (1, 3, 6-10). Volumes 2, 4-5, missing.
Records name of soldier or sailor, company and regiment, occupation, date of
demise, place of burial, name of undertaker, and cost. Chronologically arranged.
Alphabetical index by names of decedents in back of each volume. Handwritten on
printed forms. Volumes average 600 pages. 12 x 10 x 2. County Courthouse, 1907-
1921, 3 volumes, Auditor's storeroom, basement; 1922—, 4 volumes, Room 202.

Although provision was made for the relief of the county's indigent during the early days of statehood, it was not until the closing years of the nineteenth century that the legislature enacted a measure providing for separate relief for the blind. In 1898 the legislature passed an act authorizing the township trustees, who, since 1805, had provided outdoor relief for the county's indigent, to certify to the county commissioners an amount, not to exceed $100 per annum per capita, for the relief of the indigent blind. Such certification was to be made a record, listing the name of the person for whom the relief was required and the amount. (93 O. L. 270.) The county commissioners were directed to make a levy upon the townships to the amount certified by the trustees. This amount, when paid into the county treasury, was paid to the township treasurer to be used for the blind relief payments. Six years later, in 1904, the probate judge, rather than the township trustees, was authorized to certify the blind list to the commissioners. Those eligible to relief included all blind males more than twenty-one years and all females more than eighteen years of age who had no property or other means with which to support themselves. Not less than two citizens of the county, one of whom was required to be a physician selected by the court, were required to testify that each applicant had been a resident of Ohio for five years and a resident of the county for one year immediately preceding the filing of an application for relief. The probate judge was required to register the name and address of the applicant entitled to benefits, and issue to each beneficiary a certificate giving his name, address, and the amount to be drawn. (97 O. L. 392-394.)

Although the act of 1904 was declared unconstitutional for the reason that it required the expenditure for a private purpose of public funds raised by taxation (*Auditor of Lucas County* v *The State*, 75 O. S. 114-137), the act of 1908 eliminated the constitutional obstacles. This act provided for the levying of stipulated tax by the county commissioners for the purpose of creating a fund for the relief of the needy blind, and authorized the probate judge to appoint a blind relief commission. This commission, consisting of three members appointed for a three-year term, was directed to meet annually in the office of the county commissioners to examine the list of applicants properly filed in the order of filing in a book furnished by the county commissioners. Benefits to applicants were not to exceed $150 per annum, and were to be made quarterly. (99 O. L. 56-58.)

After being in operation for five years, this commission was abolished by the legislature in 1913 and its powers and duties were transferred to the county commissioners. (103 O. L. 60.) In the examination of any applicant for blind relief, determined, upon evidence furnished by a registered physician or surgeon, that the individual might have such a disability benefitted or removed by the proper surgical operation or medical treatment, and such a person entitled to relief filed his consent or such a treatment in writing, the commissioners were authorized to expend all or a part of a year's allowance for this purpose.

Six years later, in 1919, the commissioners were authorized to appoint such clerks as they might deem necessary to investigate the applications filed for relief. These clerks, known as "blind relief clerks," served at the pleasure of the county commissioners. (108 O. L. pt. i, 451-422.) The maximum benefits to applicants fixed at $150 in 1913 was increased to $200 in 1919 and to $400 in 1927. In the event both husband and wife were blind and both had made application for relief, the maximum to be paid was fixed at $600. (103 O. L. 60; 109 O. L. pt. i, 421; 112 O. L. 109.)

When in April 1936, the state of Ohio accepted the provisions of the Social Security Act (approved August 14, 1935) providing for federal grants to the states for aid to the blind, the Ohio commission of the blind was designated by the legislature has the state agency for administering the act. The county commissioners, who, in the past had been directed by the legislature to care for the blind, were made the agency for administering the act in the county. The commissioners were directed to appropriate from the general fund of the county a sufficient amount, when supplemented by federal and state grants, to provide for needy blind people a subsistence "comparable with decency and health." In the event the county commissioners failed to make such appropriations, the attorney general was directed to bring *mandamus* proceedings against them.

The act provides that any person not less than eighteen or more than sixty-five years of age who has lost his sight while a resident of the state and has resided in the state for a period of five years during the nine years immediately preceding the filing of the application for assistance, the last year of which shall have been continuous, are entitled to benefits under the act.

Applications for blind relief are filed with the county commissioners, who, by statute, are required to list such claims in books kept for that purpose in order of filing. At least ten days prior to any action on a claim, a person making applications for blind relief files with the commissioners a duly certified statement of the fact. No claims are granted by the commissioners until they receive from a registered position "skilled in disease of the eye" a certificate explaining to what extent the applicant's vision is impaired, and evidence in writing from two reputable citizens that they know the applicant to be blind, and that "he has the qualifications to entitle him to the relief asked." The commissioners may allow the examining position a fee not to exceed three dollars. They may likewise employ a registered physician to reexamine the applicant.

If, after such an inquiry, the commissioners are satisfied that the applicant is entitled to relieve, they are directed by statute to issue an order for such a sum as the board finds necessary, not to exceed $400 per annum, to be paid monthly from the fund created for such a purpose. In the event both husband and wife are blind and have made application for relief, the total relief allowance by the commission must not exceed $600 per annum. Again, as in 1913, the commissioners were authorized, upon finding that any applicant for blind relief might have his disability benefitted or removed by the proper surgical operation or medical treatment, to expend all or part of a year's allowance for such a purpose. Persons whose applications are denied by the commissioners may appeal to the Ohio commission of the blind, which may, upon its own motion, revise any decision of the county commissioners.

Both the county commissioners and the Ohio commission for the blind have power to issue subpoenas, compel the production of papers, and examine witnesses. At least once a year, and oftener if directed by the Ohio commission of the blind, the county commissioners must examine the qualifications, disabilities, and needs of all persons on the blind lists, and they may increase or decrease the amount of relief, according to the budgetary requirements within the fixed limits established by law. However, if a person is removed from such list, the commissioners are required to notify the county auditor and the Ohio commission of the blind as to their actions. (116 O. L. pt. ii, 195-200.) Blind relief records are open to the inspection of the public.

All records are located in the blind relief office, Central Parkway and Wade Streets, first floor, southeast corner.

695. MINUTES
1933—, 4 volumes (1-4).
Minutes of blind relief commission showing application number, date, action taken, and amount allowed; also financial statement of moneys received and disbursed. Chronologically arranged. No index. Typed. Volumes average 200 pages. 16 x 14 x 2.

696. ACTIVE CASES
1920—. 4 file boxes (A-Z).
Active cases where relief has been allowed showing name, address, case history, amount, also dates of payments. Alphabetically arranged by names of recipients. No index. Typed on printed forms. 26 x 16 x 16.

697. CANCELLED CASES
1920—. 4 file boxes (A-Z).'
Records of cases for payment was refused or discontinued showing name, address, Dave, case history, and cause for refusal or discontinuous. Alphabetically arranged by names of recipients. No index. Typed on printed forms. 26 x 16 x 16.

698. CORRESPONDENCE
1923—. 1 file box.
Incoming and outgoing official correspondence relative to blind relief. Alphabetically arranged by names of correspondents. No index. Handwritten and typed. 26 x 16 x 16.

Old age pensions, although well known in Europe at the end of the nineteenth and beginning of the twentieth century and in a few American States during the same period, were not provided for in Ohio until recently. (Arthur Lyon Cross, *A Shorter History of England and Greater Britain*, New York, 1925, 746-747; J. Salwyn Schapiro, *Modern and Contemporary European History 1815-1925.* New York, 1923, 295.) During the depression years the sight of thousands of aged persons who had lost their homes and savings, and as a result of such losses faced starvation, touched the sensibilities of Ohioans. Accordingly, in 1933, an "Old Age Pension" law, proposed by initiative petition, was voted upon at the general election of that year providing for the granting of aid to the aged in Ohio under certain conditions. The law was adopted by a majority of the electors voting thereon. (115 O. L. pt. ii, 431-439.) The act, as amended in 1936, provides, among other things, that any person sixty-five years of age or upward (unless confined in any penal or corrective institution or the state hospital) who is a citizen of the United States, who has resided in Ohio not less than five years during the nine prior to making application for aid, and who has resided in the county for application for aid is made, for one year is eligible to receive a pension, providing his income from all and every source does not exceed $360 per year. (116 O. L. pt. ii, 1st s. sess. H. 605; 116 O. L. pt. ii, s. sess. H. 558.) Moreover the applicant must be unable to support himself, and have no husband, wife, child, or other person who is legally responsible for his support. (115 O. L. pt. ii, 431-439.) In addition to this, the net value of all real and personal property of the unmarried applicant, less all incumbrances and liens, must not exceed $3,000; if the applicant is married the net value of the property of husband or wife shall not exceed $4,000. (*Ibid.*, 431-439.) It may be required that such property, as condition precedent to payment of aid, be transferred to the division of aid for the aged in trust. This provision does not, however, prohibit the applicant or his wife from occupying such property during their lifetime.

For the purposes of administering the old age pension law there was created in the state department of public welfare a division of aid for the aged. The chief of the division of the aid for the aged, appointed by the director of public welfare with the approval of the governor, is authorized to appoint all necessary assistants, clerks, stenographers, and other employees and fix their salaries, subject to approval of the director of public welfare. (*Ibid.*, 431-439.)

In each county the commissioners constitute a board for administering this act. However, if the commissioners, by a majority vote, decline to serve in such a capacity, the state director is authorized, with the consent of the director of public welfare, to appoint a board consisting of three to five members, who, like the commissioners, serve without compensation. The local boards are required to keep such reports as the division may prescribe, and are also authorized to employ, subject to the approval of the division, such investigators, clerks, and other employees as are necessary for the performance of its duties. (115 O. L. pt. ii, 431-439.)

Applications for relief are made annually to the local board. Each applicant is thoroughly investigated. In its investigations the local board is not bound by common law or statutory rules of evidence, but is authorized to make inquiries in such a manner as seem "best calculated to conform to substantial justice." For the purpose of its investigations, each county board has the power to compel the attendance and testimony of witnesses. Decisions of the local boards may be appealed to the division. (*Ibid.*, 431-439.)

After the applicants have been investigated by the local board, "certificates of aid" are granted to persons entitled to relief and conformity with the provisions of the law. Each certificate containing the applicant's name and the pension allowed, as well as the records pertaining to the investigation, is forwarded to the division. The division may approve, modify, or reject the certificate and findings of the board. (*Ibid.*, 435.)

Under the provisions of this act the state became the general guardian of public and private welfare. The pension system relieves the increasing burdens place upon county homes, which, even under the most favorable conditions, are a poor substitute for homes. Although $2,625,000 was appropriated by the legislature for old age pensions in the early part of 1935, the cost to the public in the long run, should not be much greater than that of the antiquated system of support in charitable institutions (116 O. L. 510.)

All records are located in the aid for the aged office, sixth floor, 704 Race Street, Cincinnati, Ohio.

699. APPLICATIONS FOR AID
1934—. 20 file cabinets.

Applications made by agent persons for aid giving name and address, date of birth, insurance, debts, property holdings, statements as to Residents and citizenship; also date in case number. Alphabetically arranged by names of applicants. No index. Typed. 48 x 24 x 12.

700. GENERAL FILING SYSTEM (Case Records)
1934—. 1 file cabinet.

Records name, address, and age of applicants; name of caseworker, and date assigned for investigation; also date approved and amount granted. Alphabetically arranged by names of applicants. No index. Typed. 48 x 24 x 12.

701. CASE WORKERS' INDIVIDUAL RECORDS
1934—. 1 file cabinet.

Records name, address, age, and relatives of applicant, data application, date case assigned, remarks of caseworker, grant (if any), and amount. Alphabetically arranged by names of clients. No index. Typed. 48 x 24 x 12.

702. REPORTS OUT-OF-TOWN INVESTIGATIONS
1934—. 1 file cabinet.

Detailed reports from other counties on applications showing names of relatives interviewed and reports of out-of-state agencies. Alphabetically arranged by names of states and counties. No index. Typed. 48 x 24 x 12.

703. PENDING CASES
1934—. 1 file cabinet.

Records of cases not yet assigned for investigation, check for insurance adjustments, and preliminary reports. Alphabetically arranged by names of applicants. No index. 48 x 24 x 12.

704. CLOSED CASES
1934——. 1 file cabinet.
Complete records of cases rejected and closed. Numerically arranged by case numbers. No index. Typed. 48 x 24 x 12.

705. MONTHLY STATISTICS
1934——. 1 file cabinet.
Multigraphed sheets giving number of cases investigated during each month, number of cases in process of Investigation, number of continuations, number of rejections, number of miles traveled by investigators, number of visits made, number of workers assigned, and amount of postage used. Chronologically arranged. No index. Typed. 48 x 24 x 12.

Aid to dependent children, although provided for it by the Ohio legislature in 1913 in the form of mothers' pensions, assumed a new significance when, in April 1936, the Ohio legislature accepted the provisions of the Social Security Act. With the acceptance of the act, the sections of the General Code (1683-2 - 1-683-10) relative to mothers' pensions were repealed.

The administration of the act in the state is delegated to the department of public welfare through the division of charities. The state department was authorized to prescribe forms, certificates, reports, records, and accounts to be kept by the local departments.

The administration of the act in the counties is placed in the hands of the juvenile judge or judge of the court of domestic relations, except in counties in which, by charter or by law, the powers were vested in or imposed upon "a county department, board or commission, or officer other than the juvenile judge." When he serves in the capacity of county administrator, the juvenile judge is directed to utilize the services of the employees of the court exercising juvenile jurisdiction. The act did not affect the status of any employee of the juvenile court who had qualifications under the rules and regulations of the civil service commission. In the performance of his duties the judge is authorized to compel the attendance of witnesses and of the production of books, and may institute contempt proceedings against persons refusing to testify. Otherwise, powers conferred upon a judge are administrative powers only

Those entitled to aid under the act include, among others, a child residing in the state less than sixteen years of age who has been deprived of parental support or care by reason of death, continued absence of a parent, or mental or physical incapacity of a parent. However a child more than sixteen but less than eighteen years of age may receive aid at the discretion of the county administration.

Applications for aid are made to the juvenile court by the parent or a relative with whom the child must be living. Before aid is granted, a careful examination of the home is made by the employees of the juvenile court. If the child is found to be eligible, the court may grant such amount as is deemed proper. The amount of aid payable to any child is determined on the basis of actual needs, "and shall," according to the statute, "be sufficient to provide support, and care requisite for health and decency." In the event aid is granted, the home of such a child must be visited four times during each year. Each month, the county auditor issues warrants upon the county treasurer for the payment of the warrants certified by the court. The decisions of the juvenile judge are subject to abrogation or modification by the department of public welfare. Any person attempting to receive aid on behalf of any child not entitled to such aid is deemed guilty of a misdemeanor and upon conviction may be punished by fine or imprisonment or both.

The provisions of the act are financed by federal, state, and local funds. The county commissioners are required, each year, to include in the annual tax budget and amount not less than that computed to yield a levy of fifteen one-hundredths of one mill on each dollar of the general tax list of the county. If the commissioners fail to comply with the provisions of the act relating to appropriations, the state department of public welfare is directed to request the attorney general to institute *mandamus* proceedings against them. (G. C. secs. 1359-31 -1359-45; 116 O. L. pt. ii, 188-195.)

All records are located in County Courthouse, Room 224.

706. APPLICATIONS FOR AID
1936—. 1 volume.
Applications for aid for dependent children showing name, address, date, and name of caseworker. Chronologically arranged. Alphabetical index by names of applicants in front of each volume. Typed on printed forms. 12 x 10 x 4.

707. APPLICATIONS ALLOWED
1914—. 1 volumes. (1-2).
Records name of applicant, address, case number, date investigated, caseworker's report, and amount of relief. Alphabetically arranged by names of applicants. No index. Handwritten. Volumes average 400 pages. 14 x 12 x 4.

708. POSTPONED OR REJECTED APPLICATIONS
1936—. 2 file boxes.
Record of date, case number, caseworker's report, and recommendation. Alphabetically arranged by names of applicants. No index. Typed on printed forms. 12 x 16 x 26.

709. CASE WORKERS' REPORTS
1936—. 5 file boxes.
Caseworkers' reports on all cases investigated showing data application, time of investigation, and recommendations. Alphabetically arranged by names of case workers. No index. Handwritten and typed. 12 x 16 x 26.

710. RECORD OF MOTHERS' AND CHILDREN'S AID
1921—. 20 file boxes.
Record of mothers and children receiving aid showing name of recipient, address, date, case history, and amount of relief. Alphabetically arranged by names of parents. No index. Handwritten and typed. 12 x 16 x 26.

711. MOTHERS' PENSIONS CANCELLED
1914—. 2 volumes (1-2).
Record of date, case number, and cause of cancellation. Alphabetically arranged by names of pensioners. No index. Handwritten. Volumes average 400 pages. 12 x 10 x 4.

712. PSYCHOLOGISTS' TESTS
1936—. 1 file box.
Complete report of mental tests of children receiving aid showing date of test, and report of examiner. Alphabetically arranged by names of children. No index. Typed. 26 x 16 x 32.

713. LEDGER
1921—. 1 volume.
Record of active cases of children receiving aid showing name of child and parents, address, date, and amount of relief. Numerically arranged by case numbers. No index. Handwritten. 600 pages. 14 x 12 x 6.

714. EXECUTIVE CORRESPONDENCE
1914—. 4 file boxes.
Correspondence of executive nature and case workers reports. Alphabetically arranged by names of correspondence and case workers. No index. Handwritten and typed. 52 x 26 x 16.

715. HAMILTON COUNTY MAP
1936. 1 map.

Shows roads, rivers, transportation lines, cities, villages, and townships. Prepared and published by A. C. Wagner Publishing Company, Cincinnati, Ohio. Lithographed, colored. No scale. 50 x 36.

716. GREATER CINCINNATI MAP
1936. 1 map.

Shows streets, Alice, subdivisions, public parks, and transportation lines. Prepared and published by A. C. Wagner Publishing Company, Cincinnati, Ohio. Lithographed, colored. No scale. 50 x 36.

The responsibility for supervising and conducting elections in the county is placed in hands of state deputy supervisors of elections or the county board of elections. This board, consisting of four qualified voters in the county, is appointed for a four-year term by the secretary of state, who, by virtue of his office, is the chief election official of the state. On the first Monday in March in the even-numbered years, the secretary of state appoints two board members, one of whom is from the political party which cast the highest number of votes in the state for the office of governor at the last preceding state election, and the other from the political party which cast the next highest vote at such election. (G. C. sec. 4785-8. For the method of appointment when the term of each of the four members of the board expires on the same date see G. C. sec. 4758-8a.) The board members may be removed by the secretary of state for the neglect of duty, malfeasance, misfeasance in office; for willful violation of election laws; or for other good and sufficient causes. (G. C. sec. 7585-11.) The compensation of the members is determined on the basis of population of the county and is paid by the county. (G. C. sec. 4785-18.) Similarly the expenses of the county board are paid from the county treasury, "in pursuance of appropriations by the county commissioners," in the same manner as other expenses are paid. (G. C. sec. 4785-20.)

The person's so appointed by the secretary, meeting five days after their appointment, select as chairman one of their members, who presides at the meetings, and as clerk a resident electorate of the county other than a member of the board. (G. C. sec. 4785-10.) The board is vested with authority to establish, define, and provide election precincts; fix places of registration; provide for the purchase, preservation, and maintenance of voting booths, ballot boxes, books, maps, flags, blanks, cards of instruction, and other equipment used in registration. (G. C. sec. 4785-13.) The board is authorized, further, to issue rules, regulations, and instructions consistent with the law or contrary to the rules and regulations as established by the chief election official. (G. C. sec. 4785-13.)

Besides providing places of voting and equipment, the board is authorized to appoint clerks and other officers of elections. On or before the first day of September before each November election the board by a majority vote is authorized, after careful examination and investigation as to their qualifications, to appoint for each precinct six "competent persons, for as judges and two as clerks, who shall constitute the election officers of such precinct." Not more than two of the judges and one of the clerks, states the law, "shall be members of the same political party." Precinct election officers, appointed for a one-year term, maybe removed by the board for neglect of duty, malfeasance, or misconduct in office. (G. C. sec. 4785-25.)

The board is authorized to receive and examine and certify the sufficiency and validity of nominating petitions. They receive the election returns, canvass the returns, then make abstracts therefrom and transmit to the proper authorities. They issue certificates of elections on forms prescribed by the secretary of state and report annually to the same official, on forms prescribed by him, the number of voters registered, elections held, votes cast, and such other information as the secretary of state may require. More over, the board prepares and submits to the proper authorities a budget estimating the cost of elections for the ensuing year. (G. C. sec. 4788-13.)

Finally, the board is empowered to investigate irregularities, non performance of duty, or violation of election laws by election officials. For the purpose of conducting investigations they may administer oaths, issue subpoenas, some in witnesses, and compel the presentation of books, papers, and records in connection with any investigation and report the facts to the prosecuting attorney. (G. C. sec. 4785-13.)

(The Secretary of State, in 1930, ruled that the members of the various Boards of Elections were to be considered as state officers. This had reference to appointments made under section 4785-8a of the General Code. See *Supplement to Page's Annotated General Code 1926-1935*, George C. Trautwein, ed. Cincinnati, 1935, note, page 688.)

All records are located in the board of elections office, first floor, 622 Sycamore Street, Cincinnati, Ohio.

717. MINUTES OF BOARD OF ELECTIONS
1910—. 15 volumes.
Minutes of meetings on the board of elections. Chronologically arranged. No index. Handwritten and typed. Volumes average 250 pages. 16 x 14 x 3.

718. REGISTRATION LIST
1930—. 554 volumes.
Complete list of registered voters in Cincinnati, Norwood, and St. Bernard. Numerically arranged by ward numbers; also alphabetically arranged by precincts. No index. Handwritten and typed. Volumes average 250 pages. 14 x 11.5 x 3.

719. MASTER INDEX OF VOTERS
1930—. 3,588 file boxes.
Kardex master index system of all registered voters in Cincinnati, Norwood, and St. Bernard. Alphabetically arranged by names of voters. No index. Handwritten on printed forms. 25 x 8 x 1.

720. COPY LIST OF QUALIFIED VOTERS
October 5, 1936. 1 volume.
Printer's copy of registered voters qualified to vote in 1936 election. Numerically arranged by wards; also alphabetically arranged by precincts and names of voters. No index. 33 pages. 14 x 10 x 4.

721. TRANSFER CARDS FILE
1935—. 13 file boxes.
Transfer cards of registered voters showing change of residence. Chronologically arranged; also alphabetically arranged by names of voters. No index. Handwritten on printed forms. 25 x 13 x 6.

722. SIGNATURE BOOKS
1936. 683 volumes.
Books showing signature and address of each voter who voted in the 1936 election; also names of judges of election and of witnesses and challengers. Numerically arranged by ward numbers; also alphabetically arranged by precincts. No index. Handwritten. Volumes average 28 pages. 14 x 9 x 1.

723. DEAD FILE
1930—. 65 file boxes.
Registration cards of voters who failed to vote for two consecutive years; also voters deceased, disfranchised by court decree, and those certified to hospital for insane. Alphabetically arranged by names of voters. No index. Handwritten on printed forms. 25 x 12 x 12.

724. COPIES OF NATURALIZATION PAPERS
1908—. 7 volumes.
Copies of naturalization papers filed with board of elections by naturalized citizens. Chronologically arranged. Typed on printed forms. Volumes average 500 pages. 14 x 10 x 6.

725. ABSTRACT OF VOTES
1908—. 20 volumes.
Results of votes polled in cities, villages, and county at all elections. Numerically arranged by wards; also alphabetically arranged by precincts. No index. Blueprint. Volumes average 200 pages. 29 x 28 x 2.

726. PETITIONS
1934—. 6 file boxes.
Petitions filed by candidates seeking political offices showing date and office sought; also names and addresses of voters signing petitions. Alphabetically arranged by names of petitioners. No index. 14 x 8.5 x 6.

In view of repeated requests made by the county commissioners and various other officers of Hamilton County that the state civil service commission exercise more direct supervision over the personnel of Hamilton County, theretofore an impossibility, because the staff and the organization of the commission were limited by appropriation and therefore unable to administer properly the civil service laws with respect to Hamilton County service, it became highly desirable that a more satisfactory plan, be inaugurated and put into practical application. At a number of conferences held by the state civil service commission with the Hamilton County commissioners and the state director of finance, it was determined that this commission would add to its organization a part-time examiner and a part-time secretary to the examiner, and that, as a matter of convenience, they would be located in Hamilton County.

With the arrangement approved by the commissioners of Hamilton County, the state civil service commission appointed an examiner from the eligible list for the position, and the commissioners appointed the examiner as assistant clerk to their board. A secretary to the examiner was likewise appointed, and both appointments were made effective June 15, 1932.

The local division of the state civil service commission was established under provisions of the civil service act of Ohio, passed March 24, 1935, which, amending the original section 486-5 of the General Code, authorizes the state commission to establish such local offices for the more efficient administration of the state civil service law. (111 O. L. 56.)

Since its establishment karma this office has handled all civil service affairs in Hamilton County. All matters affecting recruiting, classification of positions, pay schedules, personnel, procedure, records, and examinations have been treated locally.

727. APPLICATIONS
1932—. 35 file boxes (A-Z).

Application papers of all persons registering for civil service examinations. Alphabetically arranged by names of applicants. No index. Handwritten. 13 x 11 x 5. County Courthouse, Room 559.

728. EXAMINATION PAPERS
1932—. 1 file box.

Examination papers of all persons examined for civil service positions. Alphabetically arranged by names of examinees. No index. Handwritten and typed. 78 x 36 x 15. County Courthouse, basement.

729. EXAMINATION RECORDS
1932—. 1 volumes.

Records names of all persons examined for civil service positions. Chronologically arranged. No index. Typed. 200 pages. 24 x 18 x 2. County Courthouse, Room 559.

730. MISCELLANEOUS EXAMINATION MATERIAL
1932—. 6 file boxes.

Miscellaneous materials from which examination questions are drawn. Numerically arranged by code numbers. No index. Typed. 25 x 15 x 11. County Courthouse, Room 559.

731. REPORTS OF APPOINTMENTS
1932—. 1 file box.

Card record of all appointments under civil service. Alphabetically arranged by names of departments. No index. Typed. 15 x 6 x 5. County Courthouse, Room 559.

732. INDEX TO COUNTY EMPLOYEES
n. d. (current). 2 file boxes.

Current card index to all persons employed by county including civil service and noncivil service employees. Alphabetically arranged by names of employees. No index. Typed. 15 x 6 x 5. County Courthouse, Room 559.

733. COUNTY PAYROLL

1932—. 40 file boxes.

Kardex system giving names of all county employees approved by civil service commission and amount of payroll. Alphabetically arranged by names of departments. No index. Typed. 24 x 10 x 1. County Courthouse, Room 559.

734. CORRESPONDENCE

1932—. 2 file boxes.

General correspondence of civil service commission. Alphabetically arranged by subjects. No index. Handwritten and typed. 25 x 15 x 11. County Courthouse, Room 559.

The office of county surveyor, another English institution transplanted to America during the colonial period, became an important office in frontier Ohio where land titles and boundary lines were often in dispute. The office is purely a creature of statute, there being no constitutional provision for its establishment.

The first act of the general assembly pertaining to the surveyor was passed during the first legislative session of 1803. Under this act the court of common pleas was authorized to appoint a person well qualified to act as county surveyor. He received his commission from the governor, was required to give bond conditioned for the faithful performance of the duties of his office, and was directed to survey all lands which were sold or were to be sold for taxes. The surveyor was authorized to appoint chainmen or markers whose function it was to establish corners. The surveys made by the surveyor or his deputies were the only ones to be accepted as legal evidence in any court of law or equity. For remuneration, the surveyor was permitted to retain all fees collected by him in the operation of his office. (1 O. L. 90-93.)

Although it made no fundamental change in the duties of the surveyor, the act of 1816 fixed his term of office at five years; authorized him to appoint deputies, and made him responsible for their official acts. Moreover he was made liable to removal by the court for negligence or incompetency, and was made liable to a suit by persons believing themselves damaged by his negligence or the negligence of his deputies. (14 O. L. 424-425.) A year later, in 1817, provision was made for the appointment of a successor in the event the office became vacant because of death, resignation, or removal. (15 O. L. 65.)

The act of 1831 consolidated the previous acts, redefined the duties of the surveyor, increased the amount of his bond, and authorized him, when directed by the county commissioners, to procure from the surveyor general's office a "certified plat, together with the field notes of corners, and bearing trees to each section, quarter section, lot, or original survey in his county, and cause the same to be preserved in a book by him provided for that purpose which shall be deposited in the county auditor's office, for the use of the landholders in the county." It provided further, that the surveyor should keep "a fair and accurate record of all official surveys made by himself or by his deputies," in a suitable book to be kept by him for that purpose, and that he should number his surveys progressively. (29 O. L. 402.) More significant, however, was the fact that the office was made elective for a three-year term by the act of 1831. The term remained at three years until 1906 when it was to be reduced to a two-year period. (*Ibid.*, 399; 98 O. L. 245-247.)

During the years of the development of the office other duties have been delegated to the surveyor. Thus, in 1842 he was given the duty of ascertaining and reporting trespassing on public lands. (40 O. L. 57.) Ten years later, he was given the same powers as the justices of the peace to take and certify deeds, mortgages, powers of attorney, and other instruments affecting real estate, to administer oaths, and to take and certify affidavits. (52 O. L. 70.) In 1867 he was given authority, when directed by the county commissioners, to transcribe any at all dilapidated maps, records of plats, and field notes of surveys in other counties. (64 O. L. 216-217; 78 O. L. 258.) Similarly, in 1881, he was authorized to procure from any office in the state a certified plat together with the field notes of corners, quarter sections, lots, or original surveys and place them in a book provided for that purpose. Certified copies from his book were to be taken as *prima facie* evidence. (29 O. L. 399; 78 O. L. 285.)

With the increase in modern means of transportation, there developed a growing need for more efficient methods of road construction and maintenance. Accordingly, in 1906, the surveyor was directed to act, whenever the services of an engineer were required, in the capacity of an engineer with respect to roads, turnpikes, bridges, or ditches, except in cities of the first grade. (98 O. L. 245-247.) He was directed by statute to perform all duties in his county which would be done by a civil engineer or surveyor, to prepare all plans, specifications, and estimates of cost, and to submit forms to contracts for the construction and repair of all bridges, culverts, roads, draws, ditches, and other public improvements (except building) over which the county commissioners had authority. At the same time, he was made responsible for the inspection of all public improvements, and was directed to keep a complete list of all estimates and bids received for such work, as well as of contracts awarded for improvement. (*Ibid.*, O. L. 245-247.)

Similarly, another measure, enacted in 1919, increased the duties of the surveyor regarding road construction and road maintenance. Under this act the surveyor was authorized to designate one of his deputies as maintenance engineer. This engineer, under the direction of the surveyor, was to have charge of all "road maintenance and repair work" in his county. Furthermore, when authorized by the county commissioners, the surveyor was to appoint a maintenance supervisor or supervisors to have charge of the maintenance of improved highways within a district or districts established by the commissioners for surveyor, and containing not less than ten miles of improved country roads. (108 O. L. pt. i, 497.) Four years later, the surveyor was given the additional duty of assisting the county planning commission. (110 O. L. 312.)

Thus the general responsibility of planning and directing county road construction is vested, by statute, in the county surveyor. Because of this increased responsibility placed on this office there has been an attempt to raise the general qualifications of those seeking election to it. Accordingly, in 1935, an act was passed changing the title of the office to that of "county engineer," and eligibility to the office was restricted to "professional and registered surveyors listed to practice in the state of Ohio." (116 O. L. 283.) This act was amended in 1936 to permit the incumbent to continue in office upon reelection, regardless of a lack of these qualifications.

General Office Division

Records for the general office division are located in the County Courthouse, Room 225.

735. COUNTY ROAD CONSTRUCTION AND REPAIR CONTRACTS
1891-1934. 565 boxes (labeled by names of townships and road numbers). Specification number, type of work to be done, date of completion, final cost, name of contractor, estimate book and page number, and field book number. Numerically arranged by road numbers. Handwritten on printed forms. 16 x 10.5 x 4.5.

For subsequent records see entry 737.

736. INDEX TO COUNTY ROAD CONSTRUCTION AND REPAIR CONTRACTS
1891-1934, 20 file boxes (labeled by names of townships and road numbers).
Index listing names of township and road, beginning and ending of road, general direction of road, progress and description of work, date contract was let, contract number, date of completion, and cost. Alphabetically arranged by names of townships; also numerically arranged by road numbers. Handwritten on printed forms. 19 x 7 x 5.

For index to subsequent records see entry 738.

737. COUNTY ROAD CONSTRUCTION AND REPAIR CONTRACTS

1935—. 11 file boxes (labeled by names of villages, roads, and townships). Contracts listing specification, proposition, emergency, force account, road, and bridge numbers; also date awarded, date bond was signed, time allowance, date notified, time of expiration, extensions of time, assignment, page and volume numbers of county commissioners' minutes (entry 1), bridge fund number, work and material items, engineer's estimate of total cost, name of inspector, cost of inspection, previous estimates, total deductions, amount paid contractor, type of work, names of bitters, total bids as perform, and township and bridge fund numbers. Numerically arranged by road numbers. Handwritten on printed forms. 26 x 16 x 10.5.

For prior records see entry 735.

738. INDEX TO COUNTY ROAD CONSTRUCTION AND REPAIR CONTRACTS

1935—. 1 file of 5 shutters. Index listing name of township, name and number of road, and remarks. Alphabetically arranged by names of townships. Handwritten. 21 x 6.5.

For index to prior records see entry 736.

739. STATE HIGHWAY CONSTRUCTION RECORD

1929—. 3 file boxes (2 file boxes, 6-46; 1 file box labeled Final). Record initiated 1929. Record listing name of road, specification and force account numbers, name and address of contractor, volume and page numbers of county commissioners' minutes entry one, fund number, items, engineer's estimate, name of an inspector, cost of inspection, inspector's weekly report, amount retained, previous estimates, contractor's estimate, amount paid contractor, date received, date referred to county surveyor with authority to employ necessary labor, labor teams, material, date of engineer's estimate of materials, items, quantity, unit measure and cost, fund available, date contract was let, date referred for computation, computation report, total cost is per bids, and remarks. Numerically arranged by contract numbers. No index. Handwritten on printed forms. 24 x 16 x 10.5.

740. WPA CONTRACTS AND RECEIPTS
1936—. 1 file box.
Records cost of painting road and street markers, cost of road relocation jobs, stream pollution and sewer projects. Alphabetically arranged by project titles. No index. Handwritten on printed forms. 24 x 16 x 10.5.

741. HAMILTON COUNTY PURCHASE ORDERS
1933—. 1 file box. Prior records missing.
Records type and amount of material purchased, cost of material, unit price, total cost, and name and location of department for which purchase was made. Alphabetically arranged by names of firms supply and material. No index. Handwritten on printed forms. 24 x 16 x 10.5.

742. WPA PURCHASE ORDERS
1935—. 2 file boxes
Records cost of material and labor on WPA projects, project number, supervisory cost, itemized material purchases, cost of teams, trucks, heavy equipment, local cash expenditures, and other local expenditures. Chronologically arranged. No index. Handwritten on printed forms. 24 x 16 x 10.5.

743. CWA, FERA, WPA, MISCELLANEOUS RECORD
1933—. 2 file boxes.
Record of applications for road improvements, estimates of repair costs, job classification, finished projects, and projects underway. Numerically arranged by project numbers. No index. Handwritten on printed forms. 24 x 16 x 10.5.

744. DISTRIBUTION LEDGER
1919—. 3 volumes.
Records distribution of road repair cost, cost of engineering (a - equipment, b - maintenance) in Western Cheviot, Woodlawn, Eastern, and Sanitary divisions, total cost, voucher number, kind of material, and from whom purchased. Chronologically arranged. No index. Handwritten on printed forms. Volumes average 350 pages. 25 x 14.5 x 2.25.

745. CONTRACTORS' ACCOUNTS

1880-1911. 3 volumes. Subsequent records missing.
Records name of township, date of contract, section number, amount of contract, type of work, and name of contractor. Chronologically arranged. Alphabetical index by names of contractors in front of each volume. Handwritten on printed forms. Volumes average 200 pages. 14 x 10.5 x 1.5.

746. MISCELLANEOUS RECORD OF BILLS AND RECEIPTS

1931—. 1 file box. Prior records missing.
Records cost of gasoline, car tests, petty cash, voucher quotations for engineer's supplies, and sundry costs. Chronologically arranged. No index. Handwritten on printed forms. 24 x 16 x 10.5.

747. ROAD AND BRIDGE FUND ACCOUNT

1911—. 2 volumes.
Records road fund number, date, file number, terms of agreement, volume and page numbers of county commissioners' minutes, type of work, name of contractor, estimate of material, cost, final date of voucher, amount saved, total amount paid out, balance, and remarks. Chronologically arranged. No index. Handwritten on printed forms. Volumes average 200 pages. 15 x 11 x 1.

748. WEEKLY PAYROLL

1892-1907. 5 volumes (1-5). Discontinued.
Records name of county employee, type of work, number of days worked, amount of wages per day, total amount of wages per week, signatures of employee and clerk, total amount of weekly payroll, and date of payment. Chronologically arranged. No index. Handwritten on printed forms. Volumes average 200 pages. 13.5 x 12.5 x 1.25.

749. STATE HIGHWAY LETTERS, COMPLAINTS AND PAYROLLS

1929—. 1 file box.
Records general complaints on conditions of state highways, correspondence pertaining there too, and amounts paid to individuals for construction and repair highways. Alphabetically arranged by names of roads. No index. Handwritten and typed. 24 x 16 x 10.5.

750. ROAD AND BRIDGE DAY BOOK

1918—. 1 volume. Record initiated in 1918.

Records road maintenance fun number, date, file number, terms of agreement, volume and page numbers of county commissioners' minutes (entry 1, type of material, name of contractor, estimate of cost, date of voucher, amount paid, amount saved, remarks, and balance. No index. Handwritten on printed forms. 500 pages. 14.75 x 12 x 2.

751. ENGINEERS' AND INSPECTORS' WEEKLY REPORTS TO COUNTY COMMISSIONERS

1898-1899. 1 volume. Prior and subsequent records missing.

Miscellaneous reports on work completed each week. Chronologically arranged. No index. Handwritten on printed forms. 500 pages. 12 x 10 x 3.

752. GENERAL CORRESPONDENCE

1919—. 9 file boxes (4 file boxes labeled A-Z; 5 file boxes, 1-925).

General correspondence covering complaints, contracts, and completed work on roads, culverts, bridges, and sewers. Handwritten and typed. 24 x 16 x 10.5.

753. INDEX TO COMPLAINTS

1919—. 1 volume.

Index to complaints listing nature of complaint, name of complainant, to whom, date answered, and file number of complainant. Alphabetically arranged by names uptown chips: Bridge, and sewer numbers. Handwritten on printed forms. 800 pages. 12.75 x 10 x 4.

754. MISCELLANEOUS CORRESPONDENCE

1880-1911. 22 volumes (labeled chronologically). Discontinued.

Copies of miscellaneous letters from surveyor's office pertaining to road work. Alphabetically arranged by names of correspondents. No index. Handwritten. Volumes average 200 pages. 14 x 10.5 x 1.5.

755. HAMILTON COUNTY BLUEPRINT MAP
1935. 1 map.
Physical map showing roads, bridges, and culverts in Hamilton County. Prepared by county engineer. Blueprint. Scale, 1 inch equals 2,000 feet (Framed.) 48 x 72.

Sanitation Division

The sanitation division of the engineer's office was established under authority of General Code section 6612-1. The function of this division is to supervise the construction, repair, and maintenance of sewer and water lines, and the control and elimination of stream pollution throughout the county.

Records of this division are located in County Courthouse, Room 225.

756. SANITARY DEPARTMENT ACCOUNTS
1933——. 1 file box (A-R).
Records type and amount of materials purchased by department, quantity of units, unit price, total cost, from whom purchased, and order number. Alphabetically arranged by names of departments. No index. Handwritten on printed forms. 24 x 16 x 10.5

757. ASSESSMENT CARDS
1924——. 32 file boxes (1-149).
Records name and address of property owner, district and what numbers, amount of assessment, frontage, acreage, and total amount of assessment. Alphabetically arranged by names of property owners. No index. Handwritten on printed forms. 16 x 7 x 5.

758. CONSTRUCTION ORDERS (Y Branches, Sewers)
1924——. 4 file boxes (1-121).
Records name of street, location, grade, stake off of center line of water line, water line number, district number, office station, building station, crossovers, riser length and depth, total length, lots, and remarks. Numerically arranged by waterline numbers. No index. Handwritten on printed forms. 24.5 x 12.75 x 10.25.

759. CONSTRUCTION ORDERS (Y Branches, Water)
1924—. 2 file boxes.
Records name of street, location, grade, stake off of center line of water line, water line number, district number, office station, building station, crossovers, riser length and depth, total length, lots, and remarks. Numerically arranged by waterline numbers. No index. Handwritten on printed forms. 24.5 x 12.75 x 10.25.

760. DISTRICT LEGISLATION
1934—. 1 file box.
Records resolutions and ordinances of village councils pertaining to establishment of sewer and water districts and correspondence of county commissioners office relating thereto. Numerically arranged by district numbers. No index. Typed. 26 x 16.5 x 11.5.

761. FINANCE RECORD
1924—. 4 file boxes (labeling varies).
Financial accounts of sanitary division showing improvements, cost of labor, contracts, name of contractor, date work was done, and cost of office upkeep. Chronologically arranged. No index. Handwritten on printed forms. 26 x 16.5 x 11.25.

762. INSPECTOR'S LABOR CARDS
1924—. 1 file box.
Records distribution of labor hours, date, number of hours worked, name of inspector, location of project and type of work, classification of workers, distribution of machine hours, types of machines used, and start and finish of work. Alphabetically arranged by names of thoroughfares. No index. Handwritten on printed forms. 16 x 7 x 5.

763. INSPECTORS' MATERIAL CARDS
1924—. 2 file boxes.
Records type of work, number of workers' hours, number of machine hours, size of sewer, transfer of material from work station to location, quantity, purpose, and remarks. Alphabetically arranged by names of roads. No index. Handwritten on printed forms. 16 x 7 x 5.

764. PLANS FOR SEWERAGE
1924—. 43 volumes. (labeled by district numbers).
Records legislation by county commissioners authorizing sewer construction and extensions; also correspondence pertaining thereto. Chronologically arranged. Numerical index by district numbers in front of each volume. Typed. Volumes average 200 pages. 11.5 x 9.5 x 1.5.

765. PLANS FOR WATER LINE INSTALLATION
1924—. 29 volumes (labeled by district numbers).
Authorizing water main construction and extensions also correspondence pertaining thereto. Chronologically arranged. Numerical index by district numbers in front of each volume. Volumes average 200 pages. 11.5 x 9.5 x 1.5.

766. SEWER RECORD
1924—. 8 file boxes (1-121).
Records applications for construction and extensions of sewers, legislation of county commissioners pertaining thereto, amount of work done, name of contractor, engineer's estimate, material cost, labor cost, name of subdivision, street and section, location by district, work started, date of completion, and total cost. Chronologically arranged. Handwritten on printed forms. 26 x 16.5 x 11.25.

767. INDEX TO SEWER RECORD
1924—. 2 file boxes.
Index giving names of owners of property abutting on all water and sewer lines in county, recording properties served, location record, and water and sewer line numbers. Alphabetically arranged by names of property owners. Handwritten on printed forms. 18 x 8 x 5.

768. SEWER TAP PERMITS
1924—. 48 file boxes (1-9800).
Records sewer line number, permit number, name of property owner, and cost record. Numerically arranged by permit numbers. No index. Typed on printed forms. 16 x 10.5 x 4.5.

769. INSPECTORS' DAILY SEWER REPORT CARDS
1924—. 7 file boxes (1-118).

Records number of hours worked, date, weather conditions, name of contractor, sewer and district numbers, name of subdivision, number of men, description of work done, and names of foreman and inspector. Alphabetically arranged by names of thoroughfares; also numerically arranged by sewer numbers. No index. Handwritten on printed forms. 20 x 13.5 x 4.5.

770. STATUS OF MAINTENANCE RECORD AND CWA, PWA, FERA CORRESPONDENCE
1924—. 1 file box.

Sewer maintenance correspondence between sanitation division and county commissioners relative to cost of maintenance and correspondence pertaining to CWA, PWA, and FERA sewer projects. Alphabetically arranged by names of correspondents. No index. Handwritten and typed. 26 x 16.5 x 11.25.

771. WATER WORKS AND SEWAGE
1915-1935. 88 volumes.

Record of filtration and disposal system in general. Chronologically arranged. No index. Printed. Volumes average 100 pages. 11.5 x 8.5 x .25.

772. INSPECTORS' DAILY WATER LINE REPORT CARDS
1924—. 5 file boxes (1-178).

Records number of hours worked, weather conditions, name of contractor, water line and district numbers name of subdivision, name of foreman, number of men employed, number of machines, name of street, size of pipe, description of work done, and name of inspector. Alphabetically arranged by names of thoroughfares; also numerically arranged by waterline numbers. No index. Handwritten on printed forms. 20 x 13.25 x 4.5.

773. WATER LINE RECORD
1924—. 4 file boxes (1-149).

Records applications for water main installation, estimates of cost, location by district, work started and completed, name of contractor, material and labor cost, legislation by county commissioners to allow extensions and construction, names of subdivision and street, section, and total cost. Numerically arranged by sewer numbers. No index. Handwritten on printed forms. 26 x 16.5 x 11.25

774. WATER LINE CORRESPONDENCE
1924—. 2 file boxes (1-263).
Correspondence pertaining to legislative steps between sanitary division and county commissioners relative to water line construction. Numerically arranged by waterline numbers. No index. Typed. 26 x 16.5 x 11.25.

775. SEWER LOCATION RECORD
March 1936—. 353 maps.
Records location of sewers in Cincinnati and in Hamilton County, size of sewer, grades, and depths. Prepared by county engineer. Alphabetically and numerically arranged by key letters and numbers. Drawn on photostat maps. Scale, 1 inch equals 200 feet. 30 x 22.

776. INDEX MAP TO SEWER LOCATION RECORD
1936—. 1 map.
Key map index showing location, size, and grades of existing sewers in Hamilton County. This map will record capacity and volume flow of each sewer in Hamilton County when survey is completed. Alphabetically and numerically arranged by key letters A-Z shown horizontally from bottom to top on left margin. Numbers 1-26 vertically on bottom margin. Prepared by Carl Siegrist, county engineer's office. Hand drawn with portions in color recording progress of stream pollution survey. Scale, 1 inch equals 200 feet. 30 x 15.

777. INDEX TO SEWER GAUGING RECORD
July 1936—. 1 volume.
Index to entries 778-781 showing name and number of sewer, file reference, and chart. Alphabetically arranged by names of sewers; also numerically arranged by sewer numbers. Handwritten. 2 pages. 13 x 9 x .25.

778. TYPICAL WEEKLY SEWAGE FLOW CHARTS
July 1936—. 16 sheets (A-P).
Records sewage by hour and day, graphic flow in million gallons per day, maximum, minimum, average flow for typical weeks, sewer number, location, and

file references. Chronologically arranged. For index see entry 777. Handwritten on printed forms. 32 x 20.5.

779. SEWER GAUGING RECORD
July 1936—. 22 volumes (A-1 to P-7C).

Records gauge readings on individual sewers, sewer number, location, date and hour of readings, weather conditions, name of recorder, head in by inches and feet, cubic feet per second, rates per day in million gallons, rates in million gallons for five-, fifteen-, and thirty- minute intervals. Chronologically arranged. For index see entries 777. Handwritten on printed forms. Volumes average 100 pages. 11.5 x 9 x 2.

780. TYPICAL DAILY SEWER FLOW CHARTS
July 1936—. 16 volumes (A-P).

Records average minimum and maximum readings of sewer flow in million gallons per day. Chronologically arranged. For index see entry 777. Handwritten. Volumes average 50 pages. 13 x 9 x .5.

781. SEWER FLOW CHARTS
July 1936—. 120 sheets (A-1 to P-7C).

Records graphic flow of sewage by hour and day in million gallons per day, sewer number, location, and file reference. Numerically arranged by sewer numbers. For index see entry 777. Typed on printed forms. 32 x 20.5.

782. HAMILTON COUNTY SEWER SYSTEM MAP
1914—. 1 map.

Roller type commercial map of Hamilton County upon which is recorded the sewer system of the county and showing sections, sewers, districts by numbers, fractional range, estates and owners, streets, cemeteries, parks, railroads, suburbs, and villages. Prepared by J. A. Stewart and employees of sanitation division. Published by C. E. Stewart Company, Cincinnati, Ohio. Printed with districts and sewers in color. Scale, 1 inch equals 1,000 feet. 48 x 72.

783. HAMILTON COUNTY WATER DISTRIBUTION MAP
1914—. 1 map.

Roller type commercial map of Hamilton County upon which is recorded the water distribution system of the county and showing sections supplied with water, water tanks and their capacity, water mains and their size, district numbers, fractional ranges, estates and owners, streets, cemeteries, parks, railroads, suburbs, and villages. Prepared by J. A. Stewart and employees of sanitation division. Published by C. E. Stewart Company, Cincinnati, Ohio, printed with districts in color and water lines and mains in heavy ink. Scale, 1 inch equals 1,000 feet. 48 x 72.

784. MISCELLANEOUS CORRESPONDENCE AND CONTRACTS
1924—. 1 file box.

Correspondence between county commissioners and sanitary division, Village councils, and other county officials relative to sewer contracts and water distribution. Alphabetically arranged by subjects. No index. Handwritten and typed. 26 x 16.5 x 11.25.

Surveying Division

The surveying division, established by statute (G. C. 2788-1), is in charge of all surveys made under the supervision of the county engineer.

All records of this division are located in County Courthouse, Room 209.

785. HAMILTON COUNTY ATLAS
1869-1884. 3 volumes.

Records townships and villages of Hamilton County, section numbers, fractional ranges, townships of Ohio, and separate outline and railroad map of United States. Alphabetically arranged by names of townships. No index. Printed with sections in color. Prepared by county engineer's office. Published by C. O. Titus, Philadelphia, Pennsylvania. Scales vary. Volumes average 120 pages. 22 x 19 x 3.

786. CINCINNATI ATLAS
1883-1884. 1 volume.

Civil and topographical maps of Cincinnati listing wards, schools, public buildings, and business firms. Numerically arranged by ward numbers. No index. Printed with wards in color. Scale, 1 inch equals 1,000 feet. 56 pages. 20 x 15.5 x 1.

787. MISCELLANEOUS MAPS, SUBDIVISION OF LOTS IN HAMILTON COUNTY
1864-1890. 1 volume

Maps showing lot numbers; also names of agents, owners, and streets. Numerically arranged by ward numbers. No index. Printed, handwritten, and blueprints with sections in color. Scale, 1 inch equals 1,000 feet. 150 pages. 23 x 16.5 x 3.

788. HAMILTON COUNTY PLAT BOOKS
1876-1885. 5 volumes (1-5).

Topographical maps of streets and roads in Cincinnati and Hamilton County listing grade, scale, elevation, name of owner of estate, name of surveyor, and field book and file numbers. Numerically arranged by ward numbers. Handwritten. Scale, 1 inch equals 1,000 feet. Volumes average 130 pages. 34 x 18 x 4.5.

789. INDEX TO PLATS, PLANS, AND PROFILES
1876-1885. 2 volumes.

Index to plat books of Hamilton County listing plat book number, plan number, description, and remarks. Alphabetically arranged by names of townships. Handwritten on printed forms. Volumes average 225 pages. 16 x 11.5 x 3.

790. HAMILTON COUNTY ROAD RECORD
1793—. 15 volumes (1793-1871, labeled chronologically; 1884—, 1-4). 1872-1883, destroyed in courthouse fire of 1884.

Records petitions for roads, surveyor's reports, plats, and minutes of county commissioners. Chronologically arranged. Handwritten on printed forms; some late entries, photostats. Volumes average 250 pages. 18 x 12.5 x 2.5.

791. INDEX TO HAMILTON COUNTY ROAD RECORD
1793—. 2 file boxes.
Card index showing name of road, name of surveyor, and volume and page numbers of road record. In index does not include missing record of 1872 - 1883. Alphabetically arranged by names of roads. Handwritten on printed forms. 17 x 7 x 5.

792. SURVEYOR'S RECORDS
1857—. 30 volumes. (1-30).
Records showing plants, surveys of streets, highways, and estates. Alphabetically arranged by names of townships. Handwritten on printed forms. Volumes average 500 pages. 18 x 14.5 x 2.5.

793. INDEX TO SURVEYOR'S RECORDS
1857—. 4 volumes (1 volume labeled City; 3 volumes labeled A-Z County). One volume is an index to city surveys listing name of street, description of survey, for whom surveyed, plat book and page numbers, and remarks. Three volumes are an index to county surveys listing name of township, section and number, for whom surveyed, range, name of surveyor, description of survey, and plat book and page numbers. Index to city surveys, alphabetically arranged by names of streets. Index to county surveys, alphabetically arranged by names of townships. Handwritten on printed forms. Volumes average 200 pages. 18 x 13 x 3.

794. BID AND ESTIMATE BOOK
1884-1917. 12 volumes. (00-11).
Records bids for road and bridge construction, repairs, date bid was received, type of work to be done, and date of completion. Chronologically arranged. Alphabetical index by name of townships. Handwritten on printed forms. Volumes average 500 pages. 19 x 11.5 x 2.

795. INDEX TO BID AND ESTIMATE BOOK
1884-1917. 2 volumes (1, 1).
Index recording volume and page numbers of bid and estimate record, specification number, type of work, and date of completion. Alphabetically arranged by names of townships. Handwritten on printed forms. Volumes average 200 pages. 18.25 x 12.5 x 2.

796. COMPLAINT BOOKS
1901-1916. 3 volumes. (labeled chronologically). Discontinued.
Records complaints, date received, to whom referred, by whom investigated, date of investigation, and action recommended. Chronologically arranged. Thumb tab index by names of townships. Handwritten on printed forms. Volumes average 300 pages. 19 x 12 x 2.

797. COUNTY ENGINEER'S [Surveyor's] LEDGER
1899-1913. 12 volumes. (1-12). Discontinued.
Records payments to employees of engineer's office. Chronologically arranged. Alphabetical index by names of employees in front of each volume. Handwritten on printed forms. Volumes average 450 pages. 14 x 9 x 2.

The regional planning commission of Hamilton County, an official organization, financed by public funds which are prorated among the seventeen participating municipalities and the county, on the basis of their proportionate area, was organized March 21, 1929, in accordance with provisions of section 4366-13 of the General Code of Ohio, as enacted on April 17, 1923.

The original planning commission is composed of eight members, appointed by the board of county commissioners, to serve for a term of three years. The reason for establishing a regional planning commission was to create an agency which would coordinate physical improvements undertaken by the numerous local subdivisions, in accordance with comprehensive plans to be prepared by such a commission for the entire region, with a view toward promoting a more harmonious and integrated development of such improvements.

The powers and duties of the regional planning commission, as defined by law, are to draw plans and maps of the region, and the county, which shall indicate the commission's recommendations for systems of "transportation, highway, park and recreational facilities," the water supply, sewerage, and garbage and sewage disposals. The commission is empowered and required also to provide maps and plans which shall indicate civic centers, and such other public improvements which may affect the development of the region or county and which do not begin or terminate within the boundaries of any single municipality. (G. C. sec. 4366-15.)

Whenever a regional plan is adopted by a city planning commission, or by the county commissioners, the fact is certified to the regional planning commission. A copy of so much of the plan as is affected by such adoption is deposited by the regional planning commission with the county recorder. When the plan recommends the location of a sewage or garbage disposal plant, a copy of the plan is not deposited with the county recorder until six months after its adoption, and when so deposited, the copy states at the action or non-action of the appropriating authority with respect to the purchase or appropriation of property for the required plant. (110 O. L. 310.)

All records are located in the County Courthouse, Room 409.

Topographic Survey Maps

798. GOVERNMENT TOPOGRAPHIC MAP, HAMILTON COUNTY AND VICINITY
1931. 1 map.
Enlargement of sectional maps made by the United States Coast and Geodetic Survey covering period 1898-1931. Shows topographical changes of area, as determined from government surveys over a period of years; also lists townships, cities, Villages, highways, waterways, electric and steam railways, section and school numbers, fractional range, and altitude of elevated area. Prepared and published by United States Coast and Geodetic Survey, Washington, D. C. Photographic prints with mounted portions in color. Scale, 1 inch equals 62,500 feet. 48 x 36. In metal map file.

799. GOVERNMENT SECTIONAL TOPOGRAPHIC MAPS, HAMILTON COUNTY AND VICINITY
1898-1931. 107 maps.
Sectional maps made by the United States Coast and Geodetic Survey showing topographical changes of area as determined from government surveys over a period of years. Author and publisher: United States Coast and Geodetic Survey, Washington, D. C. Photostats, with topographical changes shown in color. Scale, 1 inch equals 62,500 feet. 34 x 17. In metal map file.

800. TOPOGRAPHIC SURVEY MAP, HAMILTON COUNTY
1929. 1 volume.
A sectional map of topographical surveys of Hamilton County showing townships, Corporation lines, sections, ward boundaries, steam and electric railways, highways, thoroughfares, waterways, parks, estates, fractional range, and altitudes of elevated areas. Author: Planning Commission, Cincinnati, Ohio. Publisher of basic map, C. E. Stewart Company, Cincinnati, Ohio. Publisher of basic map, C. E. Stewart Company, Cincinnati, Ohio. No index. Printed on glazed linen, with portions in color. Scale, 1 inch equals 400 feet. 48 pages. 33 x 27 x 1.5.

Political Maps

801. ZONING DISTRICT MAPS, HAMILTON COUNTY
1929-1935. 322 maps.
Showing all district divisions in Cincinnati, and villages of Hamilton County, excepting the city of Norwood. Author: Planning Commission, Cincinnati, Ohio. Hand drawn on glazed tracing linen in black and white. Scales vary. 20 x 15. In metal map file.

Ethnic Maps

802. DISTRIBUTION OF POPULATION MAPS
1929—. 3 maps.
Shows distribution of population in townships, cities and villages in Hamilton County. Author: Planning Commission, Cincinnati, Ohio. Hand drawn on glazed tracing linen in black and white. Scales vary. 1 map, 96 x 72; 2 maps, 48 x 36. In metal map file.

Communication Maps

803. WATERWAY MAPS, HAMILTON COUNTY
1929-1935. 8 maps.
Showing rivers, canals, creeks, and bridges in Hamilton County. Prepared by planning commission. Hand drawn on glazed tracing linen in black and white. Scales vary. 2 complete maps, 48 x 36; 2 complete maps, 96 x 72; 4 sectional maps, 20 x 15. In metal map file.

804. THOROUGHFARE MAPS, HAMILTON COUNTY
1929-1935. 423 maps.
Showing all highways and county roads in Hamilton County, Cincinnati, and vicinity. Prepared by planning commission. Hand drawn on glazed tracing linen in black and white. Scales vary. 17 complete maps, 96 x 72; 406 sectional maps, 48 x 36. In metal map file.

805. STREET MAPS, HAMILTON COUNTY
1929-1935. 75 maps.
Showing County and village roads, and streets in Cincinnati, by name and number. Prepared by planning commission and county engineer. Printed, black and white. Scales vary. 31 basic maps of county and village roads, 96 x 72; 14 sectional maps of county and village roads, 48 x 36; 30 maps of Cincinnati streets, 20 x 15. In metal map file.

806. CAR AND BUS ROUTE MAPS OF HAMILTON COUNTY
1929-1935. 35 maps.
Showing street car and bus transportation routes in Cincinnati, Norwood, Milford, and Hamilton, Ohio. Prepared by planning commission. Printed, black and white. Scales vary. 3 basic county maps, 96 x 72; 32 sectional maps, 48 x 36. In metal map file.

807. SECTIONAL ROAD MAPS, HAMILTON COUNTY, CINCINNATI, AND TOWNSHIPS
1929. 1 volume.
Sectional map of county, city, and townships, showing roads and thoroughfares in the county, electric and steam railways, waterways, bridges, parks, and estates. Prepared by planning commission. No index. Printed on glazed linen with roads in color. Scale, 1 inch equals 2,000 feet. 45 pages. 42 x 27 x 1.

808. PLANS, MAIN THOROUGHFARES
1930. 1 map.
Showing those sections of main thoroughfares in Hamilton County to be opened, widened, or of sufficient width. Prepared by planning commission. Basic map published by E. E. Stewart Company, Cincinnati, Ohio. Printed, with thoroughfares in color. Roll map. Scale, 1 inch equals 2,000 feet.

Miscellaneous

809. REGIONAL PLANNING MAPS, HAMILTON COUNTY
1929-1935. 57 maps.

Plans for Hamilton County drawn by the planning commission since establishment of this office. Prepared by planning commission. Hand drawn on glazed tracing linen in black and white. Scales vary. 48 x 36. In metal map file.

810. SCHOOL DISTRICT MAPS, HAMILTON COUNTY
1929-1935. 211 maps.

One complete map showing all school districts in Hamilton County, and sectional maps of each school district. Prepared by planning commission. Hand drawn on glazed tracing linen in black and white. Scales vary. Complete map, 96 x 72; 185 sectional maps, 48 x 36; 25 sectional maps, 20 x 15. In metal map file.

811. PARK PLANS, HAMILTON COUNTY
1935-1935. 346 maps.

Maps of Sharon Wood, Burnet Woods, Eden Park, Mt. Airy Forest, and all athletic fields and playgrounds in Cincinnati and vicinity. Prepared by planning commission. Hand drawn on glazed tracing linen in black and white. Scales vary. Maps of 4 parks 96 x 72; others, 20 x 15. In metal map file.

812. MISCELLANEOUS MAPS, PRINTS, AND TRACINGS
1929. 32 cardboard filing tubes.

Copies of all maps, prints, and tracings made by the planning commission which show the nature of regional improvements recommended, made, and discarded. Photostats, printed, and hand drawn, with sections in color. Scales vary. Tubes average 48 x 5.

813. PHOTOGRAPHS
1929—. 1 steel file box.

Kodak pictures of schools, playfields, churches, cemeteries, and parks in Hamilton County. Mounted on separate cardboards. Alphabetically arranged by subjects. No index. 17 x 12.5 x 9.5.

814. REPORT OF REGIONAL PLANNING COMMISSION
1929-1931. 1 volume.

Published report covering all activities of the planning commission. Alphabetical index by subjects in front of each volume. Printed. 31 pages. 11 x 8.5 x .25. On shelf, east wall.

815. CUMULATIVE REPORTS
1931—. 12 street file boxes (A-Z).

Official correspondence pertaining to work of the commission, pamphlets from other planning commissions, and news clippings pertaining to parks, boulevards, Parkways, and subways. Alphabetically arranged by names of correspondents or organizations. No index. Printed and typed. 44.5 x 15 x 13.

816. ROAD INFORMATION
1929—. 1 steel file box.

Record of information on Hamilton County roads, compiled by the commission on seasonal tours. Alphabetically arranged by names roads. No index. Handwritten and typed. 17 x 12.5 x 9.5.

817. MAILING LIST
1935—. 1 steel file box.

Record of invitations from the planning commission to individuals to attend meetings of the commission and correspondence pertaining there too. Alphabetically arranged by names of individuals. No index. Handwritten and typed. 17 x 12.5 x 9.5.

818. GENERAL CORRESPONDENCE
1935—. 1 steel file box.

Business correspondence pertaining to the office and work of the commission. Alphabetically arranged by subjects. No index. Handwritten and typed. 17 x 12.5 x 9.5.

BOARD OF PARK COMMISSIONERS 277

Provision for the establishment of the Hamilton County park district was made by the city council of Cincinnati up on the filing of an application in the probate court of the county on April 5, 1929. After the necessary hearings, the probate court, as provided by the Ohio Park District Act, established the district on July 17, 1930, and appointed the first board part commissioners for the county, consisting of three members, to serve terms of three years, as provided by law. (107 O. L. 66.) The board is required to keep "an accurate and permanent record of all its proceedings." (G. C. sec. 2976-6.)

The purpose of the park district, is defined by the legislature in 1919, is "to encourage forestry, to provide for the converting into forest reserves lands acquired for that purpose and to provide for the conservation of the natural resources of the state, including streams, lakes, submerged and swamp lands." (108 O. L. pt. ii, 1097.) The districts, has created by the prophet judge, may include such parts of any county or counties as might be logically converted into a metropolitan park district. (107 O. L. 65.)

The legislative act passed March 6, 1917, provided for the creation of park districts to encourage forestry by converting into forests reserve lands acquired for that purpose and to provide for the conservation of the natural resources of the state, including streams, lakes, and submerged and swamped lands. The act provided that districts could be created upon proper application to the probate court, and that such districts might include such parts of any county or counties as might be logically converted into a metropolitan park district. (*Ibid.*, 65.)

The work of the commission is financed by public taxation. The legislature made provision for a maximum revenue of one-tenth of one mill on each thousand dollar valuation for park purposes, and for a referendum vote on an extra levy not to exceed one-tenth of one mill, which amounts to an annual tax of ten cents per thousand dollars valuation. (*Ibid.*, 67.) The county treasurer and the county auditor are ex officio members of the board.

The purpose and aim of the board of park commissioners of the Hamilton County park district is to acquire, develop, and maintain parks or reservations for the use and enjoyment of all citizens, benefitting particularly those men and women who live in crowded city quarters.

278

BOARD OF PARK COMMISSIONERS

Topographic Surveys

819. STUDIES, HAMILTON COUNTY TOPOGRAPHY
1921. 14 maps (1-14).
Studies and plans submitted by regional planning commission of land tracks in Hamilton County proposed for use as playgrounds or parks. Prepared by regional planning commission engineers. Hand drawn and mounted on cardboard. Scale, 1 inch equals 1,000 feet. 40 x 62. County Courthouse, Room 522.

820. TOPOGRAPHY OF HAMILTON COUNTY
1914. 1 map.
Map showing entire area of Hamilton County. Prepared by United States Engineering Survey, Washington, D. C. Hand drawn. scale, 1 inch equals 1,000 feet. 30 x 24. County Courthouse, Room 522 in steel filing cabinet for aerial photography.

821. MAPS, TOPOGRAPHICAL SURVEY, CITY OF CINCINNATI
1912. 48 sheets. (1-48).
Topographical maps showing thoroughfares. Prepared by Colonel H. M. Waite. Published by United States Engineering Department, Washington, D. C. Photostatic prints. Scale, 1 inch equals 400 feet. 42 x 32. County Courthouse, Room 522.

822. PARK STUDIES, GENERAL
1928—. 26 drawings. (1-26).
Topographical studies of Hamilton County parks. Prepared by regional planning commission. Hand drawn. Scale, 1 inch equals 1,000 feet. 36 x 30. County Courthouse, Room 522 in steel filing cabinet.

Aerial Surveys

823. AERIAL SURVEY, HAMILTON COUNTY
October 1931. 2 volumes, 1,000 photographic prints (Volumes 1-2).
Volumes contain photographic survey. There are included in survey 1,000 overlapping photographic contact prince for public use with aerial stereoscope. No systematic arrangement. No index. Made by Bowman-Park Aero Company.

Louisville, Kentucky. Scale for atlases and prints, 1 inch equals 1,000 feet. Volumes average 52 pages. 22 x 18. Prints, 6.5 x 8.5. County Courthouse, Room 522 in steel filing cabinets.

824. AERIAL SURVEY, HAMILTON COUNTY
1931. 2 volumes.
Showing topography of Hamilton County roads, streets, parks, rivers, and creeks. No systematic arrangement. No index. Prepared by Hamilton County park board. Printed. Scale, 1 inch equals 1,000 feet. Volumes average 50 pages. 51 x 39. County Courthouse, Room 522 in steel filing cabinet.

825. AERIAL PRINTS, SHARON WOODS
1931. 50 prints (1-50).
Photographic prints showing location of dam, shelter-houses, streams, roads, and trails. Numerically arranged. Photographed by Hamilton County park board. Printed. Scale, 1 inch equals 1,000 feet. 51 x 39. County Courthouse, Room 522 in steel filing cabinet.

826. ENLARGEMENTS, AERIAL
1931. 6 volumes. (1-6).
Enlargements of aerial photographs of proposed park areas. No systematic arrangement. No index. Printed and mounted on cardboard. Scale, 1 inch equals 1,000 feet. 52 x 39. County Courthouse, Room 522 in steel filing cabinet.

Maps, Plats, and Plans

827. PLANS, CONSTRUCTION DETAILS, SHARON WOODS
1931—. 145 drawings (1-145).
Plans for shelter houses, club houses, residences, outbuildings, fireplaces, and other work drawings for construction in Sharon Woods. Numerically arranged by plan numbers. Prepared by Hamilton County park commission. Hand drawn. Scale, 1 inch equals 1 foot. Sizes vary from 8 x 12 to 32 x 42. County Courthouse, Room 522 in steel filing cabinet.

828. ROAD CONSTRUCTION MAPS
1921. 26 maps (1-26).

Eight studies and plans for construction of roads in Hamilton County showing accessibility to parks and playgrounds; also to roads leading to Sharon Woods. Numerically arranged by road numbers. Prepared by Hamilton County engineers. Hand drawn and mounted on cardboard. Scale, 1 inch equals 1,000 feet. 36 x 42. County Courthouse, Room 522 in steel filing cabinet.

829. PLATS, COUNTY AUDITOR'S
1919. 14 volumes (1-14).

Plats furnished by auditor's office of grounds proposed for park sites or playgrounds. Alphabetically arranged by names of proposed parks. No index. Prepared by Hamilton County engineers. Hand drawn and mounted on cardboard. Scale, 1 inch equals 1,000 feet. 40 x 62. County Courthouse, Room 522.

830. PROPOSED PLANS, PARKS AND PARKWAYS
1914——. 3 maps, 45 drawings (maps, 1-3; drawings, 1-45).

Proposed plans for parks and Parkways. Numerically arranged. Prepared by United States Geological Survey, Washington, D. C. with additions to date by park commission engineers. Hand drawn and mounted on cardboard. Scale, 1 inch equals 1 mile. 36 x 30. County Courthouse, Room 522 in steel filing cabinet.

831. TRAIL MAP, SHARON WOOD
1936. 1 map (original).

Map showing location of Sharon Woods and various trails, shelter houses, and other accommodations. There have been 50,000 reprints made from this map. Prepared by Hamilton County park commission. Hand drawn and mounted on cardboard. Scale, 1 inch equals 100 feet. 14 x 12. County Courthouse, Room 522.

832. TOWNSHIP SHEETS
1929. 36 sheets (1-36).

Drawings and plans of vacant property or acreage in Hamilton County townships being studied for possible acquisition by park commission. Numerically arranged. Prepared by Hamilton County park commission. Hand drawn and mounted on cardboard. Scale, 1 inch equals 1,000 feet. 32 x 42. County Courthouse, Room 522 in steel filing cabinet.

833. HISTORICAL MAPS OF OHIO
1928—. 18 maps (1-18).
Showing park commission studies of roads, trails, fields, and woodlands in Hamilton County. Prepared by park commission engineers. Hand drawn and mounted on cardboard. Scale, 1 inch equals 1,000 feet. 62 x 42. County Courthouse, Room 522.

Models

834. MODEL OF DAM, SHARON WOODS
December 1935, 1 model
Model of dam made of plaster, hemp, and steel which is painted in natural colors. Made by WPA model-makers. Scale, .25 inch equals 1 foot. 48 x 48 x 18. County Courthouse, Room 522.

835. MODELS, SHARON WOODS TOPOGRAPHY
1935. 3 models.
Models showing woodlands, roads, creeks, trails, hiking and bridal pads, office, pavilion, baseball diamond, clubhouse, boathouse, shelter-house, police and superintendent's residences, lake, dam, and wading pool; made of plaster, hemp, and steel and painted in natural colors. Made by WPA model-makers. Scale, 1 inch equals 100 feet. 84 x 72 x 12. 1935, 1 model. County Courthouse entrance; 1 model, Sharon Woods' office; 1 model, County Courthouse, basement.

Business Administration of Office

836. JOURNAL OF PROCEEDINGS
1931—. 2 volumes (1-2).
Record of official business of semimonthly meetings. Chronologically arranged. No index. Typed. Volumes average 150 pages. 11.5 x 8.5 x 1.5. County Courthouse, Room 522.

837. GENERAL CORRESPONDENCE
1931—. 12 file boxes.
General correspondence, contracts, orders for supplies, requisitions for merchandise, permits, advices of goods received and gasoline receipts including

WPA and PWA records in miscellaneous information on parks. Alphabetically arranged by subjects. No index. Handwritten and typed. 18 x 12 x 24. County Courthouse, Room 522.

838. CASH JOURNAL
1921—. 7 volumes (1-7).
Daily entries of cash and miscellaneous receipts allocated by budget commission. Chronologically arranged. No index. Handwritten on printed forms. Volumes average 150 pages. 14 x 11 x 1. County Courthouse, Room 522.

839. INFORMATION AND REPORTS ON CITY AND COUNTY PARKS
1931—. 16 file boxes.
Miscellaneous information on city and county parks, forestry conservation, and historical material; incidental data on national parks, state parks, regional planning, and roads. Alphabetically arranged by items. No index. Handwritten and printed. 13 x 10 x 6. County Courthouse, Room 522 in steel filing cabinet.

At its 1914 session the legislature, following the disastrous floods of the previous year, made provision for the establishment in Ohio of conservancy districts, to prevent floods, to protect cities, villages, farms, and highways from inundation. This act, authorized by the constitutional amendment of 1912 (Art. II, sec. 3), was upheld by the courts as a valid exercise of the police power of the state. (*County of Miami* v. *Dayton*. 92 O. S. 223-24, 236.) The conservancy districts, according to the act, may be established not only to prevent floods but to regulate streams, reclaim overflowed lands, provide irrigation, regulate the flow of streams, or divert water courses.

The court of common pleas of any county in the state or any judge in vacation is authorized, after a petition signed by either 500 freeholders or by a majority of freeholders has been filed with the clerk of courts, to establish a conservancy district which may be within or without the county where the court is located. After conducting hearings on the petition as to the purpose of the district, the court may declare the district organized and give it a corporate name. The clerk of courts, within thirty days after the district has been declared a corporation by the court, transmits to the secretary of state, and to the county recorder in each county having lands in the district, copies of the finding and the decrees of the court incorporating the district. The districts, according to statute, are considered as political subdivisions.

Within thirty days after the decrees of incorporation, the court is authorized to appoint as a board of direction of the district three persons at least two of whom are freeholders in the district, who serves three, five, and seven years respectively. After the expiration of their terms, the tenure of office is five years. The directors, after taking an oath that they "will not be interested directly or indirectly in any contract led by the district," organize by selecting one of their members president. They may select some person, not a member of the board, as secretary. The board is authorized to employ a chief engineer, who may be an individual, copartnership, or corporation; an attorney; and such other engineers and attorneys as maybe necessary or carrying on the work. The board may provide for their compensation, which, with all other necessary expenditures, shall be taken as a part of the cost of improvement. While the chief engineer prepares plans and specifications of work, all contracts which exceed $1,000 are let by competitive bidding.

For the purpose of its work, the board or its agents are authorized to enter upon lands within or without the district for the purpose of making surveys. They are authorized to exercise the right to eminent domain; condemn property, after an appraisal, for the use of the district; and make regulations to protect their work by prescribing the method of building roads, bridges, or fences. Moreover, they may remove bridges, cemeteries, or other structures impeding their work. The commission may cooperate with the federal government, persons, railways, corporations, the state government of Ohio or other states for assistance in drainage, conservancy, or other improvements.

To finance such improvements the board is authorized to levee upon the property of the district a tax not to exceed three-tenths of a mill on the assessed valuation. Certified to the county auditor, and to the various treasurers of the counties within the district, this tax is used to pay the expenses of organization, surveys, and plans. The commission is authorized, further, to borrow money at a rate not to exceed six percent per annum in assessments for a bond. (104 O. L. 13-64.)

The board is required to "keep in a well-bound book a record of all its proceedings, minutes of all meetings, certificates, contracts, bonds given by employees and all corporate acts, which shall be open to the inspection of all owners of property in the district, as well as to all other interested parties." The secretary, who may serve also as treasurer, is designated as the "custodian of the records of the district and of its corporate seal."

(Hamilton County is in the Miami Conservancy District. The records of this board are housed in Dayton.)

The superintendent of buildings in Hamilton County (an office originating in 1904) is appointed by the board of county commissioners. His appointment is made from a list prepared by the civil service commission, and he is subject to removal only after a hearing before that body–and then only by the county commissioners. (*Opinions, Attorney General*, 1930, sec. 2106.)

Provision for the appointment of a superintendent of county buildings by the county commissioners is made under section 2410 of the General Code. The county commissioners are thereby authorized to "employ a superintendent of county buildings, and such watchmen, janitors, and other employees as it deems necessary for the care and custody of the courthouse, jail, and other county buildings, and of bridges, and other property under its jurisdiction and control." (G. C. sec. 2410; R. S. sec. 845.)

All records are located in the County Courthouse, office of superintendent of buildings.

840. JOURNAL

1902-1912. 3 volumes. Discontinued.

Journal entries of superintendent's office showing dates, names, amounts, Appropriations, and balances. Chronologically arranged. No index. Handwritten on printed forms. Volumes average 300 pages. 16 x 7.5 x 1.

841. LEDGER

1918-1924. 2 volumes. Discontinued.

General service and building maintenance accounts. Alphabetically arranged by names of funds. No index. Handwritten on printed forms. Volumes average 370 pages. 14 x 9 x 1.

842. REQUISITIONS

1933—. 4 file boxes. Prior records destroyed.

Requisitions on county purchasing department for supplies showing name of person or department requesting supplies, requisition date and number, date of delivery, item number, quantity required, description, code number, purchase order number, and signature of official in charge of agency requesting supplies. Chronologically arranged. No index. Typed on printed forms. 26 x 18 x 9.5.

843. BILLS ALLOWED

1878-1903. 7 volumes. Discontinued.

And entries of bills allowed for payment by County Commissioners giving date allowed, account number, name of firm or individual presenting Bill, and amount of bill. Chronologically arranged. No index. Handwritten. Volumes average 300 pages. 18 x 12 x 1.5.

844. SUPERINTENDENT'S RECEIPT BOOK

1932—. 1 volume. Prior records destroyed.

Record of Maintenance supplies received by superintendent showing dates, names, description of supplies, and quantity received. Chronologically arranged. No index. Handwritten. 50 pages. 17 x 15 x .5.

845. ADVICE OF GOOD RECEIVED OR SERVICES PERFORMED

1933—. 2 file boxes. Prior records destroyed.

Record of goods received by county agencies through requisitions on purchasing department showing name of agency, date, by whom counted and inspected, certificate of purchasing agent's inspector, item number, quantity, unit, description, remarks, date received by purchasing department, date assigned to inspector, date received an auditor's office, and by whom checked. Chronologically arranged. No index. Typed on printed forms. 26 x 18 x 9.5.

846. INVOICE BOOK

1885-1901. 7 volumes. Discontinued.

Original invoices posted on sheets showing dates, names, description of merchandise, and amounts. Chronologically arranged. No index. Volumes average 600 pages. 16 x 12 x 6.

847. COURTHOUSE SUPERINTENDENT'S RECORDS

1889-1900. 11 volumes. Discontinued.

Itemized entries of supplies furnished by superintendent of buildings for building maintenance. Chronologically arranged. No index. Handwritten. Volumes average 50 pages. 17 x 15 x .25.

848. WEEKLY PAYROLLS
1889—. 28 volumes.
Weekly payrolls of employees under supervision of superintendent of buildings showing names of employees, kind of service, number of days worked, amount of wages per day, total wages per week, and signature of employee. Chronologically arranged. No index. Handwritten on printed forms. Volumes average 200 pages. 19 x 13 x .5.

849. COURTHOUSE MESSENGERS' PAYROLL
1890-1906. 5 volumes.
Weekly payroll entries of courthouse messengers showing names of messengers location, total wages per week, and signature of messenger. Chronologically arranged. No index. Handwritten on printed forms. Volumes average 200 pages. 17 x 12 x .75.
For subsequent records see entry 1.

850. MEMORIAL HALL AND ARMORY
1909-1925. 1 volume.
Rental engagements of memorial hall in armory giving dates of rentals, names of organizations renting building, and amounts charged for rentals. Chronologically arranged. No index. Handwritten. 300 pages. 12.5 x 6 x 1.5.
For subsequent records see entry 1.

The Hamilton County agricultural society, and aggregate corporation whose object is the promotion of agriculture in the county, was established in 1855 under provisions of sections 9880-9921 -1c of the General Code authorizing such county societies and defining their powers and duties.

County agricultural societies in Ohio were provided for by statute as early as 1846. On February 28 of that year the legislature passed an act authorizing the forming of such societies and making provisions for their aid by the counties. On February 15, 1853, the legislature declared such societies to be bodies corporate and politic, capable of suing and being sued, and of holding in fee simple such real estate as they might purchase for sites where on to hold fairs, to be paid for by the county commissioners. (51 O. L. 333.)

By act of the legislature passed February 20, 1861, county agricultural societies were required to report annually to the state board of agriculture, and to meet with the state board at Columbus once each year. (58 O. L. 22.) In 1883 the legislature provided for the organization of district or county agricultural societies. The act making this provision stipulated that when thirty or more persons, residents of any county or district embracing two counties, organized themselves into an agricultural society under the rules and regulations of the state board of agriculture, the county might aid this society with a grant not to exceed $400 per year. (80 O. L. 142.) By act of April 21, 1896, provision was made for representation in a county society of thirty or more residents of any county or district embracing two or more counties. (92 O. L. 205.) In 1900 the legislature extended the amount of county aid to $800 per year. (94 O. L. 395.) Later, on May 6, 1902, the legislature passed an act authorizing thirty or more persons, residents of a county or district embracing *one or more counties,* to organize themselves into an agricultural society. (95 O. L. 403.)

On April 17, 1919, the legislature made provisions for the organization of county and independent agricultural societies; provided for the payment of class premiums; defined the duties of persons competing for premiums; prescribed the publication of treasurers' accounts in the list of awards by societies; designated who might be a member of a county agricultural society; authorized the election of a board of directors by a society consisting of eight members; and prescribed their term of office and the manner of their election. The act further stipulated how such societies might obtain state aid, and authorize the county commissioners to insure all buildings belonging to agricultural societies. (108 O. L. pt. i, 381-385.)

The legislature in 1921 passed an act stipulating that the total amount of county aid to county agricultural societies should not exceed 100 percent of the amount paid by the society in regular class premiums. (109 O. L. 240.) By act of March 27, 1925, the county commissioners were authorized to purchase or lease, for a term of not less than twenty years, real estate whereon to hold fairs under the management of county agricultural societies, and to erect thereon suitable buildings. (111 O. L. 238.) On March 10, 1927, the legislature authorized the county commissioners annually to appropriate, on the request of the agricultural society, a sum not less than $1,500 or more than $2,000 from the general fund for the purpose of "encouraging agricultural fairs."

The most recent legislation effecting agricultural societies was that of March 19, 1935. This act provides that where no duly organized county agricultural society exists, and when no fair was held by a duly organized county agricultural society which had held an annual exposition for three years previous to January 1, 1933, the county commissioners, on the request of the independent society, should appropriate annually from the general fund a sum not to exceed $2,000 nor less than $500, for the encouragement of independent agricultural fairs. (116 O. L. 47.)

Carthage Fair

All records are located in the County Courthouse, Room 410.

851. BUILDING CONTRACTS
1908—. 3 file boxes.
Record of repairs and improvements to properties on Carthage fairgrounds. Chronologically arranged. No index. Handwritten. 18 x 9 x 6.

852. ENTRY BOOK
1908—. 28 volumes.
Exhibitors' book containing names and addresses of exhibitors; also numbers assigned. Numerically arranged by assignment numbers. No index. Handwritten. Volumes average 100 pages. 16 x 10.5 x 1.5.

853. JOURNALS

1908——. 5 volumes.

Journal of cash received and expenditures. Chronologically arranged. No index. Handwritten on printed forms. Volumes average 98 pages. 17 x 14.5 x 1.

854. MINUTE BOOKS

1855-1935. 8 volumes.

Combination treasurer's account and minute books, including record of meetings, and awards. Chronologically arranged. No index. 1855-1930, handwritten; 1931-1935, typed. 5 volumes average 350 pages. 14 x 9 x 2; 3 volumes average 250 pages. (loose-leaf) 11.25 x 9.25 x 1.5.

855. PAID BILLS

1908——. 4 file boxes.

Bills which have been paid. Alphabetically arranged by names of vendors. No index. Handwritten. 25 x 13 x 11.

856. RETURN VOUCHERS

1906——. 11 file boxes.

Canceled checks. Chronologically arranged. No index. Handwritten on printed forms. 18 x 9 x 6.

857. STATE RECORDS

1890——. 1 file box.

Report of the society to state on general activities showing receipts, expenditures, and bank balances. Chronologically arranged. No index. Handwritten. 18 x 9 x 6.

858. TREASURER'S ENTRY BOOK

1908——. 5 volumes.

Treasurer's account book of receipts and disbursements. Chronologically arranged. No index. Handwritten. Volumes average 300 pages. 14 x 8.5 x 2.

859. ROLL BOOK

1908——. 38 volumes.

Record of exhibitors' contest numbers, their exhibits, and awards achieved. Chronologically arranged. No index. Handwritten. Volumes average 75 pages. 14.5 x 8.25 x 1.

860. MISCELLANEOUS

1855——. 17 file boxes.

General record of all fair activities. Chronologically arranged. No index. Handwritten. 18 x 9 x 6.

The county dog warden, appointed or employed by the county commissioners, has as his duty the enforcement of the provisions of the General Code relating to licensing dogs, the impounding and destroying of unlicensed dogs, and pain of compensation for damages to livestock inflicted by dogs. This officer, like other county officials, is required to give bond conditioned for the faithful performance of his duties of his office. This bond, in the sum of not less than $500 or more than $2,000 is filed with the county auditor. His compensation and tenure, like that of his deputies, is determined by the county commissioners.

The warden is required to make a record of all dogs owned, kept, or harbored in his county to patrol the county; and to seize and impound dogs more than three months of age found not wearing a valid registration tag. The last provision does not apply, however, do dogs kept in a regularly licensed kennel. Moreover, he is required to present to the commissioners weekly written reports of all dogs seized, impounded, redeemed, and destroyed, and to report all claims for damages to livestock inflicted by dogs.

In the performance of their legal duties, the dog warden and his deputies have the same police powers as are conferred by statute upon sheriffs and police. They may summon the assistance of bystanders in performing their duties, and serve writs and other legal processes in any court in the county with reference to enforcing the provisions of the laws relating to dogs. (G. C. sec. 5652-7.)

All records are located in the dog warden's office, 3949 Colerain Avenue, Cincinnati, Ohio. Records prior to 1927 missing.

861. DOG RECORD
1927——. 5 volumes.
Complete record of all unlicensed dogs taken in Hamilton County showing location, name of owner, time taken, height, weight, sex, color, breed, hair, how taken, and name of deputy. Numerically arranged by case numbers. No index. Handwritten. Volumes average 250 pages. 18 x 12 x 2.

862. DOG LICENSES

1927—. 60 volumes.

Records name of owner, date license issued, the charged, and description of dog. Numerically arranged by application numbers. No index. Typed. Volumes average 200 pages. 12 x 4 x 4.

863. ANIMAL CLAIMS

1927—. 1 file box.

Report of claims for animals killed by dogs showing name of persons registering claim, date of loss, type of animal, amount of claim, report of investigator, recommendation by warden, and all correspondence relating to case. Numerically arranged by case numbers. No index. Typed. 30 x 16 x 12.

864. FINANCIAL RECORD

1927—. 5 volumes.

Complete record of all unlicensed dogs taken in county showing where found, date, sex, these charge, and final disposition of the case. Numerically arranged by case numbers. No index. Handwritten. Volumes average 300 pages. 18 x 12 x 3.

865. CORRESPONDENCE

1927—.1 file box.

Correspondence relating to general business of the office, excepting correspondence relating to animal claims. Alphabetically arranged by names of correspondents. No index. Handwritten and typed. 30 x 16 x 12.

Governmental

All addresses refer to Cincinnati unless otherwise noted

Auditor
138 East Court Street
https://www.hamiltoncountyauditor.org/

Board of Elections
138 East Court Street
https://votehamiltoncountyohio.gov/

Clerk of Courts
1000 Main Street
https://www.courtclerk.org/

Commissioners
138 East Court Street
www.hamiltoncountyohio.gov/government/county_commissioners/index.php

Conservation District
138 East Court Street
www.hamiltoncountyohio.gov/government/departments/soil_and_water/ind
ex.php
see also: 2702 East Kemper Road
Sharonville, OH
https://www.hcswcd.org/

Coroner
138 East Court Street
https://www.hamiltoncountyohio.gov/government/departments/coroner/

Dog Warden/Animal Services
138 East Court Street
www.hamiltoncountyohio.gov/government/departments/dog_warden_anim
al_services/index.php

Engineer
138 East Court Street
https://www.hamiltoncountyohio.gov/government/departments/engineer/

Park District
138 East Court
**https://www.hamiltoncountyohio.gov/government/departments/park_distric
t/index.php**

Public Health
138 East Court Street
**www.hamiltoncountyohio.gov/government/departments/public_health/inde
x.php**

Recorder
138 East Court Street
www.hamiltoncountyohio.gov/government/departments/recorder/index.php

Sheriff
138 East Court Street
https://www.hcso.org/

Treasurer
138 East Court Street
www.hamiltoncountyohio.gov/government/departments/treasurer/index.php

Veterans Service Commission
138 East Court
**https://www.hamiltoncountyohio.gov/government/departments/veterans_se
rvice_commission/index.php**

FamilySearch
https://www.familysearch.org/search/catalog
    FamilySearch is a free website with digitized records. Court records located for Hamilton County include: Auditor, Circuit Court, Common Pleas Court, Hamilton County Health Department, Probate Court, Recorder. Other records listed include abstracts of records published by an individual or society.

Hamilton County Genealogical Society
A chapter of the Ohio Genealogical Society
P. O. Box 15865
Cincinnati
https://www.hcgsohio.org/
    A very good website. As an example the listing for Local Records has links to Cemeteries and Burials, Court Records, Death Records, Land Records, Marriages and Divorces, Naturalizations, and more. For Wills, links can give a searchable chronological listing of every name found in Hamilton County Wills from 1791-1850. Local record repositories offers seven other websites leading to other collections in the Cincinnati area.

University of Cincinnati
Blegen Library, 8th Floor
2602 McMicken Circle
https://libraries.uc.edu/libraries/arb.html
    A note on the websites indicates the old, large volumes in fragile condition which patrons are not permitted to handle. Call at least a week prior to visiting to make an appointment.

Cincinnati History Library and Archives
Located in the Cincinnati Museum Center
1301 Western Avenue
https://www.cincymuseum.org/cincinnati-history-library-archives/
    While a very limited days and hours, (Thursday and Friday, noon-4pm *by appointment only*), the website offers "a new inclusive search engine for their collections." An index to local history resources contains over 69,000 entries from 21 sources. The manuscript collection houses approximately 11,300 collections which encompasses churches, societies, institutions, charities, etc.

Cincinnati and Hamilton County Public Library
(Formerly the Public Library of Cincinnati and Hamilton County)
800 Vine Street
https://chpl.org/
 Genealogical databases are available for CHPL card-holders which includes: Findmypast, Fold3, HeritageQuest, and others. The Genealogical and Local History Department, located on the third floor, is one of the five largest genealogical collections in the United States. A note mentions the Department is temporarily housed in the Cincinnati Room with a limited number of books on view. It is suggested to make an appointment and request needed material.

Ohio Genealogical Society
611 State Route 97 West
Bellville, OH
ogs.org
 The Samuel D. Isaly Library is Ohio's "top repository for Ohio genealogical information." The extensive collection includes: 70,000 volumes arranged by state, county, and subject matter; original 1880 census for all 88 Ohio counties; 250,000 ancestor cards by surname; 4,000 Bible records; over 23,000 high school and college year books; and over 5,000 lineage society applications. OGS offers lineage societies for First Families of Ohio, Settlers & Builders of Ohio, Century Families of Ohio, The Society of Civil War Families of Ohio, and the Society of Families of the Old Northwest Territory. The library also contains over 5,000 family histories.

Maintenance
  Building Accounts, 811
  County Home and Chronic Disease
    Hospital, 585
Maps of
  Alleys, 716
  Altitudes of Elevated Areas, 800
  Annexations to Cincinnati, 41
  Athletic Fields, 811
  Boundary Lines, Cincinnati, 45, 233,
    234
  Bridges, 755, 803, 807
  Buildings, 42, 786
  Burnet Woods, 811
  Business Firms, Cincinnati, 786
  Bus Routes, 45, 233, 806
  Cemeteries, 38-40, 42-44
  Change of Area, 798, 799
  Churches, 42
  Cincinnati, 370, 512
  Cities, 370, 512, 715, 798
    Population of, 802
  Corporation Lines, 800
  Culverts, 755
  Districts, 234, 539, 801, 810
  Eden Park, 811
  Estates, 43, 46, 47, 800, 807
  Fire Stations, 45
  Highways, see Maps of Roads
  Historical, Ohio, 833
  Insurance, 513
  Interurban Lines, 233
  Kentucky, Section of, 42, 44
  Land, 372
  Longview Hospital, 39
  Lots, 787
  Miscellaneous, Copies of, 812
  Norwood, 512
  Ohio Congressional District, 234

Maps of, continued
  Parks, 38-40, 42-44, 716, 800, 807,
    811, 822
  Park Sites, 829
  Parochial Schools, 45
  Playgrounds, 811
  Police Stations, 45
  Population of Cities, Townships, and
    Villages, 802
  Railroads, 38, 42-46, 387, 785, 800,
    807
  Ranges, 46, 47, 800
  Real Property, 73, 387, 512
  Regional Improvements, 812
  Rivers, 715
  Roads, 233, 234, 715, 755, 789, 798,
    800, 804, 805, 807, 828
  School Districts, 539, 810
  Schools, 45, 786, 798
  Section of Kentucky, 42
  Sections, 38, 40, 42, 43, 798-800
  Sewer System, 782
  Sharon Woods, 811, 831
  Street Numbers, 45
  Street Railway Routes, 45, 808
  Streets, 233, 716, 788, 8805
  Subdivisions, 716
  Suburbs, 39, 40, 42, 233
  Thoroughfares, 38-44, 46, 47, 800,
    807, 808, 821
  Townships, 39, 40, 42-44, 46-49, 538,
    715, 785, 798, 800
  Trails, Sharon Woods, 831
  Transportation Lines, 715, 716
  Villages, 44, 46, 48, 715, 785, 801
  Wards, 38, 786, 800
  Water Systems, 783
  Waterways, 798, 800, 803, 807

Naturalization
Applications, 215, 218, 236
Certificate Duplicates, 218
of Minors, 219
Papers, Copies of, 724
Record, Index to, 217
Newspaper Clippings, 16, 815
Northern Kentucky, see Maps
Norwood, City of
Atlas of, see Maps
Map of, see Maps
Official records, 512
Plats of, see Plats
Survey of Real Property, 512
Notary Public Commissions, 66
Notice, Waivers, 198
Notices
Newspaper, 16
of Sales, 304
to Taxpayers, 509
Nurses, Certificate of Registered, 225
Nurses' Reports, Hillcrest School Hospital,
549

Oaths of Allegiance, Minors', 219
Oaths of Office, Judges', Common Pleas
Court, 96
Office Returns, Common Pleas Court, 83
Officers' Payrolls, Election Board, 485
Offices, County, see each Office
Official Records
Cincinnati, 512
Norwood, 512
Ohio Congressional Districts, see Maps
Ohio, Historical Maps of, 833
Ohio State Institutions, Inmates Committed
to, 606
Ohio State Medical Board, Certificates
Issued by, 223, 224, 226
Ohio State Penitentiary Sentences, 319

Ohio State School Survey Commission
Reports, 530
Ohio Survey Maps, see Maps
Oil Assessments, see Taxes, Assessments
Opinions
Court of Appeals, 154
Rendered, 279
Requests for, 278
Optometry Licenses, 68
Orders
against Funds, Public Welfare
Department, 620
Court, 237, 240, 302
Decennial Board of Equalization, 506
Merchandise, Purchasing Department,
516, 520, 522
Park Commission Supply, 837
Purchase
for County, 741
Public Welfare Department, 632,
633
Vendors', 343
WPA, 742
to Receive (Warrant Stubs), 409
Relief, 619, 624
for Sale of Rel Estate, 295
for Sales, Sheriff's, 302, 304
Sewer Construction, 758
Sheriff's Court, 290
Supply, County Home and Chronic
Disease Hospital, 586, 587, 590
for Water Lines, 759
Ordinances of Village Councils, 760
Original Deeds, 24
Original Wills, 175
Original Wills, Not Probated, 176

Pamphlets, Regional Planning Commission,
815
Papers, Naturalization, 724

Heritage Books by Jana Sloan Broglin:

*Additions and Corrections to the W.P.A. Inventory
of Adams County, Ohio: West Union*

*Additions and Corrections to the W.P.A. Inventory
of Allen County, Ohio: Lima*

*Additions and Corrections to the W.P.A. Inventory
of Ashland County, Ohio: Ashland*

*Additions and Corrections to the W.P.A. Inventory
of Athens County, Ohio: Athens*

*Additions and Corrections to the W.P.A. Inventory
of Belmont County, Ohio: St. Clairsville*

*Additions and Corrections to the W.P.A. Inventory
of Cuyahoga County, Ohio: Cleveland*

*Additions and Corrections to the W.P.A. Inventory
of Fulton County, Ohio: Wauseon*

*Additions and Corrections to the W.P.A. Inventory
of Geauga County, Ohio: Chardon*

*Additions and Corrections to the W.P.A. Inventory
of Hamilton County, Ohio: Cincinnati*

*Additions and Corrections to the W.P.A. Inventory
of Hancock County, Ohio: Findlay*

*Additions and Corrections to the W.P.A. Inventory
of Lake County, Ohio: Painesville*

*Additions and Corrections to the W.P.A. Inventory
of Lorain County, Ohio: Elyria*

*Additions and Corrections to the W.P.A. Inventory
of Lucas County, Ohio: Toledo*

*Additions and Corrections to the W.P.A. Inventory
of Medina County, Ohio: Medina*

*Additions and Corrections to the W.P.A. Inventory
of Montgomery County, Ohio: Dayton*

*Additions and Corrections to the W.P.A. Inventory
of Muskingum County, Ohio: Zanesville*

*Additions and Corrections to the W.P.A. Inventory
of Seneca County, Ohio: Tiffin*

*Additions and Corrections to the W.P.A. Inventory
of Trumbull County, Ohio: Warren*

*Additions and Corrections to the W.P.A. Inventory
of Washington County, Ohio: Marietta*

*Additions and Corrections to the W.P.A. Inventory
of Wayne County, Ohio: Wooster*

Hookers, Crooks and Kooks, Part I: Hookers

Hookers, Crooks and Kooks, Part II: Crooks and Kooks

Lucas County, Ohio, Index to Deaths, 1867–1908

Mason County, Kentucky Wills and Estates, 1791–1832, Second Edition

www.ingramcontent.com/pod-product-compliance
Lightning Source LLC
Chambersburg PA
CBHW071831270326
41929CB00013B/1959

* 9 7 8 0 7 8 8 4 4 9 3 2 1 *